Central America and the Reagan Doctrine

Central America and the Reagan Doctrine

Edited by Walter F. Hahn

Introduction by Jeane J. Kirkpatrick

The Center for International Relations at Boston University *in association with* *United States Strategic Institute* *Washington, D.C.*

Copyright © 1987 by

United States Strategic Institute

Printed in the United States of America

University Press of America
4720 Boston Way
Lanham, MD 20706

3 Henrietta Street
London WC2E 8LU England

Distributed by arrangement with
University Publishing Associates, Inc.

British Cataloging in Publication Information Available

Library of Congress Cataloging-in-Publication Data

Central America and the Reagan doctrine.

Bibliography: p.
1. Central America—Politics and government—
1979-   . 2. Central America—Foreign relations—
United States. 3. United States—Foreign relations—
Central America. 4. United States—Foreign relations—
1981-   . 5. Geopolitics—Caribbean Area. I. Hahn,
Walter F.
F1439.5.C452   1987   327.730728   87-2037
ISBN 0-8191-6178-0 (alk. paper)
ISBN 0-8191-6179-9 (pbk. : alk. paper)

This book is produced on acid-free paper
which exceeds the minimum standards set by the
National Historical Publication and Records Commission.

Contents

Preface

This volume represents a compilation of articles published in *Strategic Review*. It also reflects a unique confluence of two institutions.

Strategic Review is the quarterly journal of the United States Strategic Institute, founded in Washington in 1972. The driving spirit behind USSI's creation was its Chairman, Dr. Arthur G. B. Metcalf, industrialist, aviator, scientist, and pioneer in the field of aeronautics, who served in the U.S. Army in World War II.

The idea of USSI and the journal was born in the turmoil at the height of the Vietnam war and its devastating repercussions on the American scene. Dr. Metcalf and a group of equally concerned former military leaders and strategists — including prominently General Ira C. Eaker, who created the mighty Eighth Air Force and commanded the victorious U.S. air offensive against Nazi Germany in World War II — looked about them at an American political-intellectual landscape torn by confusion over fundamental national values and goals, and at governmental leadership seemingly drained of strategic thought and purpose in coping in an ever more explosive world. They decided that a new, independent, nonpartisan forum was needed to help restore clarity of national vision both of the enveloping dangers and of the imperative means — physical as well as intellectual — to deal with them. *Strategic Review* was established with the declared dedication to "the advancement and understanding of those principles and practices — military and political — which serve the vital interests and security of the United States."

The journal quickly grew in fulfillment of this dedication. It attracted outstanding contributions from military professionals and civilian authorities. Notwithstanding a fundamentally hostile environment of media and policy forces throughout the 1970s, it gained stature for the solidly anchored and clear analyses conveyed by its articles and editorials. *Strategic Review* was acknowledged as a salient in what may be characterized as an American "strategic reawakening" in 1979–1980.

With that progressive "reawakening" — and its expression at the policy levels in Washington — has come a deliberate broadening of *Strategic Review*'s vistas. In the 1970s, the journal's priority focus was on America's dangerously deteriorating defense posture, and strategic self-delusions, in the face of the accumulating military power and global advances of the Soviet opponent. While not neglecting the realms of military strategy, doctrine, tactics and hardware, progressively since 1981 *Strategic Review* has directed its searchlight outward onto the global determinants of a coherent U.S. Grand Strategy — onto the historic forces of geopolitics, the sinews of alliance systems, the cockpits of regional conflict, and the less distinct but increasingly critical arenas of insurgency, terrorism and political-psychological warfare.

This shift in — or rather extension of — emphasis in the journal's coverage has been responsive not simply to an urge to plow new ground, let alone to a sense of "previous mission accomplished." Rather, it has proceeded from recognition of a verity concerning the global struggle. The verity is that so long as the United States and its major allies can sustain the necessary ramparts of defense and deterrence at the strategic and conventional levels of the East-West confrontation, the pivotal struggle will rage with ever greater intensity within the strategic but vulnerably unstable regions flanking that confrontation, and in the shadowy dimensions of "subconventional" and political-psychological warfare.

The strategy of the "indirect approach" is as old as the precepts of the ancient Chinese philosopher-strategist Sun Tzu. No serious student of the history of the Soviet Union and of the clearly and persistently iterated doctrine of its leaders can avoid the conclusion that this has been the principal, designated battleground ever since the Bolshevik regime consolidated its hold on Russia and embarked on the "historic, global mission of socialism" — but a battleground endowed with new meaning in the nuclear age. No serious analyst of the tides of developments in Asia, Africa and the Middle East since World War II — and particularly since the 1970s — can ignore either the driving vectors of Soviet strategy in those regions or the common denominators of strategic design. And no serious observer of events in Central America, the "strategic backyard" of the United States, during the past decade can still take refuge behind the comfortable notion that the progressive intrusion of Soviet arms and strategy into the region has been the function of accident or expedience, let alone the expression of strictly local developments.

This broadening of *Strategic Review*'s mandate, with an immediate focus on Central America, coincided with growing ties between the United States Strategic Institute and the Center for International Relations of Boston University.

The Center for International Relations was founded in 1982 with the central purpose of establishing in the Boston area, under the aegis of Boston University, an academic institution that provides for, and encourages, realistic study and understanding of the forces that shape the global environment and affect the foreign and security policies of the United States. It thus seeks to inculcate on the academic level an understanding of the same basic values that USSI has advanced in the professional and policy arenas. Under the direction of Professor Hermann Eilts, a former U.S. Ambassador to Egypt and Vice Commandant of the U.S. Army War College, the Center has grown rapidly in faculty, students and stature.

In December 1984, USSI and the Center for International Relations joined in an association. This arrangement formalized and strengthened personal links between the two organizations. Dr. John R. Silber, President of Boston University, to whose vision we are indebted, is a Vice President of the Institute. Professor Eilts is a member of the Editorial Board of *Strategic Review*. Professor H. Joachim Maitre, Associate Director of the Center, joined *Strategic Review* as its Foreign Affairs Editor.

This book is an expression of, and testimonial to, this cooperative relationship. Indeed, the idea of the book originated with Gerald J. Gross, Vice President for Arts, Publications and Media at Boston University.

In setting about to implement the idea, we encountered some genuine and pleasant surprises. When we first began to direct a sharpened focus on Central America and relevant U.S. policy issues, we did so without any preconceived idea of methodical coverage, let alone of ultimately combining the various contributions. Yet, we now find that not only do the various articles fit together, but they do so compatibly without the "forced harnessing" that so often marks anthologies. It attests to consistency in our coverage.

A caveat is in order in this connection. The reader who opens this book with the expectation of finding a comprehensive treatment of Central America's geography and countries — and of their political and socioeconomic structures and problems — will be disappointed. The focus in *Strategic Review* has been on the strategic content of the Central American phenomenon, on the core elements of conflict in the region, and on their relevance to U.S. policy. The coverage is thus geopolitically and functionally oriented rather than regionally comprehensive, with Cuba, Nicaragua, El Salvador and Mexico as the focal geographical points.

A second surprise concerned the durability of the contributions to this volume. Even though they date back to as early as spring of 1982 (in the case of Chapter 12 by David C. Jordan), without exception they have withstood the tests not only of time but of veritable rapids of developments. The updating that needed to be undertaken, in the texts themselves and in the form of postscripts by the authors, was minimal. This reflects again upon the fundamental nature of the coverage.

Especially since the various contributions were not designed originally to march in tandem, there is inevitably some overlap between them. Rather than surgically eliminate redundancy, however, we decided that it serves in most cases a useful purpose — not only in terms of emphasis, but also in illuminating differing vantage-points on the same phenomenon. This applies markedly to Chapters 4 and 5 on Nicaragua by Arturo J. Cruz and Nestor D. Sanchez, respectively. Both treat some of the same features of that subject, but the one looks at it through the spectacles of a participant in (and victim of) the events, while the other contemplates it from the policy levels of Washington.

Because the contents of this volume span the efforts of several years, it is particularly difficult to extend due credit to the many who, at one time or another, contributed to the overall product. An obvious place to start, however, is at the "foundation level," in both its practical and institutional connotations. *Strategic Review* would not exist — and this volume would not have materialized — without the generous and enduring support of the Scaife Family Charitable Trusts, the Carthage Foundation, Boston University, and others whose policies of modesty prevent us from documenting our gratitude.

Abigail DuBois, Managing Editor of *Strategic Review,* and Chantale Shepard, Editorial Assistant, toiled with professional dedication in the vineyards of the original harvests as well as their present blending — and did so while somehow coping with the caprices of a peripatetic Editor-in-Chief. Dr. H. Joachim Maitre, Foreign Affairs Editor, was my alter ego in the seeding and nurturing of the articles (now chapters). And the members of the Editorial Board of *Strategic Review* not only provided advice, but kept us honest.

For the production of the book itself, our thanks go to the staff of the Office of Publications Production at Boston University — to Robert Frost, Director of Publications Production; Dorothy Snowman, University Editor; and Jerome Schuerger, Director of Graphic Design. The role of Boston University Vice President Gerald J. Gross in conceptualizing and helping to shape the volume has already been noted.

But the ultimate credit belongs to the authors who are represented in this volume. It is their product. They gave of themselves not for remunerative reward, but out of a sense of dedication to the national interest, concern over a crucial and flaming problem area at our very doorstep, and the urgent need for a unified, redressive U.S. strategy.

Walter F. Hahn
Editor-in-Chief, *Strategic Review*
Adjunct Professor, Boston University

Introduction

JEANE J. KIRKPATRICK

The history of the Americas can be read as a record of the effort to escape tyranny and establish liberty. Our forebears came to this hemisphere in search of freedom from oppression and hardship. Simon Bolivar, whose bicentenary we celebrated two years ago, defined our vocation: to resolve here in the Americas the "great problem of mankind, the problem of how to live in freedom."

That effort — to solve the problem of liberty — continues to this day. It dominates the politics of our world, and especially the lives of the people of Central America. In Central America today there is a momentous struggle between two conceptions of human life — two conceptions of culture, economics and politics. Each conception has its distinctive end, its distinctive method. One leads to tyranny; its method is violence. The other leads to freedom; its method is consent. There never has been as much evidence as today that the way of freedom leads to peace, creativity, development and well-being, and that tyranny leads to violence, economic stagnation and war.

As Jose Napoleon Duarte, President of El Salvador, has said repeatedly, two revolutionary movements seek today to replace the old dictatorships and old oligarchies of Central America. One is a democratic revolution whose goal is constitutional democracy, with its associated rights and freedoms. The other is a Marxist-Leninist revolution, which seeks to replace traditional dictators with new-style, Castroite dictators with the help of arms, advisers and doctrines from the Soviet Bloc. The struggle between the traditional Latin military regime and the two revolutions has dominated the politics of Central America during the last twenty years.

Now, however, this three-sided struggle has become essentially a two-sided one. The recent inauguration of a democratically elected

xiii

government in Guatemala may mark the final demise of "traditional" military-oligarchical rule in the region. Democratic institutions had already taken root in El Salvador and Honduras, and have been firmly established in Costa Rica since 1948. Traditional autocrats are finished in this region. Democratic revolution vies with the new *caudillos* for supremacy.

Each revolution has distinctive means as well as ends. The method of democracy is freedom. The method of the Marxist-Leninist revolution is force. In El Salvador, the FMLN resorts to kidnapping women, attacking North Americans, destroying crops, dams and power plants, and murdering peasants whose only sin is seeking to protect themselves. In Guatemala, the guerrillas continue their war against organized society and threaten the country's new, fragile democratic institutions. In Nicaragua, the guerrillas-turned-rulers relentlessly tighten the vise of repression, prohibiting virtually all free activities, forcibly relocating the inhabitants and imposing ever more suffocating censorship. All this repression is justified in the name of "social discipline" and blamed on the Contras — just as Soviet representatives blame the continuing war against Afghanistan on those who resist conquest.

The essays in this volume not only analyze the conflict in Central America, but they also illuminate its international and geopolitical context. Even today, some argue that the problem of Central America should be viewed from an exclusively "regional" rather than an "East-West" perspective. In Managua today, a visitor must stare fixedly at his own feet to avoid seeing Soviet weaponry, Cuban advisers, East German security experts and other so-called *internationalists* of the Soviet Bloc. The Soviet and Cuban factors give Central American problems their distinctive dimensions and special contemporary urgency. Without the Soviet and Cuban factors, there might still be instability and strife in Central America, but of a kind and extent that could, in fact, be dealt with in a strictly "regional" context.

It is astounding that there should be lingering illusions about the Soviet offensive in Central America. Soviet aspirations and expansionist projects on the American continent are no longer a secret.

It has been some time since Soviet strategists determined that in Latin America only armed struggle has been successful as a means to establish Marxist-Leninist governments and to spread the revolution. In the *Soviet Military Encyclopedia* of 1978, for example, an article on Latin America noted: "The change in the balance of power in the international arena in favor of socialism" — that is, the strengthening of the Soviet Union — "has led to the activation of the struggle of the people of Latin America, which opens up the road to socialism in the Western Hemisphere."

Or read on: "The struggle for national liberation is a form of war carried out by the colonial peoples and dependencies, or, formerly, colonial territories, in which the socialist countries are the decisive factor when those peoples launch a struggle against the backward reactionaries." This is a *very* straightforward formulation, which makes clear the role the Soviets assign to force — Soviet force — in such areas as Central America today. Wherever a minority instigates an internal struggle, the military support of the Soviet Bloc becomes the pivotal instrument. The Soviets mask their strategy with terms like "national liberation" and "popular revolution" because, as Robert Strausz-Hupé observed many years ago, the Soviets are the "scavengers of revolution."

They have developed a simple formula for local conquest, which was amply demonstrated in Nicaragua and is poignantly described in this volume by Arturo J. Cruz, a Nicaraguan democrat who became a prominent victim of the strategy of deception and now is one of the leaders of the anti-Sandinista forces. First come acts of terrorism carried out by a small Marxist-Leninist "vanguard" that hides its true identity under nationalist and democratic facades. The process gathers momentum and guerrilla warfare develops, which is fanned into full civil conflict featuring a broad popular alliance against the targeted regime. Finally, in the heady aftermath of victorious popular revolution, the Marxist-Leninist "vanguard," by dint of superior arms, organization and discipline, seizes the levers of power.

The Soviets run no risks in the process. Once their "vanguard" is in control, the Soviets open the pipelines of assistance to make that control permanent. This is when the strange international brigades appear, providing advice and services, helping to extend and consolidate the regime's hold over the country.

The whole process demonstrates that Marxism-Leninism does not trust the laws of history to achieve its objectives — does not trust the laws of history to prevent defeat. It relies on the laws of force.

What should we, who live on this continent, do in the face of the penetration of the hemisphere by Soviet imperialism? We must face it. We must face the fact that it is a hemispheric problem. There are not zones of immunity. The problem of El Salvador is not merely a Salvadoran problem, nor one belonging only to its immediate neighbors. The huge arms cache discovered in Chile amid the unfolding crisis in that country is a strident reminder that the problem is continental and demands our attention.

We have come to a new, crucial moment in the history of Central America, of the United States, and of the hemisphere. It is not the first such crucial moment, and it will not be the last, but its consequences are likely to be long-lived and far-reaching.

The U.S. Government has responded to the challenge with an evolving set of policies and principles that have been called the Reagan Doctrine. It is argued in this book — and was evidenced in the Administration's hard-fought battle to obtain Congressional approval of even a modicum of assistance to Nicaragua's freedom-fighters — that public understanding of the Reagan Doctrine is still weak.

The crisis in Central America, and its stakes for the United States and the hemisphere as a whole are clear. Any veils that may still seem to obscure the true nature and import of the crisis have been woven by the disinformation of those who seek to deceive us and the confusion of those who sincerely, but naively, take refuge in wishful thinking. It is to be hoped that this book can help rend those veils and point the way to the urgently needed bipartisan understanding and consensus that are so eloquently argued by John R. Silber in his concluding chapter.

PART I

The Strategic Setting

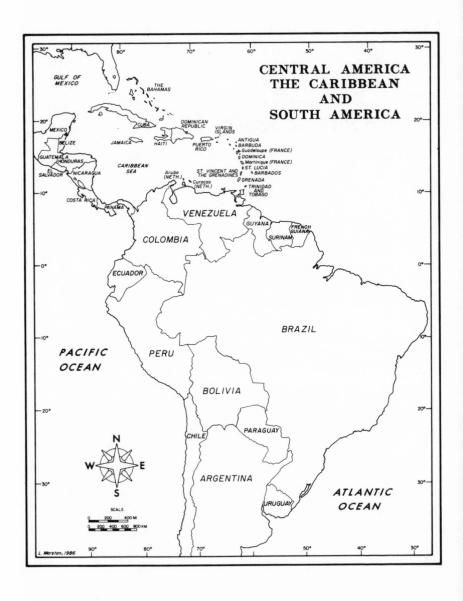

1 Central America: The Larger Regional Scenario

R. Bruce McColm

Leonid Brezhnev, speaking before the Congress of Soviet Trade Unions in Moscow on March 16, 1982, warned that NATO's deployment of Pershing-2 missiles in Europe "would compel us to take retaliatory steps that would put the other side, *including the United States itself, its own territory,* in an analogous position."[1] A year and a day later, Georgi A. Arbatov, Director of the Institute for the Study of the USA and Canada, reiterated the threat and was seconded by Defense Minister Dimitri Ustinov and the Commander-in-Chief of the Warsaw Pact, Marshal Kulikov. Asked where such threatened Soviet missile deployments would occur, a member of the Soviet negotiating team in Geneva told the Spanish news agency EFE that the site could be either Cuba or Nicaragua.[2]

In the spring of 1983, both Costa Rica's Foreign Minister, Fernando Volio Jimenez, and the American Ambassador to the United Nations, Jeane Kirkpatrick, reported that the Sandinista government in Nicaragua had signed a secret agreement with the Soviet Union for the construction of a sea-level, interoceanic canal across the San Juan River and Lake Nicaragua. America's sovereignty over the Panama Canal is due to expire in the year 2000. Against this background, politically the reported project would become the Soviets' Latin American version of the Aswan Dam. Geopolitically, it would have the effect of severing the hemisphere, clamping a vise of Soviet naval power projection around the Caribbean.[3]

This chapter appeared as an article, entitled "Central America and the Caribbean: The Larger Scenario," in the Summer 1983 issue of Strategic Review.

Such are the harbingers of a fundamental geostrategic transformation — at a time when the American public debate is fixed almost obsessively on narrower currents of events in El Salvador, on human rights issues, on analogies with Vietnam, and on the comforting notion that the trends we are witnessing are reflecting factors and forces "indigenous" to the region that will eventually right themselves into a new stability. For a variety of reasons lodged in their history and traditions, Americans tend to shy away from a geopolitical framework of analysis. The danger is that the geopolitical lessons relevant to the Caribbean Basin, Central America and Latin America generally will sink in only then when it will be too late to act upon them.

THE GEOPOLITICAL STAKES

From the vantagepoint of the United States, the geopolitical contours of the Caribbean Basin are clear enough — or should be clear enough. By virtue of its sovereignty over Puerto Rico and the U.S. Virgin Islands, the United States is a Caribbean nation. It is an area where a host of vital U.S. interests intersect. Prominent among these are the maintenance of stable, trouble-free national borders and unhampered access to the vital sealanes that flow into the Caribbean Sea. The Soviet Union understands the price of maintaining a standing army on its borders. We do not. Yet, if our southern borders should become unstable, we would be forced to divert American defensive strength from Europe and Asia in order to mount an immediate defensive shield where today there is none.

The primary thrust of long-term Soviet strategic objectives in the region seems equally clear: namely, to create through a Soviet naval and air presence and enhanced Cuban forces an offensive interdiction capability effective enough to block sealanes and disrupt NATO's "swing strategy." This strategy calls for the airlift, in the event of war, of three reinforcing U.S. divisions to Europe, where some of their equipment is prepositioned. Other equipment and five or more additional divisions would be moved aboard Military Sealift Command vessels and merchant ships of the National Defense Reserve Fleet and NATO countries. The optimal embarkation port for three of those U.S. Army divisions — the 2nd Armored,

1st Mechanized and 5th Infantry — is Beaumont, Texas, on the Gulf of Mexico. Three others — the 7th, 9th and 25th Infantry Divisions, based in Hawaii, Washington and California — would normally be moved by sea through the Panama Canal, thence eastward south of Cuba.[4]

Modernized Soviet naval and air forces operating from bases in Cuba, Nicaragua and Grenada could effectively harass such reinforcements. Soviet surface and submarine fleets could close the four major choke-points in the region's sealanes. The Soviet Backfire bomber fleet, with a 4,000-kilometer range, can now be accommodated on at least three — and perhaps as many as ten — bases in Cuba, thence to threaten mid-Atlantic searoutes. It should be recalled that during World War II, German U-boats operating in the Caribbean without the benefit of friendly regional ports or air-cover managed within six months to sink 260 merchant ships, half of them oil tankers.

To counter such an interdiction threat, the United States would have to invade Cuba. Defense planners suggest that this operation alone would require 100,000 troops — in other words, the strength of our reinforcements for NATO — and more aircraft carriers than are currently available.

Even short of such worst-case scenarios, the strategic significance of the Caribbean Basin is patent. The region hosts critical links in the network of American listening posts monitoring ship and submarine activities in the Atlantic Ocean and the approaches to the Caribbean, as well as other vital communications, tracking and navigational facilities. The Navy's Atlantic Underseas Test and Evaluation Center in the Bahamas and the Virgin Islands is critical to the development of U.S. anti-submarine capabilities.

The Panama Canal, although termed obsolete by some defense planners, during the Korean War funnelled 22 per cent of all troops and materiel for that conflict, and currently remains the key to allowing a three-ocean presence for the one-and-a-half ocean fleet of the U.S. Navy. Only 13 of the Navy's 475 ships are too large to transit the Canal. It is also vital, of course, to the economies of Australia, New Zealand and Japan in their trade with Western Europe.

America's economic health is increasingly at stake also in the mounting traffic of strategic and raw materials through the 13 maritime routes of the Caribbean. The U.S. Department of Commerce has calculated that imported raw materials will rise from the present 20 per cent of total U.S. consumption to nearly 50 per cent by the year 2000. The bulk of these materials are and will continue to be transshipped through the Caribbean Sea.

Most of the supertanker traffic from the Middle East and Africa requires the lightering facilities in the Bahamas, the Virgin Islands, Trinidad, Curacao and Aruba for the transfer of crude oil to standard craft. These routes carry more than 50 per cent of U.S. oil imports to domestic markets, and refinery facilities in the area account for 12.5 per cent of our total processed oil. Oil from Alaska and Ecuador passes through the trans-Panamanian pipeline, augmenting the tanker routes through the Canal. Add to this some proven 45 billion barrels of oil in Mexico, and 6 billion or more in Guatemala and the Venezuelan reserves, and the aggregate importance of the Caribbean for American oil imports can be said to rival that of the Persian Gulf area.[5]

The Caribbean Basin itself is a principal source of U.S. raw material imports. After Canada, Mexico is the second most important supplier of critical raw materials to the United States, and the principal supplier of silver, zinc, gypsum, antimony, mercury, bismuth, selenium, barium, rhenium and lead. Over 50 per cent of U.S. bauxite imports have traditionally come from Surinam, Guyana, Haiti and Jamaica, and iron ore from Brazil and Venezuela is important to our industrial requirements. The availability of these mineral imports represents an important economic convenience for the United States today; in the event of a major global conflict, their availability would be crucial.

THE SOVIET UNION'S STRATEGIC SHIFT IN THE 1970s

There is not the space here to detail the interplay of Soviet-Cuban and American strategies in Central and Latin America since the advent of Fidel Castro in Cuba in 1960 and the establishment of that country as the Soviet Union's first strategic foothold in the Western Hemisphere. Suffice it to say that the stage for the currently unfolding and possibly climactic clash of those strategies was set in the early 1970s. It was then that the United States shifted from a previously active policy in the Southern Hemisphere to one of "benign neglect," screened by U.S.-Soviet detente and the so-called Nixon Doctrine.

In 1974 the United States tacitly abandoned its policy of economic denial against Cuba and, indeed, made ostensible tries at normalizing relations with Havana, even after the onset of the Cuban intervention in Angola. This encouraged Latin American and Caribbean Basin countries to enter into expanding relations with both Cuba and the Soviet Union.

Soviet theoreticians, such as Central Committee member Boris Ponomarev, waxed enthusiastic about Soviet opportunities in the region in the early 1970s. Writing in 1971, Ponomarev argued:

> Seemingly quite reliable rear lines of American imperialism are becoming a tremendous hotbed of anti-imperialist revolution. A tremendous revolutionary movement is developing by the side of the main citadel of imperialism, the United States. These changes are having and, unquestionably, will continue to have a strong impact on further changes in the correlation of world forces in favor of the international working class and socialism.[6]

Under Brezhnev the Soviet Union encouraged local communist parties to join broad electoral fronts and to infiltrate the trade unions, while Moscow put its emphasis on the pursuit of diplomatic and commercial ties with the countries in the region. From 1964 to 1975, the Soviet Union expanded trade relations with Latin America to include 20 countries and through its Council for Mutual Economic Assistance (CMEA) entered into several multilateral economic agreements with organizations such as SELA (The Latin American Economic System). Meanwhile populist military coups in Ecuador, Bolivia, Panama and Peru gave Moscow inroads into the Latin American military, an institution which had previously been relatively immune to communist influences. The military, according to Soviet theoreticians, was the only stable institution in an often chaotic political environment that could serve as the likely generator of change toward socialism.

By the mid-1970s, the Soviets had large diplomatic, economic, cultural and scientific missions throughout the Caribbean and Central America such as in Costa Rica, Venezuela, Trinidad and

Tobago, Guatemala, Nicaragua and Jamaica. These missions, besides cultivating indigenous cadres through an extensive KGB infrastructure, sought on a more practical level to encourage the governments in the area to play a more active role in the politics of the Third World at large, with particular attention to coordinating commodity export prices, policies toward multinational corporations and Third World debt, and advocating "anti-imperialist" and "anti-colonial" positions in various international organizations.

Before the 1970s, Soviet theoreticians had believed that the region must first pass through a "popular democratic" revolutionary phase before reaching the portals of "scientific socialism." This strategy was now modified. Local communist parties were urged to play a prominent role in left-wing coalitions, even within so-called "progressive military regimes."

The defeat of the Broad Front in Uruguay in 1971, the military coup that toppled Salvador Allende in Chile in 1973 and the small turnout for the leftist alliance in the 1973 Venezuelan elections forced Moscow to reconsider the merits of the electoral path to power. The year 1975 brought a watershed for Soviet strategy in Latin America. The pro-Soviet Belasco government in Peru fell, and a spate of right-wing takeovers took place in Uruguay, Bolivia and Argentina in what the Soviets called "a reactionary counteroffensive unprecedented in Latin American history."

Thereafter, Moscow discreetly financed through Cuba and East European countries urban terrorist groups such as the Tupamaros and Montoneros in the Southern Cone countries — more in an effort to foster political insecurity and to isolate the governments internationally than actually to topple them. The urban terrorist campaigns of the mid- and later-1970s throughout the Southern Cone were simply well-orchestrated reminders that the revolutionary spirit was still alive.

THE BOLDER CUBAN CONNECTION

Meanwhile, encouraged by the passiveness of the successive Nixon, Ford and Carter Administrations in Washington, Cuba began to break out of its diplomatic and economic isolation and to knot stronger ties with regional countries, particularly in the English-speaking Caribbean. With American influence waning throughout the Caribbean Basin during the 1970s, Havana established relations with a growing number of left-leaning governments in the Caribbean. Primarily through the good offices of Michael Manley, the leftist Prime Minister of Jamaica, the Cubans forged links with the small, Marxist-leaning Black Power parties in the eastern Caribbean.

This political offensive by Castro reaped some early practical benefits. During the Angolan conflict, Cuba was able to refuel its Africa-bound aircraft in Guyana, with which it had established relations in the early 1970s. Cuba's participation in regional organizations helped shape more strongly anti-American positions, and through its program of scholarships and guerrilla training Havana gained a great deal of credibility among younger political elites in the region. At one point, 500 Cuban advisers were assigned to Jamaica to train its security forces, and in the bitter Jamaican electoral campaign in 1980 the Cuban Ambassador, Ulises Estrada, was implicated in an arms smuggling plot to destabilize the island. During this period Havana also gained influence with the governments of Saint Lucia, through former Deputy Prime Minister George Odlum and the Progressive Labor Party, and Grenada after the March 1979 coup that brought Maurice Bishop and his New Jewel Movement to power.

The 1970s featured not only a quickening of the Soviet-Cuban political and clandestine offensive in the Southern Hemisphere, but also a busy learning period. By dint of their growing presence, Soviet analysts were able to study the inter-American defense system and maritime navigation. Cuban and Soviet trawler fleets gathered intelligence and mapped the geology and topography of the area in a systematic way. Moscow thus was preparing its eventual challenge to America's "hegemonic presumption" in its strategic backyard.

THE SOCIO-ECONOMIC BACKDROP

The Soviet Union and its Cuban surrogates, in casting their strategy toward the Caribbean Basin, no doubt were keenly sensitive to the pull of socio-economic forces that were opening opportunities for wedges of influence. Central America in particular beckoned as a prime target area. By and large, the "city-states" in this region are in the process of capital formation, in contrast with their South American counterparts which generally boast relatively sophisticated, if inequitable, capitalist systems. This process means that the small but growing middle class in most Central American states can be divided because of competing aspirations within it vis-a-vis the traditional agrarian producers, and that a large number of marginal and, for the most part, culturally homogeneous farm workers are ripe for radicalization.

During their modernization throes, these small nations cannot sustain rapid changes in the social dynamics of the traditional society without suffering political upheaval. And, more often than not, the countries of the Central American isthmus have depended on the military to protect national security and order. But, as this institution is traditionally miniscule in these countries and represents more a political than a fighting force, it is hard-put to cope with a war of attrition waged by urban and rural guerrillas.

Moreover, the year 1978 brought about a rapid deterioration in the economics of the region. Export commodity prices such as coffee, cotton and bananas plummeted. At the same time, the costs of imported oil and borrowed capital escalated, while the slowed economic growth in the industrial countries reduced tourism in the region, a major generator of capital. Widening credit deficits turned inexorably into severe foreign exchange shortages and national bankruptcies. The elites created during the previous periods of rapid economic growth still expected participation within the political structures of the society but were, by and large, excluded from the decisionmaking spheres.

Political instability exacerbated the economic decline. The Central American Common Market had been crippled by the brief 1969 Soccer War between Honduras and El Salvador. But this episode proved minor when compared to the economic consequences of increased political terrorism in the 1970s. After the Nicaraguan civil war ended, the expanding guerrilla strategy of economic warfare cancelled the large strides toward industrialization made by El Salvador, Guatemala and Honduras.

The cumulative effect of the late 1970s to the Caribbean Basin is a persistent and generalized economic depression. Since 1980 economic growth in the Caribbean has fallen far behind population growth. Unemployment and underemployment throughout the region stand between 25 and 50 per cent, with the major impact falling on the young people that make up the majorities of the populations. In some cases, inflation rates have soared over 100 per cent, and import quotas have seriously squeezed the once-growing middle class. This has resulted in a full-scale flight of capital and the middle class from the Caribbean Basin.

On the Caribbean island-states, the newly emergent leftist forces, which still view Cuba as a viable economic model, have profited from the social problems that come from population growth and increased urbanization. Over 50 per cent of the island populations are young — below the age of 18 — and associate the economic depression in the Caribbean with an overdependence on the economies of the Western industrialized countries and with the legacy of colonialism.

The Caribbean, in addition to suffering economic depression, is also experiencing a transition from the old labor-based, populist governments modeled after the British Labor Party. The genera-tion of such leaders as Eric Williams of Trinidad, Vere Bird of Antigua, Milton Cato of St. Vincent and the Grenadines and "Skipper" Barrow of Barbados, who combined a Fabian socialism with a pro-Western orientation, is rapidly disappearing from the political landscape.

The micro-Marxist parties, once independent outgrowths of the New Left and Black Power movements in the local universities, gained additional legitimacy after the success of Maurice Bishop in overthrowing the regime of Eric Gairy in Grenada in March 1979. Groups such as the Dominica Liberation Movement, the Antigua Caribbean Liberation Movement and splinter factions of local labor parties have gained legitimacy and strength by dint of military train-ing in Libya and Cuba, even if they have not scored heavily in democratic elections. In the future, these political forces will repre-sent destabilizing factors throughout the eastern Caribbean.[8]

THE EXPANDING SOVIET MILITARY PRESENCE

In a 1975 article General I. Shavrov, Chief of the Soviet General Staff Academy, wrote that regional conflicts in the developing world were "epicenters" of the global struggle between East and West.[9] In the aftermath of the communist victory in Vietnam, Shavrov and other Soviet strategists noted a definite relationship between the strategic nuclear balance and the incidence of local wars. He observed that by the mid-1970s the West was experiencing a crisis at the hands of irregular warfare and had not succeeded in gaining one major victory through the use of military force. Shavrov went on to suggest that Soviet aid now was the most important factor in determining the outcome of such a conflict and remarked that the Soviet Union's bluewater navy and growing airlift capability permitted it to inhibit Western influence in regional conflicts while supporting those forces and regimes allied with the Soviet Union.

Beginning in 1975, the Soviet Union embarked on an aggressive policy addressed to the peripheral theaters of the developing world — in Angola, South Yemen, Ethiopia, Kampuchea, Laos, the Shaba invasions of Zaire and Afghanistan. The general offensive grew bolder against the background of passive and confused reaction from the United States to the accelerating tempo of conflicts in the Third World, climaxed by the image of American powerlessness in the Iranian Revolution. The successful use of Soviet military intervention evidently convinced Moscow to downgrade economic ties with the developing world in favor of the more successful and quicker-results policy of military assistance.

This policy of military assistance has entailed the expanding muscles of Soviet power in a "screening" mode while the local surrogates of that power are being strengthened. Both prongs of this strategy have been clearly in evidence in the Caribbean.[10]

Since early July 1969, when a seven-ship Soviet squadron entered the Caribbean, a new chapter has unfolded in the political evolution of the hemisphere. For the first time since the destruction of the Spanish fleet off Santiago de Cuba on July 3, 1898, the naval force of a rival great power entered the Caribbean. The construction of a nuclear submarine docking facility in Cienfuegos on the southern shore of Cuba in the summer and fall of 1970 signalled a permanence of the Soviet naval presence in the region, plus a logistical capability of servicing nuclear submarines which would operate within striking range of half the United States.

THE ARMS BUILDUP IN CUBA

At the same time, since the Cuban combat intervention in Angola in 1975 the Soviet Union has engaged in a remarkable effort to strengthen the Cuban armed forces.[11] From 1980 to 1981 alone, Soviet arms shipments to the island tripled, totaling about $2.5 billion worth of military materiel. Some 63,000 metric tons of Soviet arms were shipped to Cuba in 1981, more than in any year since the 1962 Cuban Missile Crisis. Some of these arms were to replace equipment used by Cuban forces deployed in various missions throughout Africa. But they were clearly aimed as well at upgrading and enhancing the island's offensive military capabilities.

During the past decade the Cuban military has been steadily professionalized, with estimates of some 120,000 men in the regular standing forces, 60,000 ready reserves, 175,000 to 200,000 second-line reserves, and about 100,000 members of the Army of Working Youth. In addition, since 1981 the Cuban Government has created a 500,000-man Territorial Militia to guard the island against attack.

The Cuban military has modeled its organization, strategy and tactics on those of the Soviet military. Ready reserves can be called up on four hours notice and train at least 45 days a year. Half of the Cuban troops sent to Angola and Ethiopia were reserves, and the Cuban military thus has recourse to a large pool of personnel with combat experience. In addition, the Cubans have developed a dual command structure, which allows them to rotate high-ranking members of the armed forces between Angola and Cuba.

We may recall the revelation in September 1979 that a Soviet combined arms combat brigade of between 2,000 and 3,000 men had been spotted in Cuba. The obvious role of such a force would be of implanting a tangible Soviet deterrent against any possible American strikes on Cuba in reprisal for Cuban actions elsewhere in the region. In the larger scheme of things, therefore, the Soviet brigade carries clear offensive connotations.

The upgrading of Cuba's air and naval forces now gives Havana the capability of quick strikes from the island into the Caribbean. Previously dependent on the Soviets for their logistical lines of support to Africa, Cuba now possesses the capacity to transport medium to heavy weaponry off the island and can rapidly deploy some 5,000 special forces within 24 hours anywhere in the Caribbean Basin. In a low-level conflict such a force could mean the margin of victory.

Part of the Soviet aid package to Cuba in recent years has included 15 to 20 MIG-23 Floggers (bringing the combined Cuban MIG force to between 200 and 225), MI-8 helicopter gunships, AN-26 medium-range transports, Foxtrot diesel-powered attack submarines, T-62 tanks and a number of BM-21 multiple rocket launchers. Counting fixed-wing combat airplanes and helicopters, Cuba deploys an Air Force of 555 planes. Besides the aforementioned submarines and Koni-class frigate, the Cuban Navy has ten large patrol boats and 26 fast-attack craft armed with Styx surface-to-surface missiles. The Navy also deploys another 40 fast-attack craft of the Turya and Zhuk classes, which are ideal for amphibious landings.

In late May 1983, Cuba began practicing amphibious assaults around Mariel, deploying a contingent of 400 Marines, four light tanks and eight armored personnel carriers. Using Soviet-made Polnocny-class ships capable of carrying six tanks, the Cubans demonstrated a capability of projecting force particularly against vulnerable eastern Caribbean states.[12]

The Soviets also supplied Cuba in 1979 with batteries of modified SA-2 anti-aircraft missiles, as well as mobile SA-6 launchers. These large missiles, which in the Soviet inventory are often equipped with nuclear weapons, can be employed quickly in a surface-to-surface mode by the simple addition of a booster.

Since 1978, the Soviet Union has provided Cuba also with MIG-27s, which are frequently flown by Soviet pilots and have a range of 1,500 miles and the capability of carrying either conventional or nuclear payloads. At least three and possibly as many as nine Cuban airfields have recently been upgraded to handle the Soviet TU-95 Bear heavy intercontinental bombers, capable of carrying nuclear air-to-surface missiles. Since 1970, these long-range bombers have been traveling from the Kola Peninsula to the Cuban airfields without any U.S. protests. In the spring of 1983, nearly ten TU-95s were sighted in Cuba, at least two of them with operational bomb bays.[13]

CUBA AS THE FOUNTAINHEAD OF INSURGENCIES

The military buildup of Cuba has served not only the creation of a platform for extending a conventional military threat to NATO's "swing strategy" and other American vital interests in the area. Clearly, an equally important — and more immediate — purpose behind the buildup has been the establishment of a staging area for support of guerrilla movements in Central America and the Caribbean and the creation of a protective shield for the revolutionary governments in Grenada, Nicaragua, Surinam and others still to follow. Indeed, the acceleration of Moscow's arms supplies to Cuba during the past several years may well reflect also the Soviet leaders' recognition of the revolutionary potential in the region that was expressed in the leftist coup in Grenada in March 1979 and even more dramatically in the July 1979 Sandinista overthrow of the Somoza regime in Nicaragua.[14]

It should be noted that in previous years the Soviet Union had been more skeptical of the success of guerrilla attack in the region — a skepticism that was expressed in contemptuous Soviet references to the failure of the Che Guevara mission in Bolivia in 1967. Castro in the early years had felt shackled by Soviet reluctance to countenance Cuban adventures in Latin America. To be sure, in December 1964, at the Havana Conference of Communist Parties, Moscow had relented somewhat, allowing Cuban support of armed struggle in Venezuela, Colombia, Guatemala, Honduras, Paraguay and Haiti in return for Castro's promise to pursue peaceful change elsewhere in the hemisphere. At the 1966 Tricontinental Conference in Havana, which was conceived and coordinated by Moscow to undercut Communist China's inroads in the Third World, an elaborate network was established among national liberation movements in Africa, Asia and Latin America. The Latin American Solidarity Organization (OLAS) headquartered in Havana cultivated revolutionaries who recognized Cuba as "the vanguard of the Latin American revolution." Yet, the failures of Castroite guerrilla movements during the late 1960s further convinced Moscow of the unproductiveness of this approach.[15]

This Soviet view changed sharply in the late 1970s with the Sandinistas' success in Nicaragua. Soviet theoreticians who previously had heaped scorn on Cuban concepts of revolution now indulged in revisionist payments of respect to Guevara's theory of guerrilla warfare and declared that armed struggle was the only option in the hemisphere. Local pro-Moscow communist parties from Uruguay to Guatemala ritualistically endorsed such a strategy and formed alliances with Castroite guerrilla movements and the broad political fronts opposing the standing governments in the region. The formula of a diverse political front combined with factional guerrilla forces now was considered capable of substituting as the "revolutionary vanguard" for communist parties.[16]

The Nicaraguan revolution produced a sophisticated synthesis of popular-front techniques previously used by the Soviets in Latin America and guerrilla tactics. Since 1978 the key Soviet-Cuban tactics have included the unification of traditionally splintered radical groups behind a commitment to armed struggle in return for promises of training and material assistance; the placement of ideologically committed cadres trained since the 1960s in pivotal positions of the guerrilla command structure; the development of secure logistical supply-lines; and the insertion of Cuban advisers in the strategy planning sessions of the guerrilla movements to ensure control of the movements — and of their governments once they have achieved power. This process, aided by a huge intelligence and political infrastructure built up since the late 1960s, tightens Soviet-Cuban control over insurgencies.[17]

Significantly from the American vantagepoint, the strategy of unifying the democratic left with the guerrillas increases pressures on those center-left forces that traditionally have been aided covertly by the United States to counter insurgencies in the area. This strategy was reflected in Nicaragua in the formation of the Broad Opposition Front, a coalition of democratic political parties and representatives of labor and the private sector, and it is also evident in El Salvador in the presence of certain democratic elements in the FDR. The inclusion of Social-Democratic and Christian-Democratic forces in the guerrilla-controlled opposition creates a Spanish Civil War scenario in which substantial outside support is attracted to the guerrilla cause.

Salient targets of this popular-front mobilization have been the Catholic Church and elements of the Christian Democrats, traditionally bulwarks against communism in the hemisphere. Jesus

Montane Oropesa, a member of Cuba's Politbureau Secretariat and the Director of the General Department of Foreign Relations of the Cuban Communist Party, summarized the new strategy at the International Theoretical Conference in Havana on April 3, 1981:

> The fruits and knowledge we gain from the temporary strategic unity, achieved by Marxist-Leninists and Christians, are of profound importance. We must exploit the possibilities of this interesting and promising opportunity: Using this intelligent policy of *temporary strategic unity,* we must reach out to patriotic elements within the armed forces, the intellectuals of different political backgrounds, the middle class, and include sectors of the bourgeoisie. It has been demonstrated that without *undermining* or *impairing* the firmness of our purpose and convictions, we can cooperate on the basis of similar concrete objectives with Social Democrats, and we can reach even to Christian Democrats (Social Christians notwithstanding) and their reactionary bureaucratic hierarchy. . . . This is only a temporary strategy. We cannot always advance as rapidly as we want. We have to consider not only national but international factors as well. Sometimes this advance can be fast; in other instances, to ensure a strategy that would allow us eventually to be more expeditious, we opted to move cautiously and slowly.[18]

The unification of the guerrilla movements began in earnest in 1978 when Castro spent 48 hours to weld together the diverse groups that constituted the Sandinista forces. In the following year, the first of many unity pacts between the rival guerrilla forces in El Salvador were signed in Havana, and eventually the Farabundo Marti Liberation Front was established in 1980, coordinating four guerrilla forces and the Salvadoran Communist Party. The same process was applied to the Guatemalan guerrillas in 1980 and to the miniscule Honduran terrorist squads this past spring in Managua.

Most of these operations are planned and coordinated by the Americas Department of the Cuban Communist Party headed by Manuel Pineiro Losada. After a purge of the General Directorate of Intelligence (DGI) by the Soviets in the early 1970s, the Americas Department emerged in 1974 to coordinate and centralize all operational control of Cuban support for guerrilla movements. The operation brings together the expertise of the Cuban special forces and the DGI into a network of training camps, the covert movement of personnel and material between Cuba and abroad, while sponsoring propaganda support for the insurgents.

By and large the cadres of these insurgencies are veterans of the 1966 Tricontinental Conference and the Junta de Coordinacion Revolucionaria (JCR) established in 1974 in Paris to coordinate Latin American terrorist organizations. This network of organizations such as the Sandinistas, the Argentinian Montoneros, the Colombian M-19 and the Uruguayan Tupamaros has, in turn, established links with European and Arab terrorist organizations.[19]

Military training is conducted in far-flung areas from Cuba to the Middle East. Several camps in Cuba are dedicated exclusively to military training, including one in Pinar del Rio and another near Guanabaco, east of Havana. In the past three years alone, groups from nearly every country of the Caribbean Basin have been trained there in military strategy, sabotage, explosives and special commando operations. Since the late 1960s, the Sandinistas received training from the Libyans and the PLO in Lebanon, Syria, South Yemen, Libya and Algeria. Various Central American guerrilla cadres, according to Palestinian sources, fought with the PLO against Israel in past Middle Eastern wars and joined with West European terrorists in the early 1970s in acts of terrorism in Europe. An example of this international cooperation can be found in Tomas Borge Martines, the current Minister of Interior of the Nicaraguan Government, who in the 1970s acted as Castro's emissary to the PLO. Documents captured by Israeli forces during the invasion of Lebanon record training for Salvadoran and Haitian guerrillas as late as 1982.[20]

THE NICARAGUAN FUNNEL

With the triumph of the Sandinistas in Nicaragua, camps for the training of Central American guerrillas, as well as terrorist groups such as the Basque ETA, have been established in Esteli, Montlimar, Somotillo, Ocotal, Tamarindo, Puerto Cabezas, the island of Soletiname in Lake Nicaragua and several others in the Punta Cosequina area immediately across the Gulf of Fonseca from El Salvador.

Today Nicaragua has become a solid base for insurgencies in neighboring countries. An elaborate supply network extends from Nicaragua to the Salvadoran and Guatemalan guerrillas. The logistical support systems are arranged by a trusted Communist Party leader such as Shafick Handal, the Secretary-General of the Communist Party of El Salvador, from a variety of arms depots. To hide their hand, the Soviets encourage the use of the surplus American arms stockpiled in Libya, Vietnam and Ethiopia, and reconditioned weapons from World War II available in Eastern Europe. At the initial stage of the insurgency these arms are channeled through an elaborate and flexible network of routes that literally criss-cross Central America.

In the case of El Salvador, the arms, once deposited in Nicaragua or Cuba, are broken down into small lots and transported over land in trucks or on vessels down the estuaries of the coastal regions in Belize and Guatemala and directly into the Usulutan Department of El Salvador. The acquisition by Nicaragua of some 100 planes from Vietnam enhances the ability of the Sandinistas to maintain airdrops to the Salvadoran guerrillas on small bush strips in the remote rural areas of the country. As was demonstrated in North Korea and Vietnam, interdiction of such arms flows is an almost impossible task. Currently the Salvadoran guerrillas receive supplies nearly every night, including heavy artillery by overland routes through Honduras. According to the Department of Defense, the Salvadoran guerrillas are reinforced every 48 to 72 hours.[21]

FOOTHOLDS IN GRENADA AND SURINAM

Immediately after the coup in Grenada by Maurice Bishop and his New Jewel Party, the Cubans under the guidance of Ambassador Julian Rizo, a DGI agent whose previous experience included cooperating with the New Left in the United States, offered assistance in creating a 2,000-man Grenadan army, along with a popular militia. In 1982, Maurice Bishop visited Eastern Europe, Libya and the Soviet Union. Agreements between Grenada and the communist countries in effect integrated the island into the military communications system of the Soviet Bloc. Prior to the U.S. intervention, Grenada served as a transit point for Caribbean radicals destined for guerrilla training in Libya and Cuba.

A subsidiary target of the Soviet Union has been Surinam, the former Dutch colony on the northeast coast of South America. After a group of sergeants toppled the democratic government in February 1980, the strongman, Lieutenant Colonel Daysi Bouterse, a 38-year-old former physical education instructor, has been steadily courted by the Cubans and the Soviets.

By 1981, Bouterse in a secret meeting with Fidel Castro received promises of Cuban military and economic assistance. There are reports that Cuban and Nicaraguan advisers entered Surinam to help create a popular militia to protect Bouterse's regime against possible threats from Surinam's 2,000-man army. This first pro-Soviet government on the mainland of South America since the fall of Allende in Chile has publicly pledged to send an international brigade to fight in Nicaragua. The Cubans immediately introduced Oswaldo Oscar Cardenas, a confidant of Castro, as ambassador to aid in the training of the militia and the police. After the Dutch Government terminated its aid, Surinam signed a friendship treaty with Libya and pledged to defend "Cuba, Nicaragua and Grenada." The Cubans maintain their influence through the small Cuban-trained group of intellectuals of the Revolutionary People's Party who determine policy.[22]

The Soviets after reaching an agreement to establish an embassy in Surinam, finally sent Igor Bubnov, an ideologue from the Washington Embassy, to supervise the adoption of the "correct ideology" of the government.

NICARAGUA AS A MAINLAND PLATFORM

After the Sandinistas' triumph in Nicaragua, Cuba took effective control of Nicaragua's military and security forces. The number of military and security advisers to the new regime increased steadily after 1979, doubling in 1981 to some 2,000 within a total Cuban presence that may have reached as high a number as 11,000.[23]

The Nicaraguan military buildup and the consolidation of Sandinista control over that society clearly is aimed at creating an extension of Cuba's military shield in support of guerrilla struggles in neighboring countries. During the 1979–1982 period, the Managua Government received an estimated $125 million of military equipment and supplies from the Soviet Union alone. According to the Department of Defense, the Nicaraguans have some 50 to 60 Soviet T-54/55 tanks, 1,000 East German trucks and armored personnel carriers and 7,000 French surface-to-air missiles. The buildup has been fed from Libya's huge stockpile of arms purchased from the Soviet Union in the 1970s and from the equally large supply of weapons left behind by the United States in Vietnam. In addition to the $100 million of economic assistance provided Managua by the Libyan Government in 1980, another $200 million of weapons from Kaddafi's stockpiles have been pledged for use in Central America.

Responsibility for the control of certain institutions in Nicaragua has been assigned according to a division of labor among Communist Bloc personnel. Between 100 and 200 East German advisers are said to be reorganizing the country's internal security apparatus and intelligence system, as well as developing the elaborate military communications network linking Managua, Havana and Moscow. Fifty or more Soviet advisers supervise the reorganization and Sovietization of the economy under Moscow-trained economic planner Henri Ruiz, as well as overseeing the whole control effort. Some 70 Nicaraguan pilots have been trained in Bulgaria, and Bulgarian technicians are helping to organize the trade union movement. Training and instruction at the guerrilla camps is apportioned according to specialty and function among the Cubans, the PLO, the Libyans, the Vietnamese, North Koreans and Latin American revolutionaries.

The Nicaraguan Army has already grown to a combined force of 75,000 regulars and reservists. In addition, a force of unknown size is attached to the Ministry of Interior: it is believed to include specialized border troops and an elite commando detachment. Nicaragua's goal is to fashion a 200,000-man army, which would be roughly three times the military forces of the other Central American countries combined. The Nicaraguan military, with Cuban and Soviet technicians, has added 36 new military installations to the 13 remaining from the Somoza years and has extended the airfields at Puerto Cabezas and Bluefields on the Atlantic Coast and Montlimar on the Pacific to handle MIGs. The smaller airfields such as Papalonal, 23 miles northwest of Managua, were extended to facilitate the shuttle of arms to the Salvadoran guerrillas.

While the current Nicaraguan Air Force reveals a dependence on small, mobile gunships such as retrofitted Cessna-185s, T-33 jets and several reconverted trainers, South Yemen apparently has sold 10 Soviet-built MIG-17s to the Sandinistas, the addition of which would neutralize neighboring Honduras' present air superiority.

The Guerrilla Campaigns

It is against this larger background that the guerrilla wars in neighboring countries should be assessed, particularly the conflict in El Salvador. The inability of the Salvadoran guerrillas in 1981 and 1982 to mount a decisive offensive and their lack of popular support should not obscure basic trends in that war.

The Salvadoran guerrillas have recourse to a reliable base next door in Nicaragua, where Cuban advisers in a command head-quarters outside Managua can map strategy and provide consistent and reliable logistical support.[24] Operating from rural base areas near this logistical support line, the Salvadoran guerrillas, number-ing between 7,000 and 8,000 — plus a popular militia of around 12,000 and the "internationalist brigades" — have moved from a traditional hit-and-run strategy to one of coordination of brigades in semi-regular fighting. As of January 1983, certain guerrilla units have made the transition to a classical positional war, with the ability to pin down and hold regular army forces, while mobile units have encircled and in many cases destroyed the Government formations. The strategy of a "continuous offensive" by the guerrillas compels the Government troops to act in dispersement, unable to consolidate durable control over war-torn areas.

Unlike the Nicaraguan conflict, the Salvadoran battle is a classic war of attrition. The Soviet-Cuban strategy in this war is based on the premise that the Salvadoran Government cannot sustain a lengthy internal war financially, psychologically or politically. Since the initiative in the Salvadoran fighting continues to be on the side of the guerrillas, the Government is under constant and growing pressure, exacerbated by economic sabotage and uncertain popular morale. Moreover, the perceived stalemate tightens the Govern-ment's isolation in international forums and, as we have seen, fur-thers the erosion of support from the United States.

While the Vietnamese model has conventional forces sweeping into the capital for the final victory, neither Havana nor Moscow wants to tempt the United States with such a blatant pretext for possible military intervention. Instead, the drum-beat for negotiations by the guerrilla forces becomes an effective, if slower, road to victory. The ultimate goal of engaging in negotiations is to 1) allow the guerrilla forces to secure their military positions, 2) split the democratic elements in El Salvador by disagreements over tactics and the desire to end domestic violence and 3) lead to a coalition government that will pave the way for a guerrilla victory and/or control of the government.

A MATRIX OF DEVELOPMENTS

The foregoing have been at best strokes on a broad canvas. But that is precisely one of the main points of the preceding pages: namely, the breadth of the phenomenon that has been unfolding at the very strategic doorstep of the United States. It is a phenomenon, moreover, that has barely made an imprint on U.S. media reporting, let alone on U.S. public opinion.

How did it come about? We have tried to sketch the major causes and circumstances. Perhaps the best way to summarize them is in the form of a rough matrix.

On one side of the matrix stands the relative neglect by successive U.S. administrations of the areas, peoples and problems south of our borders. Notwithstanding occasional, usually belated and often myopic "initiatives," we have tended to take the region for granted in terms of our strategic priorities. We have been preoccupied by conflicts and crises elsewhere on the globe and by problems at home.

On the opposite side of the matrix is the extensive operational groundwork laid in the area by the Soviet Union and Cuba over the past two decades. Although their admixture has varied, there has been nothing really new in the techniques that have been applied: the careful creation of an expanding infrastructure of intelligence, recruitment and subversion; the nurturing of radical splinter groups; the cooption of key political figures; the schooling and training of revolutionaries; the infusions of weapons; etc. If there has been a novel touch to the combination of these time-honored techniques in the Southern Hemisphere, this has been the success of the Soviets and the Cubans in welding a "popular front" model that links guerrillas and terrorists with a broad diversity of democratic elements, including even those of the traditionally conservative Catholic Church and Christian Democracy. And while the perspectives in Havana and Moscow have not always been harmonious, the latest phase has featured a triumph of Soviet-Cuban unity of action over synthesis of doctrine.

On the third side of the matrix are the revolutionary opportunities in the region. They vary from sub-region to sub-region, but a common denominator relates to the disruptive effects of economic modernization upon societies whose frail political institutions have been largely incapable of accommodating to or even cushioning these effects. And although the Marxist-Leninist model has not, in demonstrated practice, offered the promised land, nevertheless it is particularly seductive to a youthful majority of the area's population who feel estranged from the established political processes of their societies.

The final side of the matrix represents the shifts in the global environment, notably the changes in what the Soviets call the "correlation of global forces." The trends in the overall balance of military power in favor of the Soviet Union — at the strategic and tactical nuclear levels, in the conventional arena and in the wider realm of power-projection — have been amply described and need not be repeated here. The relevance of the changing "correlation of forces" to our hemispheric scenario is that not only has it provided the Soviet Union with vastly improved means of projecting power over long distances and with a greater willingness for risk-taking: it has also clothed the expanding Soviet intervention in remote places with a contrived "legitimacy" that supposedly attaches to the global presence of a global superpower. This is reflected, in part, in the signal lack of support the Reagan Administration has been receiving in its Central American policies from our European allies. Furthermore, this "legitimacy" theme, which is persistently invoked by Soviet propaganda to cover their global adventures, also creeps into some American attitudes toward the unfolding hemispheric scenario.

This returns us to the more general subject of prevalent American attitudes toward the developments in Central America and the Caribbean. We noted at the outset that the larger picture of what is transpiring has been neglected partly because of the concentration of the U.S. media, and of the public debate, on events in El Salvador. Yet, one suspects that the failure to grasp the larger picture has to do also with a reluctance to contemplate that picture and with some lingering myths from the past. One of these involves the image of a "tiny Cuba" that is able to foment mischief in neighboring countries but, in the final analysis and despite Soviet help, will be incapable of mounting a direct threat against the overwhelming power of the United States.

It is this myth that obscures the realities of the remarkable qualitative escalation of the regional arsenals and conflict potential — of an accelerated buildup of modern, conventional forces and armaments that are directed ultimately against vital American lifelines and interests. The developments trace the prospective scenario of America's global strategy becoming hostage to its own backyard. As was suggested, this may be precisely the central objective of the Soviet Union, abetted by its willing surrogates who are looking for their own regional spoils.

NOTES

1. *Pravda,* March 17, 1982.

2. Associated Press, March 17, 1983, and April 14, 1983, and *New York Times,* April 26, 1983.

3. The Nicaraguan canal plans were first disclosed by Volio in *La Prensa Libre* (San Jose, Costa Rica) on March 25, 1983. This report came after the pro-Government newspaper *El Nuevo Diario* of Managua announced on March 10, 1983, that the Soviets were establishing a floating dock at the southern Nicaraguan port of San Juan del Sur. It is believed that Soviet technicians assigned to this project are also involved in the canal planning. Ambassador Kirkpatrick at a press conference claimed that the canal was part of the Soviet plan to accelerate its power projection into the Western Hemisphere. Only the *Washington Times,* on April 29, 1983, reported the Ambassador's remarks.

4. Much has recently been written about NATO's contingency plans in the area. The specifics of the "swing strategy" were outlined by John Cooley, *Christian Science Monitor,* October 11, 1979.

5. For a short overview of the oil traffic in the Caribbean Basin, see Lewis Tambs' testimony before the House Sub-Committee on Inter-American Affairs, "Guatemala, Central America and the Caribbean: A Geopolitical Glance," July 30, 1981.

6. Boris Ponomarev, "Topical Problems of the Theory of the Revolutionary Process," *Kommunist,* October 1971, p. 75.

7. The detentist line of local communist parties is best exemplified by the Declaration of the Conference of Communist Parties of Latin America and the Caribbean, Havana, June 1975 (reprinted as "Latin America in the Struggle Against Imperialism," *New Outlook,* December 1975). The short analysis of conditions in Latin America recommends close cooperation with "progressive elements" within the church and tactical alliances with other political parties. Despite the overthrow of Salvador Allende in 1973, the Conference still held that the Chilean model was valid. Armed struggle was reserved for Haiti, Nicaragua, Guatemala and Paraguay. This followed the line in defense of peaceful coexistence established by Leonid Brezhnev in Havana on January 30, 1974, where he proclaimed Cuba to be in the "socialist" camp and its revolution irreversible. Yet, Brezhnev praised the peaceful road to power and the warming of relations with the United States. James D. Theberge, *The Soviet Presence in Latin America* (New York: National Strategy Information Center, 1974), presents the best overview of Soviet policy toward the region during the detente era.

8. A good summary of the diversity of Caribbean socialist parties is W. Raymond Duncan, "Caribbean Leftism," *Problems of Communism,* May-June 1978, pp. 37–57. This article, however, was written before local parties received military and financial assistance from Havana and other radical states.

9. A lengthy analysis of I. Shavrov's article, "Local Wars and Their Place in the Global Strategy of Imperialism," is contained in David Holloway, *The Soviet Union and the Arms Race* (New Haven: Yale University, 1983), pp. 83–94.

10. Soviet strategists in the late 1970s began a reevaluation of the role of the Soviet Army in Third World conflicts. Admiral Sergei Gorshkov, the architect of the Soviet bluewater navy, in *Naval Power in Soviet Policy* (Moscow: Voyenizdat, 1979) stressed the strategic importance of creating capabilities to paralyze or deter the West in secondary theaters — in other words, a policy of strategic denial. *War and Army,* by D.A. Volkogonov

(Moscow: Voyenizdat, 1977), pp. 354–355, stressed the new role of the Soviet military in deterring aggression against and strengthening the "progressive forces" in the developing world.

11. Rand Corporation analysts Stephen Hosmer and Thomas Wolfe in *Soviet Policy and Practice Toward Third World Conflicts,* (Rand Corporation, Lexington, MA: Lexington Books, 1983), pp. 79–109, have outlined the strategy behind the Soviet-Cuban alliance since Angola, terming the Soviet use of a proxy "cooperative intervention." The authors stress that there are convergent, but not identical, interests between the Soviet Union and Cuba to intervene directly in the Third World. In *A Strategy for Dealing with Cuba in the 1980s* (Rand Corporation, September 1982), Edward Gonzalez emphasizes the heightened strategic importance of the militarization of the island and the conventional threat it poses to the Caribbean Basin nations. Although the author takes the position that the Cuban military buildup is simply a defensive measure, Carla Anne Robbins in the chapter, "Cuba," in *Security Policies of Developing Countries* (Lexington Books, 1982), edited by Edward Kolodziej and Robert E. Harkavy, details the professionalization and modernization of the Cuban military and the Cuban Government's sensitivity to the change in the "correlation of forces."

Details about the recent improvements in weaponry can be found in Christopher Whalen's "The Soviet Military Buildup in Cuba," *Backgrounder* (Washington, DC: Heritage Foundation, June 11, 1982) U.S. Department of State, "Cuban Armed Forces and the Soviet Military Presence," *Special Report,* No. 103, August 1982, and *New York Times,* March 28, 1983. Soviet conventional capabilities and their large intelligence operation at Lordes, Cuba, are reviewed by Jay Mallin and Ralph Konney Bennett in *Washington Times,* July 13 and 26, 1983.

12. *Washington Post,* May 27, 1983.

13. The possible presence of nuclear weapons on the island of Cuba and questions about Soviet compliance with the series of agreements over such matters has provoked a controversy between the U.S. Senate and the Department of State. For Senators Helms' and Symms' documentation of TU-95 and Soviet missile installations on the island, see *Congressional Record — Senate,* Vol. 129, No. 53, S5233–37.

14. Soviet theoreticians overhauled much of their doctrine on guerrilla warfare and the revolutionary potential of the Caribbean Basin with the triumph of the Sandinistas in Nicaragua and of the New Jewel Party in Grenada. For samples of this new Soviet enthusiasm for revolution, see O. Ignat'yev, "The Victory of the People of Nicaragua," *Kommunist,* No. 13 (September 1979, p. 95ff); Boris Koval "La Revolucion, Largo

Proceso Historico," *America Latina,* No. 3, 1980; Sukhostat et al., "A Continent in Struggle," *World Marxist Review,* March 1981, p. 47ff., and the article by the leading Soviet Latin Americanist, Sergei Mikoyan, "Las Particularidades de la Revolucion en Nicaragua y sus Tareas Desde el Punto de Vista de la Teoria y la Practica de Movimiento Liberador," *America Latina,* No. 3, 1980.

15. Several accounts exist of the Tricontinental Conference and early Castroite efforts at spawning guerrilla warfare in the Western Hemisphere. The latest are Carla Anne Robbins, *The Cuban Threat* (New York: McGraw Hill, 1983) pp. 29–33, Maurice Halperine, *The Taming of Fidel Castro* (Los Angeles: University of California, 1981), p. 185ff., and Claire Sterling, *The Terror Network* (New York: Holt, Rinehart and Winston, 1981), p. 14ff.

16. The major treatise on the theory of vanguard parties and the creation of Third World armies modeled after the Soviet Union is Yu. V. Irkin, "Revolutionary Vanguard Parties of Working People in Liberated Countries," *Voprosy Istorii,* No. 4, April 1982, pp. 55–67.

17. The combination of a unified guerrilla structure and a political front composed of diverse, sometimes democratic elements is not peculiar to Central America. In Haiti, the pro-Moscow Communist Party PUCH in a 1981 Panama meeting sought to unify Christian Democrats, Social Democrats and the Haitian Fathers, a Catholic order, for armed struggle against the Duvalier regime. After the meeting, a terrorist group, the Hector Riobe Brigade, named after a guerrilla killed in the communist-sponsored uprising in 1969, was created and is supported by Libyan funds ("International Outlook," *Business Week,* April 18, 1983). This policy has recently failed in the Dominican Republic and Colombia, where the left is more divided.

18. *Granma,* April 4, 1981.

19. Claire Sterling, op. cit., p. 247ff.

20. Training camps and their curricula are detailed by the Department of State in "Cuba's Renewed Support for Violence in Latin America," *Special Report,* No. 90, December 14, 1981, and in "Cuban and Nicaraguan Support for Salvadoran Insurgency," *Congressional Record — Senate,* May 6, 1982.

Radical Arab support of the international terrorist network and the Central American guerrillas is extensively documented. A review of Arab and Southern Cone support for Central American revolutionaries is contained in "The PLO in Central America" by Shoshana Bryen, *Newsletter,* Jewish Institute for National Security Affairs. Vol. III, No. 21, June 1983. Libyan and Cuban cooperation in providing logistical support for revolutionaries and terrorists is discussed in John K. Cooley's account of the Libyan revolution in *Libyan Sandstorm* (New York: Holt, Rinehart and Winston, 1982), p. 227ff., and Claire Sterling, op. cit., p. 267ff.

The Israeli invasion of Lebanon produced a wealth of documents from the PLO's library. A selection of these have been presented in *PLO In Lebanon,* edited by Raphaeli Israeli (London: Weidenfeld and Nicolson, 1983). Pertinent documents on the Latin American and Caribbean connections are on pages 144–158 and 169–170.

21. The use of Nicaragua as an arms depot has been documented by the Department of State's *Special Report,* No. 80 and No. 90. The most detailed view of the flexibility and complexity of the logistical supply-lines to the Salvadoran guerrillas is George Russel's article in *Time,* May 9, 1983.

22. Author's interviews with former Surinamese Prime Minister Chin-A-Sen and "International Outlook," *Business Week,* February 14 and April 25, 1983. The degree of Cuban and Soviet involvement in consolidating the Bouterse regime was confirmed by *Time,* May 30, 1983.

23. The Nicaraguan military buildup has been documented in *New York Times,* March 10, 1982, which ran the transcript of the press briefing by John Hughes, Deputy Director for Intelligence and External Affairs in the Defense Intelligence Agency. In the briefing, Hughes showed satellite photographs of base enlargements and the extension of runways to accommodate MIGs. The Department of State in a White Paper entitled "Nicaragua: Threat To Peace in Central America," April 12, 1983, documented the arms buildup within the country and Managua's assistance to the guerrillas in neighboring countries. Independent assessments of the Nicaraguan arms buildup and the sources of supplies appeared in the *New York Times* on March 29 and April 27, 1983. Libyan supplies to the Nicaraguan regime were reported by the *Washington Post,* April 25, 1983.

The internationalist division of labor is confirmed in Shoshana Bryen's "PLO in Central America," ibid., and various State Department White Papers on the subject.

24. For a detailed analysis of the makeup of the Salvadoran guerrillas, see the author's article, "El Salvador's Guerrillas — The Winning Side?," *Freedom at Issue,* Fall 1983.

2 The Geopolitical Stakes in Central American Crisis

ASHLEY J. TELLIS

The U.S. foreign policy establishment is deeply divided today by differing perceptions of Central America.[1] "Doves" tend to view the problems in that region as stemming from indigenous structures of poverty, injustice and oligarchic, closed political systems, rather than Soviet interventionist activity. In contrast, "hawks" argue that the core issue revolves around Soviet-Cuban-Nicaraguan covert intervention and a Soviet effort to advance into and destabilize America's southern flank.

Both views seem only partially accurate. The dovish interpretation, while pointing to the need for a comprehensive solution embracing economic and social causes of instability, fails to grasp the crucial element of predatory Soviet actions. While hawks tend to be incisive chroniclers of Soviet tactics in the region, they generally fail to present a clear and compelling picture of the strategic purposes behind Soviet behavior.

It is hardly a surprise, therefore, that U.S. Caribbean-Central American policy ever since the Cuban revolution has been exemplary for its vacillation. While this has reflected partly the lack of an internal American consensus on the nature and gravity of the problem, it seems more significantly a product of the bureaucratic mentality permeating American political-military institutions, inhibiting their ability to think strategically.

Hence, U.S. perceptions of the Caribbean-Central American crisis have evinced dominant attention to the technical mechanics

This chapter appeared as an article in the Fall 1985 issue of Strategic Review.

of insurgency and subversion, the quantities and methods of covert transmission of arms to insurgents, and other manifestations of the "export of revolution." The surfeit of such information has made interesting grist for press briefings and Senate committee hearings, but has actually turned out to be a liability by obscuring an understanding of how this extensive and sophisticated regional infrastructure of arms flows and training is tied to a unified Soviet geopolitical strategy that, inter alia, incorporates vast logistic networks of surrogate and terrorist forces.

What follows below is an effort to transcend the contemporary analyst's preoccupation with details pertaining to logistics and insurgency,[2] and to sketch out instead the larger geopolitical stakes that underwrite such operations from Moscow's perspectives. In doing so, one argues *a fortiori* for renewed American attention, beyond operational details, to the broad canvas of Soviet strategic objectives.

HISTORICAL BACKGROUND

Soviet strategic purposes are best understood against a backdrop of U.S. policy in the Caribbean-Central American region. For a better appreciation of the problem, one must briefly return to the early 1970s.[3]

The ushering in of detente and the Nixon Doctrine in that period marked a shift from an activist American policy in the region to one of benign neglect. Influenced by the apparent successes of detente, the United States tacitly abandoned in 1974 its policy of economic denial against Cuba and attempted to normalize U.S.-Cuban relations, notwithstanding its unhappiness with Cuba's African adventures. Especially since the Nixon Doctrine implicitly banked on the emergence of influential regional actors, these developments encouraged Latin American-Caribbean nations to enter independently into expanding ties with Cuba and the Soviet Union, while Soviet theoreticians saw in such developments potent opportunities for the achievement of Soviet strategic objectives.[4]

In a larger sense, such developments served to raise Moscow's hopes of mending its previous breach with Cuba over the doctrine of "geographic fatalism," which held that the United States would react harshly (and adversely for Soviet-Cuban interests) to strong inroads of Soviet influence within the former's proximate geographic domain.[5] The doctrine of "geographic fatalism" certainly underlay the Cuban-Soviet disagreement in the 1960s over strategy and tactics associated with communist evangelization. The Soviets sought to restrain their adventure-seeking Cuban clients — who held the primacy of armed struggle to be indispensable to the success of revolution — because Soviet ideologues then perceived Central America neither as consisting of capitalist states nor as being an area ripe for "wars of national liberation." A series of American interventions, beginning with Guatemala in 1954 and culminating with the Dominican Republic in 1965, provided validation of "geographic fatalism."

The sudden loosening of intra-American relations in the early 1970s opened the way for a new, two-tiered Soviet policy: Latin American communist parties were encouraged to infiltrate trade unions and other parts of the political mainstream, while at the interstate level Moscow plied the normalization of diplomatic and commercial ties. Meanwhile, populist military coups in Ecuador, Bolivia, Panama and Peru were perceived by Moscow as elevating the objective of influencing regional armed forces, an institution hitherto immune to communist influence.[6] This unexpected bonanza, however, quickly disappeared with a spate of right-wing military takeovers in Uruguay, Bolivia and Argentina. Thus, the Soviet theoretical contrivance — "progressive military regimes can aid socialism" — hastily erected to take advantage of opportunity, collapsed as well.

With right-wing military takeovers having thwarted Moscow's bid to influence Latin American political outcomes through manipulation of domestic factions — a phenomenon the despairing Soviets termed "a reactionary counteroffensive unprecedented in Latin American history" — the path was now set by the early and middle 1970s for Moscow to resurrect Cuba as the revolutionary funnel through which to fuel such terrorist groups as the Tupamaros in Uruguay and Montoneros in Argentina. The victory of the Sandinistas in Nicaragua in 1979, however, proved to be the conclusive ideological victory for Havana over Moscow. Besides touting it as a historic watershed reversing the dismal trends that had afflicted communist fortunes since the ouster of Allende in Chile in 1973, the Soviets perceived in the event the first real opportunity in two decades to bury the doctrine of "geographic fatalism."

Thus, a 1983 Soviet pamphlet on Nicaragua asserted that "the victory of the Sandinista people's revolution has materially shaken the foundations of the system of American imperialism's sway which had taken shape in Central America."[7] Soviet theoreticians who had previously heaped scorn on the Castro-Guevara-Debray concept of the efficacy of armed struggle now began to pay deference to the Castroist logic. This significant doctrinal shift, reversing the Soviet position of the 1960s, was confirmed when the Soviet journal *Latinskaya Amerika,* in its first three 1980 issues, gave initial approval to the hitherto rejected views of Che Guevara on the primacy of armed struggle. This affirmation was further supplemented by a report that a "WMR Commission on Problems in Latin America and the Continent" had concluded that "far from impeding armed struggle, as some petty bourgeois theorists contend with reference to the experience of the 1960s, the present international situation largely predetermines its favorable outcome."[8] Thus the world was introduced to the familiar Cuban tactics which have since acquired even stronger notoriety.[9]

SOVIET ARMS FLOWS AND PRESENCE

Since 1975, the Soviet Union has engaged in the lavish rearming of Cuba with modern weaponry utterly disparate from the mission of aiding simple insurrection. With the exception of the United States, Cuba has by far the largest and most formidable military force in the Central American Basin, a potency made manifest by massive transfusions of MiG-23 and MiG-27 aircraft, T-62 tanks, BM-21 multiple-launch rocket systems, BMP infantry combat vehicles, ZSU-23-4 SP anti-aircraft guns, MI-24 helicopter gunships, SA-2 and SA-6 surface-to-air missiles, Turya and Zhuk missile and torpedo-armed fast-attack craft, Foxtrot class submarines, Osa/Komar class missile boats and a Koni class frigate, as well as other stores amounting to a record 66,000 tons transferred annually to Cuba since 1981 — all this in conjunction with Soviet basing facilities at Cienfuegos and a heightened Soviet military presence on the island.[10]

This Soviet military presence includes a ground forces brigade of about 2,600 men, a military assistance group of 2,000, and the largest intelligence collection and electronic monitoring facility outside the Soviet Union, at Lordes. Cienfuegos itself boasts of protective submarine pens, advanced surface-to-air missiles, sophisticated electronic intelligence, electronic warfare systems and squadrons of MiG-21 and MiG-23 fighters. Indeed, Cienfuegos represents the linchpin of Soviet strategy in the Caribbean.

What is of serious concern, therefore, is not the possibility that the United States may be surrounded by numerous nation-states professing ideological orientations alien to our own; the United States has coexisted with such regimes and can continue to do so. Rather, the picture becomes unsettling from the U.S. vantagepoint when states discard their national independence to align themselves so closely to the Soviet Union as to assume the latter's foreign policies and objectives as their own.

Thus, what is really important is not simply the rearmament of Cuba per se — or, for that matter, of Nicaragua — as much as the goals embodied by the quality and nature of the armaments so transferred and the military facilities established in the wake of Soviet-aligned partisan victories. The bulk of Soviet arms transfers to both these states does not consist merely of infantry and personnel arms which might be construed as "defensive" in orientation; instead, power-projection, amphibious and transport assets, and high-quality strike/interceptor aircraft constitute the bulk of Soviet generosity.[11] It is logical to conclude that massive transfers of such weapons hardly mark the wherewithal with which insurgencies are ignited or stoked.

LOGISTIC INFRASTRUCTURE

Even more sinister than the arms transfers are the growing logistic networks that the Sovies have sponsored in both Cuba and Nicaragua. In Cuba at least three, and possibly nine, airfields have been upgraded to host the Soviet TU-95 Bear heavy bombers capable of carrying nuclear air-to-surface missiles. Since 1970 these have been routinely transiting from the Kola Peninsula to Cuban airfields in the absence of any U.S. protest. In Nicaragua, aircraft revetments to handle high-performance fighters have been completed at Sandino airfield; the runways at Puerto Cabezas and Bluefields on the Atlantic coast and Montlimar on the Pacific have been extended to host MiG fighters; and a new airfield at Punta Huete, when completed, will have the longest runway in Central America (3,200 m) capable of accommodating Soviet jet fighters, heavy transport aircraft and Backfire bombers.

Further, in addition to their massive numerical increases in military forces, since the revolution the Sandinistas have added 36 new military bases built to Cuban specifications.

Equally troublesome is the reported secret Nicaraguan-Soviet agreement for the construction of an interoceanic canal across the San Juan River and Lake Nicaragua, and the signed agreement for Soviet repair and use of the Pacific port of San Juan del Sur, which certainly opens the way for Soviet naval surveillance, basing and other military purposes.[12] When considered in tandem with the development of a major port facility at El Buff on the Caribbean coast near Bluefields scheduled for completion in 1986, with facilities that include a 1,000-foot pier and the ability to handle ships up to 25,000 tons, it is easy to perceive a strategy to sever the hemisphere and clamp a vise of Soviet naval projection around the Caribbean.

A GEOPOLITICAL DESIGN

Despite the obvious conclusion that such Soviet presence is immediately threatening to American interests in Central America, Soviet goals are in reality even more ambitious. They include nothing less than an elaborate encampment designed to effect "hemispheric denial" via a flanking movement directed against the sea lines of communications of Europe and Japan in case of conflict.[13] In their preoccupation with Central American "revolution," American analysts generally fail to take heed of the much larger implication of the Soviet presence in Cuba and Nicaragua: namely, that it signals a wedge being driven against the wartime reinforcement of Western Europe — and that this, in turn, is part of a broader design of global hegemony.[14]

Only geopolitical analysis can competently illuminate the fact that the principal threat to American power issues not from the minor alterations in the regional power balances, but from ambitious initiatives that project Soviet geopolitical thinking. The most useful geopolitical framework that demonstrates this fact is the Mackinder-Spykman formulation,[15] which suggests that the "World-Island" of Eurasia and Africa is the decisive arena of conflict for global control between a landlocked "Heartland" power (USSR) and a maritime "Insular" power (U.S.). This perspective of geopolitical realities led Mackinder to argue that the World-Island was not made up of three ostensibly separate continents, but instead could be meaningfully conceived of as a single landmass — "effectively, and not merely theoretically an island"[16] — with several "Rimlands" lying between the Heartland and the "Outer Crescent," the latter comprising the Insular power of the New World and other offshore continents and islands.

Conceived in geopolitical terms, the contemporary superpower conflict is essentially reduced to a conflict between a landlocked Heartland power and a maritime Insular power for control of the peninsular European Rimland, which has acquired particular importance within the World-Island because of certain historical, economic and cultural factors. When perceived in this context, the Insular strategy confronts a threefold task. The first task is to ensure that the Heartland power never succeeds in maneuvering itself into a position from which it could exercise effective control over the Eurasian-African World-Island. The second task of Insular strategy is that of maintaining permanently the requisite balance of power, both locally and globally, that ensures the defensibility of the peninsular European Rimland dike. Third, it is to ensure that the lines of communication linking the Insular power with its Rimland dikes are perpetually kept open for political, economic and military reasons.

Mackinder clearly understood that both the Marginal and Insular powers were doomed to slow political asphyxiation if they were unable to contain the Heartland power from progressively appropriating the World-Island within its hegemony. If such a situation were to come to pass, the Heartland, with all its internal assets comprising geographical location, manpower (with the related Mackinderian connotations) and natural resources — coupled with political control of the World-Island — would be decisively advantaged in terms of ultimate global hegemony. Conversely stated, the control of the peninsular European Rimland by the Insular power serves as a vital prerequisite that denies the Heartland power ultimate hegemony over the World-Island.

In this perspective, the Soviet strategic salient is to detach the peninsular European Rimland from the United States by force, by diplomacy, or by a combination of both, and toward that end to create a pattern of investments that would facilitate denial of access to the World-Island in general, and the peninsular European Rimland in particular, by the military forces of the Insular American power. The disadvantages of the Insular power are exacerbated when, in the event of conflict, the lines of communication linking the Soviet Heartland to the peninsular European Rimland are far shorter and more secure than the reinforcing sea lines of communication between the maritime Insular power, the United States, and the European Rimland.

Thus, the development of such secure internal land routes — with its associated technologies, both military and civil — between the Soviet Heartland and the marginal states on the European Rimland alters the power relations between seapower and landpower to the detriment of the the former. The crucial net consequence of this development only highlights the disadvantages accruing to the Western Alliance from the asymmetry of political-military objectives: In case of conflict, the Heartland power would commit its primary armed instrument — landpower — across relatively secure internal lines of communication to attain the primary objective of annexing and appropriating the peninsular European Rimland. The Insular power, in contrast, would be forced to commit its primary armed instrument — seapower — merely to secure uninterrupted access to the Western European bridgehead, without being able to influence the outcome of the crucial land battle in any immediate sense.

In this understanding, the Caribbean-Central American region is hardly the prized plum. The real target is, and always will be, the peninsular Rimland of Europe. With respect to the Caribbean-Central American region, the crucial question, as President Reagan asked almost inadvertently in his 1983 speech to Congress, is: "If Central America were to fall, what would the consequences be for our position in Asia and Europe, and for alliances such as NATO?"[17]

CUTTING THE NATO NEXUS

The primary goal, then, of Soviet political and naval-air presence in the Caribbean is to cement a series of forward investments enabling an interdiction capability effective enough to disrupt sea lines of communication that link the Insular power, the United States, with the peninsular European Rimland, and thus to impede NATO's "swing strategy" in case of conflict. Current NATO strategy calls for the airlift of three U.S. reinforcing divisions to Europe in an emergency, where they would mate with previously stored and forward deployed war materials, while simultaneously five additional U.S. divisions with heavy weapons would be moved by the Military Sealift Command and other requisitioned bottoms by sea. The optimal embarkation port for three U.S. divisions — the 2nd Armored, the 1st Mechanized and 5th Infantry — is Beaumont, Texas, on the Gulf of Mexico, whereas the other three — the 7th, 9th and 25th Infantry Divisions based in Hawaii, Washington and California, respectively — would be moved by sea through the Panama Canal and then eastward, south of Cuba.[18] Resupply would thus include shipment of some 23 million tons of military equipment required for repair, replenishment and rearming of NATO forces, besides the minimum economic requirements for the European civilian populace. Together this massive transfusion would involve some 3,000–6,000 sailings over a sea distance of some 3,000–4,500 miles in order to clear the logjam.[19]

Soviet strategy thus projects that Cuban- and Nicaraguan-based Soviet forces would engage in persistent harassment and sea denial operations, attempting to seal the four major choke points in the thirteen Caribbean sealanes through which all the reinforcements would have to pass. Both Havana and Cienfuegos offer Soviet naval and air forces a vantagepoint to interdict virtually all the sealanes connecting South America and Panama with U.S. Gulf and East Coast ports, as well as those stretching from the Panama Canal and the Gulf of Mexico to West European harbors.

In doing so, the Soviets would attempt to attenuate the American advantages of operating through the Panama Canal which, far from being obsolete, currently remains the key multiplier that enables the United States to maintain a three-ocean presence with a depleted one-and-a-half-ocean navy.[20] Since only 13 of the roughly 500 U.S. naval vessels are too large to transit the Canal, there is no reason to believe that American naval movement through the waterway in the future will be any less important than it was in the past — even though both the vulnerability of the Canal and the time-consuming transit raise serious questions about the effectiveness of such an undertaking in the face of a relatively short, yet sharp, conflict that the Soviets would opt for in a blitzkrieg drive across the European continent.

The consequences, at any rate, of such interdiction will necessarily have a more than proportionate impact, insofar as it would undercut NATO's critical advantage of superior reinforcement capability. This advantage lies in the fact that, while the maximum number of additional combat troops the Soviet Union could deploy in the European theater within a 90–120 day period could never exceed 50 per cent of its current forces, the United States, at least theoretically, would be able to more than double its combat troops within the same period, while allowing for a steady flow of reinforcements thereafter. Even if one assumes that all additional reinforcements were air-ferried to Europe, sealift would be indispensable for the transport of the heavy weapons and ammunition without which the troops could not cope in battle.

Notwithstanding the heavy U.S. investments in antisubmarine warfare (ASW) and ferry assets, it remains uncertain how a wartime American sealift would fare in the face of the growing Soviet submarine fleet and the numerous facilities that have mushroomed close to the crucial interdiction points around the Caribbean-Central American Basin. Since less than one-third of NATO's equipment is forward-deployed in peacetime, it is understandable why, particularly in the case of a short war, the rest of the materials would be urgently needed and why losses at sea would be irreplaceable for all practical purposes. Besides the fact that Soviet submarines today would confront much higher-value targets than have crossed the seas before, accomplishing the task of interdicting reinforcements to Europe is hardly dependent on destroying a large stock of Western shipping, but rather on simply destroying a high proportion of the crucial early shipments.[21]

COMBINED SOVIET LAND-NAVAL STRATEGY

The consequences of such a possibility are best appreciated against considerations pertaining to Soviet military strategy in Europe and the implications of the asymmetrical political-military objectives referred to earlier. The corpus of military thought suggests that the *Schwerpunkt* of Soviet activity would necessarily be the European Central Region, which would provide the likeliest avenue for a pre-emptive blitzkrieg-style attack emphasizing shock, mobility and intense firepower. The objective of such a rapid, sweeping campaign across peninsular Europe — with the aim of annexing it within a 10–14 day window of activity and prior to the arrival of substantial reinforcements[22] — would be to present American policymakers with a *fait accompli* legitimizing the annexation. The major operational responsibility for achieving that objective lies vested with the highly mobile Soviet land forces.

The task of Soviet naval and air force assets in the conflict is simply corollary to the objective of aiding the land elements to occupy the peninsular European Rimland expeditiously. Hence, the strategem of committing Soviet naval and air elements, together with those of their Caribbean-Central American clients, as far forward as possible is not directed at achieving command of the sea (which a Heartland power does not of necessity require in order to subdue its peripheral Rimlands) but rather at impeding the trans-Atlantic reinforcements that the American Insular power must commit if the Rimlands are to be defended.

The creativity of Soviet strategy, therefore, lies in its adaptation of that classic defense maneuver: trading a pawn to contain a knight. By using its subsidiary naval force elements in a contestational mode, it constrains the American Navy to an arduous struggle merely to secure access routes to the Rimland — a struggle that yields the requisite time for the interim Soviet conquest of critical sections of the European Rimland. Hence, even if the United States *ultimately* achieved the exigent "command of the sea" in a geopolitical sense, it would have attenuated value if the European Rimland was meanwhile ceded.

The fear that Soviet sea denial capabilities may indeed achieve their operational objectives was brought home ominously by Exercise

OKEAN '75, in which the Soviets practiced obstructing U.S. naval breakout into the South Atlantic while simultaneously interdicting convoys in the North Atlantic shipping lanes. World War II already had demonstrated the lethality of such an operation when some 50 German U-boats, without the aid of replenishment and air cover, sank over 260 ships in six short months in the face of an Allied two-to-one superiority in antisubmarine forces. Today, Soviet submarines operating from Cienfuegos not only benefit from replenishment and air cover, but also have the ratios exactly reversed to their advantage. As Admiral Robert Hanks has commented: "Taken alone, the Soviet presence in the Caribbean is of sufficient significance to warrant serious apprehension in the United States, but when coupled with other Soviet initiatives — especially in the South Atlantic — the larger pattern thus disclosed assumes even more ominous dimensions."[23]

While discussing anti-sealane missions, the consequences of Soviet operations from Nicaraguan ports must also be considered, especially in the context of the alternate shipping route that the United States may choose in order to escape Soviet interdiction. If the Soviets operate from San Juan del Sur, it is possible for them both to interdict U.S. shipping heading eastward from the Rimlands of the Persian Gulf to the U.S. West Coast and to monitor such U.S. West Coast naval installations as at San Diego, California.

However, the tactical issue of optimal interdiction of Western shipping still remains. On the one hand, the Soviet Union could choose to interdict American shipping in the Caribbean where, besides having access to prime targets at their point of departure, she would in effect draw substantial numbers of American ASW units from the European theater of operations for duty in the Caribbean. The net disadvantage of such a tactic is that Soviet units would be stretched to their operating limits.

On the other hand, the Soviets could use their electronic eavesdropping facility at Lordes, in conjunction with their intelligence auxiliaries (AGIs) and Cuban-based photographic-electronic reconnaissance aircraft, to identify suitable targets for opportunistic attacks conducted all the way along a 4,500-mile sealane from the Caribbean to the eastern Atlantic, where American escorts would generally be functioning at their operational limits. Whichever strategy is finally used, the Caribbean-Central American basin retains its pivotal importance in Soviet naval strategy.[24]

In this context, the naval ship visits program which began in 1969 was truly a landmark event in Soviet naval expansion. Since then Cuba has hosted a variety of Soviet ships, including the mammoth Kara-class cruisers. Numerous Cuban-based MiG-23 and MiG-27 sorties have been flown by Soviet pilots, and some TU-95s have been sighted with operational nuclear bomb bays, prompting intelligence sources to speculate about the possible presence of nuclear weapons on the island, as well as a furious debate between the U.S. Senate and the Department of State on this score.[25]

THE STRATEGIC NUCLEAR DIMENSION

The construction of a nuclear submarine docking facility at Cienfuegos and the regular presence of Ugra-class submarine tenders together with their associated support barges — reportedly capable of collecting radioactive effluents from Soviet submarines — gave notice of the secondary intention of Soviet presence: namely, eventually to service ballistic missile submarines (SSBNs) and nuclear attack submarines (SSNs) operating in the western Atlantic. Thanks to inhospitable geography, Soviet SSBNs departing on patrol have to traverse numerous choke points like the Bosporus, the G-I-UK Gap and the Kurile Trench before they reach their patrol areas in the Atlantic and Pacific Oceans.

It has been an article of faith among Western naval strategists that mining these choke points prior to hostilities will cause a high rate of attrition, devastating the Soviet SSBN fleet if it attempts a breakout to sea. However, the use of a forward deployment and replenishment facility like Cienfuegos preempts the need for Soviet SSBNs to traverse risky choke points in an emergency, increases their on-station patrol time and enhances their rate of survival beyond standard Western naval estimates. Hence, the Soviet Union is particularly interested in the Cuban submarine facility, both in order to reap the tangible benefits offered in terms of operational efficiency accruing to its Yankee-class SSBNs currently patrolling the Atlantic waters near Bermuda and Nova Scotia, and to service the Golf-class SSBNs which have occasionally visited the island since 1974.[26]

The Soviet conduct with respect to SSBN deployments has been highly eccentric and characterized by considerable ambiguity — thanks, in part, to the strident, albeit confused, 1970 U.S. response which culminated in the American-Soviet "understanding" over the deployment of offensive seaborne platforms. However, it is still unclear what the understanding's precise obligations are with respect to the deployment of offensive seaborne ballistic missile platforms. Both parties have interpreted the same with considerable leeway, leading the USSR to adopt an attitude of cautious probing in order to establish incremental precedents and test American resolve.[27]

Further, if the occasional visits of Soviet November- and Echo-class SSNs at Cienfuegos are harbingers of more systematic deployments — as most observers conclude — they could cause much greater trouble than is currently anticipated. American SSBNs, generally based at Kings Bay, Georgia; Charleston, South Carolina; and Bangor, Washington, are acknowledged to be invulnerable to sonar detection in open-ocean antisubmarine warfare; therefore, the ability of a Cuban-based Soviet SSN to trail continuously a departing American SSBN on patrol from its home port is fraught with ominous consequences for the American strategic posture. Although it is assumed that such trailing does not normally occur in peacetime, several American submariners have admitted privately that American SSBNs have been trailed on several occasions, but have broken trail within a few minutes of contact. It is reasonable to project that such Soviet "restraint" would not be assured during crises.[28]

What is generally overlooked is that such efforts at trailing are eminently consistent with Soviet ASW doctrine, particularly insofar as it pertains to neutralizing American SSBNs. Soviet doctrine suggests that anti-SSBN missions are best accomplished through continuous peacetime surveillance by SSNs, long-range patrol aircraft and AGIs which, when deployed off American bases, yield valuable information about the deployment schedules of their quarry and assist in deploying SSNs in ambush positions at base approaches, establishing stationary barriers in narrows and straits, and committing SSNs as mobile barriers amid the SSBN transit routes to the wider "sea rayons." Since neutralizing American SSBNs is a mission second only to safeguarding the integrity of their own SSBN sanctuaries in case of conflict, a prominent scholar has concluded that "continuous trailing of Western SSBNs after they have left their bases and are in their operating areas is one of the most important peacetime missions of Soviet ASW submarines, if not the principal one."[29]

The "fishing" activity of large Soviet AGI fleets and their "ocean investigating" units should be further reason for continued American concern, since they operate amid the critical links of the acoustic detection networks which feed the Navy Oceans Surveillance Information Center, monitoring ship and submarine activity in the Atlantic. The so-called SOSUS system has always attracted considerable Soviet attention, especially since the Cuba Missile Crisis when Moscow was forced to use SSBNs as a surrogate for IRBMs removed from Cuba. The large numbers of intelligence-gathering auxiliaries disguised as fishing vessels that forage American coastlines are likely to be deployed in a conflict to disrupt the underwater network of hydrophones, sonars and communication nets integrated into SOSUS.

Numerous instances have already been recorded when Soviet trawlers have broken SOSUS lines with grappling hooks, both to test American reactions and to collect cable samples for careful inspection.[30] In addition to other vital communication and geodesic facilities, the U.S. Navy's Atlantic Underseas Test and Evaluation Center in the Bahamas and Virgin Islands, which is critical to developing American antisubmarine warfare capabilities, is uncomfortably close to the scene of Soviet intelligence-gathering auxiliaries.

In a geopolitical sense, then, the secondary goal of the Soviet Union in the Caribbean Basin is the capability to sever the existing security sinews between the Insular power and the European Rimland, while simultaneously seeking to preserve the inviolability of its own coercive nuclear assets. The Atlantic Alliance, straddling the area Mackinder labeled the "Midland Ocean," was erected on the implicit premise that the European Rimland dike constitutes the Insular power's first line of defense — and that should this bastion ever fall to the Heartland, the Insular entity would be pushed back into erosive isolation and ultimate beleaguerment (the "Fortress America" phenomenon). It was therefore clearly understood that Insular interests on the European Rimland would be defended, if need be, by the *ultima ratio* of American strategic nuclear use directed against the Soviet Heartland.

The Soviet response to this defensive alliance was to amass gargantuan land forces astride the secure internal lines of communication in Eastern Europe, together with developing a vast arsenal of theater nuclear weapons designed to constrain the Rimland's options by increasing its dependence on the strategic nuclear reserves of the United States, the credibility of which was simultaneously mitigated by the growing Soviet strategic nuclear arsenal. The character of this strategy has now become painfully obvious: By amassing a numerical superiority in counterforce strategic nuclear systems, the Soviets seek, in effect, to neutralize the American land-based strategic nuclear forces (which alone possess time-urgent counterforce capabilities), thus pressing the United States to increase its reliance on SLBMs, which currently possess no counterforce capabilities. Should conflict ever occur, the Heartland strategy lies precisely in offering the Insular power a choice between "suicide or surrender."[31]

Far from being content with attempting to neutralize American ICBM spearheads, however, the Soviets are also actually seeking to counter and constrain America's sea-based countervalue assets as well. In an overall sense, then, the Soviet Union conforms to Mackinder's original prognosis of how the Heartland power might attempt to overwhelm the maritime alliance:

First, by building superior land forces capable of depriving the American power of the European bridgehead's ports and bases in a series of swift, decisive strokes, she seeks to deny the Insular seapower of its crucial bases by a landward attack that seizes them from the rear.

Second, by creating the requisite naval forces, she hopes to thrust onto the sea herself in a fashion that would, despite the considerable constraints of geography and operational capabilities, assist her both to deny the oceans to the Insular power's SSBNs — thus attenuating damage to the Heartland in case of conflict — and simultaneously to enhance the inviolability of her own SSBNs in order to keep the Insular power at bay and to procure political-military benefits in case of conflict. The secondary objectives in the Caribbean-

Central American Basin therefore dovetail perfectly into Soviet grand strategy.

INTERDICTION OF STRATEGIC TRADE

The *tertiary* goal of Soviet presence in the Caribbean is interdicting American strategic trade. The Caribbean sea routes carry more than 50 per cent of U.S. oil imports to domestic markets, as well as over 70 per cent of U.S. imports of strategic raw materials. That the United States is heavily dependent on sea communications for raw materials from Marginal lands is illustrated by the fact that since 1950 her ocean-borne trade has risen by over five times, in contrast to her domestic freight, which has only doubled. Quite logically, all thirteen Caribbean sealanes figure prominently among the thirty-one sea routes designated "essential" by the U.S. Government and subject to special protective concerns.[32] There is no gainsaying the fact that U.S. dependence on the Rimlands is crucially tied to her needs for resources, markets and bases — a fact recognized as early as 1954 when a Presidential commission reported that American well-being is subject to her becoming "involved increasingly with distant resources and markets."[33]

The United States is now almost wholly dependent on Rimland and Marginal nations for her consumption of columbium, mica, strontium, manganese, cobalt, tantalum, chromium, asbestos, aluminium, fluorine, bismuth, platinum group metals, tin, mercury and nickel. The Caribbean basis itself remains a principal source of many U.S. raw material imports, especially strategic minerals like silver, zinc, gypsum, antimony, mercury, bismuth, selenium, barium and rhenium.[34]

In her formative years, the United States could take refuge in isolationist stances when her industrial might was being forged in a strictly autarkical environment and when the Royal Navy was mistress of the Midland Ocean. Moreover, the Heartland was still then an expanse relatively devoid of military power and political and economic organization; hence modest naval forces could ensure the key to survival, and perhaps to empire.

Today the situation has dramatically changed on all counts. The United States has great need of the Rimlands for her own economic and political security, while the Heartland is now manned by a ruthless "garrison sufficient both in number and quality,"[35] capable of both interdicting Insular SLOCs as well as ominously reminding America's Rimland suppliers to take account of Soviet coercive power at their rear. Hence, the United States "must keep the freedom of the seas in order that, in Mackinder's terms, the vast population of the Inner Crescent may be free to interact economically with the United States."[36]

The loss of traderoutes and resource centers would be extremely detrimental to the U.S. economy. As Secretary of Defense Weinberger has noted, the United States and its Rimland allies "have sharply increased their dependence on raw materials from other parts of the world at the very time that these areas have become increasingly vulnerable to hostile actions."[37]

THE IMPERATIVE OF A STRATEGIC VIEW

Soviet aims in Central America are thus far more grandiose than "exporting revolution." Rather, Soviet strategy seems to embrace dual objectives. In the short run, the Soviet Union seeks to exacerbate the turmoil in Central America in the hope of establishing herself as a vital power broker whose acquiescence would be necessary to create a durable peace in America's own backyard — a posture consistent with the claim of Soviet ideologists that her superpower status vests her with a crucial voice indispensable to the resolution of all global problems. In the longer run, and more importantly in the context of the Heartland-Rimland relationship, the ultimate Soviet strategic objective is to mount the kind of power projection into the Caribbean-Central American region — or failing which, at least effectuate the kind of hemispheric denial — that would squarely interdict vital American interests and Western Alliance lifelines and "in effect hold America's global strategy hostage in the event of a larger conflict."[38] It is to this larger geopolitical objective that American strategic thinking must address itself.

The American policymakers' obsession with the "export of revolution" runs the risk of leading to a distraction from America's already severely strained defensive requirements in Europe and

Asia. In the process, it also obscures the three critical inadequacies — absence of superior NATO local denial capabilities, lack of globe-girding U.S. naval strength, loss of U.S. strategic nuclear superiority — which the United States must seriously confront if it is to defend its critical interests on the peninsular European Rimland dike with a fair margin of success. What is fundamentally unfortunate is that these inadequacies are as much consequences of Soviet initiatives as they are of American complacency.

The National Bipartisan Commission on Central America (the so-called Kissinger Commission) correctly argued:

> At the level of global strategy . . . therefore, the advance of Soviet and Cuban power on the American mainland affects the global balance. To the extent that a further Marxist-Leninist advance in Central America leading to progressive deterioration and a further projection of Soviet and Cuban power in the region required us to defend against security threats near our borders, we would face a difficult choice between unpalatable alternatives. We would either have to assume a permanently increased defense burden, or see our capacity to defend distant trouble-spots reduced, and as a result have to reduce important commitments elsewhere in the world. From the standpoint of the Soviet Union, it would be a major strategic coup to impose on the United States the burden of defending our southern approaches, thereby strip-ping us of the compensating advantage that offsets the burden of our transoceanic lines of communication.[39]

If viewed in strategic and temporal perspective, the intensifying Caribbean-Central American crisis was long predictable. The temp-tation of being able to hold America's global strategy hostage in her own "strategic rear" — manifest as early as 1961, when Khrushchev declared the Monroe Doctrine "dead" — was bound to become irresistible. What is intriguing, however, about post-1962 Soviet behavior is not simply that they have systematically transgressed the Kennedy-Khrushchev understanding, but that they have done so in such gradual and patient fashion — in the best tradi-tion of a longer historical view. They have been content with small and ostensibly marginal moves which in themselves have seemed unimportant enough to warrant a strong U.S. riposte, yet have cumulatively enhanced the legitimacy of the expanding Soviet presence. In this way, they have mounted a steady buildup of power in the Caribbean Basin, with the capability of projecting it to other parts of the Midland Ocean.

The time has come for the United States to recommit herself to containing the Soviet Union to the perimeter of the Hearland mass. This task can be mastered only if policymakers escape the morass of tactical details to gain a fuller strategic view of the Soviet offensive. Mackinder himself presciently perceived that "democracy refuses to think strategically unless and until compelled to do so for purposes of defense."[40] The history of this century amply bears out that the costs of complacency, if repeated, could be catastrophic.

NOTES

1. For a typical survey of the range of opinions, see "Struggle in Central America," *Foreign Policy*, No. 43, Summer 1981, pp. 70–103.

2. A copious review of such details can be found in, inter alia, "Communist Interference in El Salvador," U.S. Department of State, *Special Report*, No. 80, February 23, 1981; "Cuba's Renewed Support for Violence in Latin America," U.S. Department of State, *Special Report*, No. 90, December 14, 1981; George Russell, "Like a Sears, Roebuck Catalogue: How the Salvadoran rebels order outside help for their revolution," *Time*, May 9, 1983. The most recent report, "The Soviet-Cuban Connection in Central America and the Caribbean," U.S. Department of State and Department of Defense, March 1985, is an important improvement insofar as it confronts geopolitical considerations at the onset of its findings.

3. This section relies substantially for historical details on R. Bruce McColm's excellent survey, "Central America and the Caribbean: The Larger Scenario," *Strategic Review*, Summer 1983, pp. 28–42.

4. See "Latin America and World Revolutionary Process," *Latinskaya Amerika*, No. 2, 1971, in *Reprints from the Soviet Press*, Vol. XIII, No. 1, pp. 23–35.

5. A brief but excellent restatement of Moscow's hopes can be found in "In Support of the Struggle of the Latin American Peoples," *Pravda*, Editorial, January 26, 1971, in *Current Digest of the Soviet Press*, Vol. XXIII, No. 4, p. 12.

6. See Soviet comments on the role of the military and the Catholic Church in "Latin America and the World Revolutionary Process," op. cit., pp. 30–31.

7. I.M. Bulychev, *Nicaragua Today* (Moscow: Mezhdunarodyne Otnosheniia, 1983), p. 56.

8. "Latin America: A Continent in Struggle," *World Marxist Review,* June 1981, p. 47.

9. These details have been surveyed in *Special Report,* No. 90, op. cit. See also "Nicaragua's Military Build-up and Support for Central American Subversion," *Background Paper,* U.S. Department of State and Department of Defense, July 18, 1984, p. 17.

10. Details of Cuban rearmament can be found in "Cuban Armed Forces and the Soviet Military Presence," U.S. Department of State, *Special Report,* No. 103, August 1982.

11. A detailed survey of the numbers and particulars of such weapons can be found in *Background Paper,* op. cit. See also, "The Soviet-Cuban Connection in Central America and the Caribbean," op. cit.

12. Details about the interoceanic canal were first disclosed by Costa Rican Foreign Minister Fernando Volio Jimenez in *La Prensa Libre* (San Jose, Costa Rica), March 25, 1983, and reported in *Washington Times,* April 29, 1983. Also cited in McColm, op. cit. As part of a "bilateral trade agreement" Nicaragua leased the Pacific port of San Juan del Sur to the Soviets as "a port of call for Soviet fishing boats." Soon thereafter, however, a 7,000-ton dry dock and a 60-foot floating pier — much larger than required for fishing vessels — were towed into port.

13. Edward B. Atkeson, "Hemispheric Denial: Geopolitical Imperatives and Soviet Strategy," *Strategic Review,* Spring 1976, p. 33. That the Soviets perceive the Central American imbroglio in global reference was underscored by the World Marxist Review Commission, which (reiterating the argument of the Havana Conference) "pointed in no uncertain terms to the 'universal character of the struggle between the peoples and imperialism' and stated that 'the struggle of Latin America is a component of the worldwide political and economic battle'." "Latin America: A Continent in Struggle," op. cit., p. 49.

14. Karl Marx's insightful remark, "The policy of Russia is changeless . . . .Its methods, its tactics, its maneuvers, may change, but the polar state of its policy — world domination — is a fixed star," is cited in Taras Hunczak, *Russian Imperialism from Ivan the Great to the Revolution* (New Brunswick: Rutgers University Press, 1974), p. ix. A magnificent amplification of this theme may found in Edward N. Luttwak, *The Grand Strategy of the Soviet Union* (New York: St. Martin's Press, 1983).

15. Although Nicholas J. Spykman critiqued certain technical formulations of Mackinder's works, their perspectives were similar enough to warrant creation of a synthetic unity for purposes of anlysis. Mackinder's most important writings are collected in A. J. Pearce, ed., *Democratic Ideals and Reality* (New York: Norton, 1962), and Spykman's most useful works are *America's Strategy in World Politics: The United States and the Balance of Power* (New York: Harcourt, Brace, 1942) and *The Geography of the Peace* (New York: Harcourt, Brace, 1944). Both Mackinder and Spykman are indispensable reading for serious geopolitical analysis.

16. Halford J. Mackinder, "The Geographical Pivot of History," in Pearce, op. cit., p. 62.

17. The consequences of the European failure to perceive the Caribbean-Central American crisis as a U.S.-European problem has been illuminatingly reviewed by Irving Kristol, "A Transatlantic 'Misunderstanding'," *Encounter,* March 1985, pp. 8–21.

18. Details of NATO's "swing strategy" are reproduced in McColm, op. cit., p. 29. For a critical view of the "swing strategy," see Robert J. Hanks, *The Unnoticed Challenge: Soviet Maritime Strategy and the Global Choke Points* (Cambridge, MA: Institute for Foreign Policy Analysis, 1980), pp. 54–59.

19. As Admiral Wesley McDonald notes, "The generally accepted main threat which would be posed to this shipping by the Warsaw Pact would be torpedo and missile-armed submarines. It is well known that Soviet mining capability and environmental conditions of ports on both sides of the Atlantic make NATO's coastal waters and the use of deep-water approaches to them very vulnerable." See McDonald, "Mine Warfare: A Pillar of Maritime Strategy," United States Naval Institute *Proceedings,* October 1985, p. 49. Also, Rear Admiral S.A. Swartztrauber, "The Potential Battle of the Atlantic," United States Naval Institute *Naval Review,* 1979, pp. 115–116.

20. See Admiral Harry D. Train II, CINCLANT, *Hearings on Military Power and H.R. 5968,* DOD Authorization for Appropriations for FY 1983 before the Commission on Armed Services, U.S. House of Representatives (Washington, DC: USGPO, 1982), p. 976.

21. This crucial insight is systematically developed in Edward N. Luttwak, "European Insecurity and American Policy," in Edward N. Luttwak, *Strategy and Politics: Collected Essays* (New Brunswick: Transaction Books, 1980), pp. 3–20. An interesting operational assessment of this problem and a possible solution can be found in E.J. Ortlieb, "Should NATO Be 'Fustest with the Mostest'?" United States Naval Institute *Proceedings,* October 1985, pp. 159–162.

22. Michael MccGwire's assumption in his forthcoming book, *Soviet Military Objectives,* cited in Hugh K. O'Donnell, Jr., "Northern Flank Maritime Offensive," United States Naval Institute *Proceedings,* September 1985, pp. 42–57.

23. Hanks, op. cit., p. 22.

24. This issue is reviewed in great detail in Joseph Cirincione and Leslie C. Hunter, "Military Threats, Actual and Potential," in Robert S. Leiken, ed., *Central America: Anatomy of Conflict* (New York: Pergamon Press, 1984), pp. 173–192.

25. See *Congressional Record — Senate,* Vol. 129, No. 53, S5233-5237.

26. A potent reminder of Cuba's strategic location was provided when in November 1983 a Soviet Victor-III submarine was disabled 470 miles east of the South Carolina coast. The submarine wallowed dead in the water until help arrived from Cuba and it was finally towed to a northeast Cuban port for repairs.

27. For an illuminating exposition of the confusion surrounding the 1970 "understanding" and the consequences ensuing thereof, see James D. Theberge, "Soviet Naval Presence in the Caribbean Sea Area," in James L. George, ed., *Problems of Sea Power as We Approach the Twenty-First Century* (Washington, DC: American Enterprise Institute, 1978), pp. 181–195.

28. "Another Age?" *The Economist,* September 1, 1984, p. 16. The U.S. has often suffered demonstrable injury from this problem. In June 1983, Secretary of Defense, Caspar Weinberger admitted that the Soviet electronic sonobuoy washed up on the shores of Washington state was "capable of picking up a good bit of classified data" about the USS *Ohio* (SSBN-726) when the vessel transited into Bangor two years ago. See "Soviets Spy on Subs with a U.S.- Designed Device," *Chicago Tribune,* June 26, 1983, p. 13.

29. Milan Vego, "Submarines in Soviet ASW Doctrine and Tactics," *Naval War College Review,* March-April 1983, p. 6. See also, Milan Vego, "The Role of Attack Submarines in Soviet Naval Theory," *Naval War College Review,* November-December 1983, pp. 48–64.

30. Thomas S. Burns, *The Secret War for the Ocean Depths* (New York: Rawson Associates, 1978), pp. 152–159.

31. Henry Kissinger, *Years of Upheaval* (Boston: Little, Brown and Company, 1982), p. 256.

32. *Essential United States Foreign Trade Routes,* U.S. Department of Commerce (Washington, DC: USGPO, 1969).

33. Cited in C.F.J. Whebell, "Mackinder's Heartland Theory in Practice Today," *Geographical Magazine,* Vol. XLII, p. 634.

34. See C. Fred Bergsten, "Access to Supplies and the New International Economic Order," in Jagdish N. Bhagwati, ed., *The New International Economic Order: The North-South Debate* (Cambridge: MIT Press, 1977), p. 205.

35. Halford J. Mackinder, "The Round World and the Winning of the Peace," *Foreign Affairs,* July 1943, p. 601.

36. Whebell, op. cit., p. 633.

37. Caspar W. Weinberger, *Annual Report to Congress, FY 1983* (Washington, DC: USGPO, 1982), p. II-13.

38. McColm, op. cit., p. 28.

39. See *Report of the National Bipartisan Commission on Central America,* (New York: Macmillan, January 1984), p. 92.

40. Halford J. Mackinder, *Democratic Ideals and Reality* (New York: Henry Holt and Co., 1942), p. 23.

PART II

Focus on Nicaragua

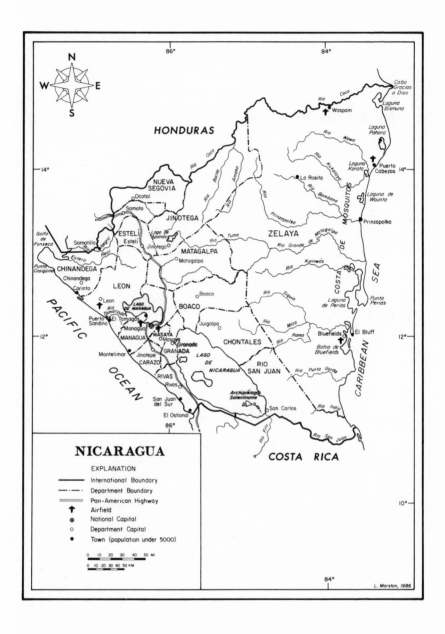

NICARAGUA

EXPLANATION

——————	International Boundary
—·—·—·	Department Boundary
══════	Pan-American Highway
✚	Airfield
⊕	National Capital
○	Department Capital
●	Town (population under 5000)

```
0  10  20  30  40  50 MI
0 10 20 30 40 50 KM
```

L. Marston, 1986

3 The "Mantos" of the Sandinistas

DOUGLAS W. PAYNE

During the Pancasan guerrilla insurgency in 1967, it was necessary for the *Frente Sandinista de Liberacion Nacional* (FSLN) to relay cadres and supplies between the *foco* base in the central mountains of Nicaragua and the FSLN underground in the cities. The routes were clogged with National Guard roadblocks as Somoza sought to isolate and eradicate the insurgents. A school bus carrying a baseball team and singing cheerleaders would drive from the city, easing through the checkpoints, then later pass by in the opposite direction. The wounded were on stretchers beneath the seats, where the outgoing supplies had been, covered with baseball gear.

The baseball team and its boosters were members of the FSLN. Once in the city, they would resume their identities as students, lawyers, salesmen, etc. The Sandinistas and other Latin American revolutionaries know this ploy as *el manto*. Literally translated, the word means "cloak" or "mantle."

THE ROOTS OF MANTO

The *manto* is one of three basic tenets of guerrilla war and revolutionary strategy with which Sandinista leaders and cadres became engrained under political-military training that began in the Soviet Union and Cuba during the late 1950s, and later extended to camps in Jordan, Lebanon, North Korea, Libya, Algeria, Yemen and inside Nicaragua.[1]

This chapter appeared as an article, entitled "The 'Mantos' of Sandinista Deception," in the Spring 1985 issue of Strategic Review.

There is *compartimentalizacion,* meaning the creation and maintenance of a cellular organization structure, each cell unaware of the others except for the fact that they exist. There is *chequero y contrachequero,* or check and countercheck, the general operating principle of gauging through maximum vigilance the relative balance between the strengths and weaknesses of your enemy and those of yourself. And there is the *manto,* or cover, which means appearing and behaving in a manner that will conceal your true nature and your real agenda.

The *manto,* like the other elements of this tactical and strategic system, is as old as war and inseparable from politics, especially for practitioners who believe in the unity of war and politics. The concept was delineated and enriched by Clausewitz, appeared in the military writings of Marx and Engels, was integrated into the doctrine of universal socialist revolution by Lenin, and has since been practiced with varying results by his students, adherents and opponents.

The successful *manto* is not perceived as such — at least not by a large enough number of influential observers to expose it — until the goals of the hidden agenda have been achieved. Stalin's abolition of the Comintern in 1943, to mask his determination to exploit opportunities for communist expansion provided by World War II, was a *manto.*[2] Castro's donning of rosary beads for the drive down from the Sierra Maestra was a *manto* — if only one facet, like one card turned over by a dealer who "plays poker while the world plays bridge by the book."[3] And during the Spanish Civil War, when the word became part of strategic language in the Spanish idiom, many perceived the lack of *manto* as a costly error on the part of the communist forces in Spain.

In the evolution of the FSLN, from its inception as a political-military organization nearly three decades ago, through the seizure of power at the head of a carefully controlled, broad-front alliance in 1979, and in its subsequent efforts to consolidate that power, there has been no lack of *manto.* The history of the Sandinistas is actually a two-tiered process: the strengthening of roots in an ideological community centered in Moscow and Havana, and the generation of a succession of *mantos* to mask a determined drive to achieve goals founded in that ideology.

To trace the fashioning and elaboration of *mantos* by the FSLN is to perceive the fundamental form of strategic deception practiced by today's Sandinista regime. As a political weapon over and above the more generally recognized tactical techniques of disinformation, it is central to the success and survival of any Marxist-Leninist revolutionary group that aims to secure and expand a foothold in close proximity to its perceived and powerful enemy.

The overthrow of Somoza appeared to be a Nicaraguan revolution. It was perceived and supported as a nationalist, Christian and social-democratic revolution by a majority of the participants and a better part of the world. Yet, for the FSLN these three labels were carefully cultivated *mantos* that camouflaged the intent of a small Leninist vanguard party, whose steadfast, uncompromising control of the military levers of the insurrection would provide the base for consolidating what it knew to be a Sandinista revolution. The intent is clear in the following passages from the May 1977 Political-Military Platform, the FSLN's blueprint for insurrection and beyond:

> The national liberation process will come about by breaking the chains that bind our country to the foreign imperialist yoke. The social liberation process will come about by breaking the yoke of exploitation and oppression imposed by the Nicaraguan reactionary classes' domination of the masses. These two historic undertakings will be indissolubly united as long as we have our Marxist-Leninist cause and a solid vanguard to provide leadership in the struggle. . . .
>
> It is a revolutionary war because, using the worker-peasant alliance with the guidance of a Marxist-Leninist vanguard, it will not only oust the Somoza clique but will create the conditions to enable the Sandinista process to *progress through the democratic revolutionary phase toward socialism.*

The *mantos* will be maintained throughout the process:

> However, strategic and tactical factors make it impossible, both nationally and internationally, to adopt socialism openly during this phase.[4]

In a January 1980 interview that appeared in the Cuban Communist Party newspaper *Granma*, Humberto Ortega of the FSLN National Directorate underscored the strategy of alliances in the successful overthrow of Somoza:

> Without a flexible, intelligent and mature policy of alliances on both the international and national levels, there would have been no revolutionary victory. . . . It was a policy that succeeded in isolating the Somoza regime, achieving nationwide anti-Somoza unity, and neutralizing the reactionary currents in favor of intervention.[5]

He stated further that the alliances could only be made

> . . .without being sectarian, and not with left-wing sectors alone, because that would have meant isolating ourselves. . . . And the only way to achieve this was to practice a mature, flexible policy by disclosing our revolutionary, democratic and patriotic program for national reconstruction.[6]

The program to which Ortega referred was first issued in an FSLN communique in early summer 1978. A year later it would be the basis for the government program recognized by the Organization of American States. In its non-ideological appeal to Nicaraguan nationalism, in its call for "a government composed of all of us," including the bourgeoisie, and in its guarantees of freedom of speech, organization and religion, the 25-point document was pure *manto*.[7]

What seemed like an ideological retreat was actually a maneuver to cement tactical alliances which the FSLN had been nurturing since its inception. The allegiance to the forces of world revolution was reconfirmed in the secret 1977 Platform, which called for "constant political–ideological reassessment using Marxism-Leninism as a guide," and pledged "to fight for the liberation of oppressed and exploited people in Nicaragua and throughout the world."[8] Meanwhile, an overlapping system of internal and international cooperation — with non-communist nationalists, Christians, and finally social democrats and sectors of the bourgeoisie — was accomplished by dissembling true beliefs in a cumulative series of appealing facades.

THE REVOLUTIONARY SEEDBEDS OF THE FSLN

The FSLN was fathered by the Moscow-line Nicaraguan Socialist Party (PSN).[9] Founded in 1944 while Nicaragua was still at war with the Axis powers and allied with the Soviet Union, the PSN organized openly until 1950, when it was outlawed in response to the increasingly anticommunist line of U.S. foreign policy. Leaders who were not imprisoned or driven into exile rebuilt the party underground and sought to strengthen its base by bidding party members in the business sector and at the National Autonomous University of Nicaragua (UNAN) to recruit for the party's youth wing. The father of Daniel and Humberto Ortega, at this time not yet in their teens, was a secret PSN member who ran his own import-export enterprise specializing in East Bloc trade. By the time Daniel and Humberto were officially integrated into the FSLN, in 1963 and 1965 respectively, both were already members of the PSN Youth, as was Casimiro Sotelo, who would lead the Sandinista delegation to the Organization of Latin American Solidarity (OLAS) in Cuba in 1967. Through the PSN, Humberto Ortega and Henry Ruiz, who is today as well a member of the FSLN National Directorate, attended Patrice Lumumba University in Moscow in the mid-1960s.

The three founding members of the FSLN — Carlos Fonseca, Silvio Mayorga and Tomas Borge — were all PSN Youth members, and by the mid-1950s operated a Marxist cell on the UNAN campus in Leon. Without advertising its identity, the organization's anti-Somoza campaign succeeded in the election of Fonseca as head of the UNAN student government in 1956. This event marked the beginning of the party's capitalization on common cause with non-communist sectors of Nicaraguan society against the Somoza regime. The following year Fonseca was the PSN's delegate to the Sixth World Youth and Student Festival in Moscow. Upon his return he wrote *A Nicaraguan in Moscow*, a glowing apology for Soviet orthodoxy that concluded: "Now the answer is the State."[10]

The ideological foundation was laid. Marxism became the idiom in which the budding vanguard rejected the reality of Somoza's Nicaragua and focused on a socialist future. Fonseca would be chief ideologue and theoretician until his death in 1976. Throughout, the goal and the tactical imperative remained steadfast: to destroy the

Somoza oligarchy while staying in the lead of the numerous other groups that opposed the regime. The line from Moscow to the PSN in the 1950s was to lie low and organize. But Fonseca and his followers, heirs to a history of political violence, yearned for revolutionary action. A model was emerging in Cuba.

Between 1958 and 1962, escalated repression by Somoza spawned over a dozen non-communist, non-Sandinista guerrilla actions against the regime. Led by members of splintering opposition parties, and in some cases by disaffected National Guard officers, they were poorly equipped, ill-conceived and easily neutralized. One group was led by Pedro Joaquin Chamorro, opposition hero and editor of *La Prensa,* who traveled to Cuba two months after Castro's victory seeking aid for an insurgency to be staged from Costa Rica. Castro turned Chamorro down for being too bourgeois. However, when Fonseca put in a request, Castro armed, and Che Guevara helped organize, a column of 55 Nicaraguans and Cubans who tried to enter Nicaragua through Honduras in the summer of 1959. When the group was intercepted and routed by the Honduran Army, Fonseca survived and escaped to Havana for further consultation with his benefactors. Tomas Borge arrived soon after, having been ousted from Nicaragua for organizing student demonstrations.

By early 1960 a plan had emerged for an armed popular insurrection based on the Cuban experience. A *foco* insurgency would be established, while the urban underground would infiltrate student groups in search of recruits. The plan caused a typical Old Left-New Left split between Fonseca and the PSN leadership, which accused him of military opportunism that endangered the party. When he tried secretly to reenter Nicaragua in the summer of 1960, the PSN announced his arrival, enabling his arrest and deportation. The dispute with the Moscow-line party was over tactics, not ideology: when the FSLN returned to civic organizing after the failure of the first *foco* attempt in 1963, collaboration with the PSN was immediately resumed.

THE MANTO OF SANDINO

The rift within the PSN led Fonseca, with Mayorga and Borge, to found in 1961 the National Liberation Front (FLN), an organically separate political-military organization with the goal of fomenting a Cuban-style revolution. By 1961, however, Fonseca was already uncomfortable with Che's pure *foquismo,* fearing that it was insufficient to galvanize the disparate and predominantly non-leftist opposition for insurrection. Perceiving Castro's success in unifying anti-Batista sentiment around a nationalist and non-ideological theme, Fonseca adopted a similar strategy by incorporating into the FLN the image of Augusto Cesar Sandino, the legendary guerrilla fighter who had driven out the U.S. Marines from Nicaragua in 1933 and become a hero for all opponents of Somoza, bourgeois as well as revolutionary socialist.

It is important to dwell at least briefly on Sandino in order to understand how *Sandinismo,* in and of itself, became a *manto* for those who have since operated under that banner. Sandino was a Nicaraguan nationalist and never a Marxist; his political goals did not extend much beyond the expulsion of U.S. forces. In the early 1930s he rejected Salvadoran Marxist Augustin Farabundo Marti's efforts to tie Sandino and his followers to the Third (Communist) International. After spending fifteen months in Nicaragua, during which time he became Sandino's personal secretary, Marti said: "His flag was only that of national independence. . . not that of social revolution."[11] But for Fonseca, that flag would furnish a thoroughly nationalist image to an organization that sought to bring the universal socialist revolution of Marx, Lenin and Che to Nicaragua. The Sandino cover would obscure the radical ideology that threatened to isolate the FLN and simultaneously provide the magnet for attracting and absorbing existing insurrectional elements in Nicaragua that merely sought the removal of Somoza.

In 1962, Fonseca officially changed the name of the National Liberation Front to the Sandinista National Liberation Front. The contradiction between Sandino's nationalism and world communism was conveniently ignored. New propaganda appeared as the FSLN began calling for all Nicaraguans to support it in a patriotic uprising in the name of Sandino. The first *manto* was on. Henceforth the FSLN would project an image of Nicaraguans seeking a purely Nicaraguan solution to Nicaraguan problems.

THE CHRISTIAN MANTO

By 1968, the FSLN was in disarray. The National Guard had destroyed the 1963 *foco* and the Pancasan insurgency of 1967. The extensive urban resistance that had been built to energize an insurrection in time with the Pancasan operation had also been smashed. The top FSLN leaders were dead, in prison or in exile. Carlos Fonseca had escaped to Costa Rica, and set about reorganizing for a prolonged popular war.

Meanwhile, in Medellin, Colombia, the Latin American Bishop's Conference was endorsing the new "theology of liberation" that had grown out of Vatican II. A wave of social and political activism was mounting among the clergy of Latin America. In Nicaragua in the late 1960s and early 1970s, Catholic religious orders, including the Jesuits, Maryknolls, Capuchins and Trappists, organized hundreds of study groups, youth clubs and Christian base communities (CEBs) to promote social action and apply political pressure against Somoza.

A major figure in the growing movement was a poet-priest, Ernesto Cardenal (today the FSLN's Minister of Culture), whose reinterpretation of the Bible called for political revolution as a prerequisite for spiritual transformation. When Fidel Castro was in Allende's Chile in 1971, he met with a conference of liberation theology priests from around the continent. His first question was: "Where is Ernesto Cardenal?"[12] Cardenal had already made two extended trips to Cuba in 1970–1971. Castro viewed him and the burgeoning liberation theology movement in general as "strategic allies of the revolution."[13] So did the FSLN.

The engineering of the "strategic alliance" began in 1969 with the FSLN's recruitment of Cardenal. As the latter himself reports:

> First, there was a letter from Tomas Borge, which he sent me from where he was hiding. Tomas said this was the first contact the Sandinista Front had had with priests, and he invited me to come see him. So I had my first talk with him. And afterward there were other talks, with him and Carlos Fonseca. Later I went to Cuba, and there I saw the Cuban revolution was love for neighbor — the gospel in action, "efficacious charity."[14]

By the time Cardenal returned from Havana, Trappist pacifism has been discarded in favor of the "divine revolution," which he proceeded to promote on journeys throughout Latin America, Europe and the United States.

Next, the FSLN recruited Jesuit priest Fernando Cardenal, Ernesto's brother (and currently Minister of Education in the Sandinista government). The FSLN was impressed by his leadership in a student occupation of the National Cathedral in 1970 to protest the holding of political (Sandinista) prisoners. Father Fernando became a clandestine member of the FSLN, stating later: "This people lay by the side of the road, and the FSLN was the good Samaritan, caring for that wounded victim."[15] He was a prime channel for FSLN access to the mass Christian activism and was instrumental in founding the Revolutionary Christian Movement (MCR) in 1972 along with Luis Carrion and Joaquin Cuadra, FSLN vanguard members whose covers had not yet been penetrated. (Today Carrion is one of the nine Comandantes, and Cuadra is the Sandinista Army Chief-of-Staff.) As a front organization, the MCR was a major source of recruits in rebuilding the FSLN guerrilla cadre and a propaganda funnel to international religious groups in Nicaragua for the portrayal of the Sandinistas as Christian revolutionaries.

In 1975, through Ernesto Cardenal, the FSLN then enlisted Nicaraguan Maryknoll priest Miguel D'Escoto (today the Sandinista Foreign Minister). Since 1970 he had journeyed throughout Latin America, Europe, Africa and the United States securing contacts as Social Communications Director of the Maryknoll Order based in New York. While Cardenal was on a U.S. speaking tour on behalf of the revolution, he contacted D'Escoto and arranged for him to meet with Front members during an FSLN international solidarity meeting in Mexico. D'Escoto became a clandestine member of the FSLN in order to spread "the cause of peace, justice and dignity for my people and all peoples, the cause I've committed myself to for Christ, as a Christian and as a missionary priest."[16] Further, he believed that Marxist analysis was the "divine whip" required to drive the Church back to the side of the poor.[17]

D'Escoto was also the director of Orbis Books, the Maryknoll publishing house and liberation theology platform. The cause of the Christian revolution began humming through the Maryknoll world distribution system, easing the way for FSLN representatives who were establishing solidarity committees in Europe and Latin America. Meanwhile, D'Escoto crisscrossed the United States arranging conferences and making presentations to American Catholic and Protestant leaders. Along the way he promoted, at the direction of FSLN commanders in Costa Rica, the spread of solidarity committees in the United States that would eventually number almost fifty and funnel, as did the committees on other continents, donated monies and material support from non-leftist as well as leftist sources to the FSLN through an office in San Jose, Costa Rica, and a bank account there in the name of Father Ernesto Cardenal.[18]

By 1976 the *manto* was solidly in place. In November, in a safehouse outside the southern Nicaraguan city of Granada, Father Fernando Cardenal met with Comandante Eduardo Contreras. Contreras, who had earlier organized, with the assistance of the Cuban DGI intelligence network, solidarity committees in Mexico that opened a pipeline of arms and materiel through Honduras, was at this time head of the Managua underground.[19] He gave Cardenal a double-bottom suitcase containing documents to smuggle out of the country, and returned to Managua, where he was killed in a shoot-out with the Guard. Cardenal traveled to Costa Rica, where the documents were edited by Comandante Luis Carrion and novelist Sergio Ramirez, by this time a secret member of the FSLN.[20] Cardenal then took the documents to Washington, D.C., where he read them to a U.S. Congressional committee. He later described the deceptive message that he presented along with his personal *manto:*

> When I accused Somoza and his regime of murder to the U.S. Congress, the lists of the missing, the tortured, and the murdered I presented were all peasant collaborators of the FSLN. The only names I gave were those of poor, lowly mountaineers, up where the guerrillas were. I did this to make things still clearer, and to be able to give an answer when I would be asked, "Fernando, for whom were you speaking when you spoke to the U.S. Congress?" The members of the committee did ask me this question.

And I told them the truth: "I am here in the name of the barefoot, lowly peasants of Nicaragua."[21]

THE ORTEGA BROTHERS AND FSLN TRAINING ABROAD

Castro's Cuba maintained an ambassador in Nicaragua until the Bay of Pigs in 1961. While Fidel and Che were supporting Carlos Fonseca's first attempt at armed incursion, the Cuban embassy in Managua sponsored open student workshops in order to inventory and cultivate promising candidates for revolutionary training. By the time Daniel and Humberto Ortega were integrated into the FSLN, Fidel was aware of their potential. In Cuba they received not only the basic guerrilla training given all FSLN recruits in preparation for the Pancasan *foco,* but also command-level Cuban Army instruction. Humberto was singled out for a final exam which called for him to plan and execute a full-scale mortar attack on a facsimile of the Nicaraguan National Palace constructed especially for the occasion.[22]

Back in Nicaragua the Ortegas became leaders of the Managua underground. Following the failed insurrection of 1967, Daniel was captured and imprisoned, not to be released until the 1974 Christmas hostage operation. Humberto escaped the crackdown, and by the fall of 1970 was in Cuba and a member of the newly restructured FSLN National Directorate.

Cuba had changed. Following the failure of Che's *foco* operation in Bolivia, the Soviet Union cut off the flow of oil and other economic necessities to Cuba in order to bring him more into line with Moscow strategic policy.[23] One result was the shutting down of the guerrilla training camps by the end of 1968. This was at the time, however, when the FSLN needed to replenish its forces for the prolonged popular war planned by Fonseca following the Pancasan defeat. Fidel had told the opening session of the 1966 Tricontinental Conference in Havana: "Any revolutionary movement anywhere in the world can count on Cuba's unconditional support."[24] Three years later the support was reciprocated for the FSLN.

Between 1969 and 1972 FSLN cadres were trained, through Cuban connections, in PLO camps in the Middle East and in North Korea.[25]

Recruits traveled from Cuba on Cuban passports through a network of safehouses provided by 4th (Trotskyist) International affiliates. During the 1960s the FSLN had developed close ties with Latin American 4th International groups that were also training in Cuba, especially the Argentine People's Revolutionary Army (ERP) led by Joe Baxter.

Through the intermediary efforts of Baxter and his European counterparts, including Pierre Frank and Alain Toussaint of the French Communist League, the FSLN was welcomed in London, Heidelberg, Cologne, Paris, Geneva, Brussels and Milan. It was during this period that the FSLN made initial contacts with the Basque ETA, the IRA of Ireland, the Italian Red Brigades and the Baader-Meinhof Gang in Germany.[26]

The first FSLN group traveled in 1969 through Europe to a camp outside Amman, Jordan, where it was joined by a group of FSLN students from Patrice Lumumba University in Moscow led by Henry Ruiz. There they received guerrilla training under the direction of George Habbash's Popular Front for the Liberation of Palestine (PFLP). The group then continued to North Korea for more advanced military training. A second group came through Europe in 1970 and was trained at a PLO camp outside Beirut, some of the cadres moving on to Algeria, Yemen and Syria before returning home through the network.

The third and largest group was led by Humberto Ortega in 1971-1972. It included not only recruits from the FSLN student front organization, the Revolutionary Student Movement (FER), which was directed by Bayardo Arce before he went underground, but also a harvest from the Front's efforts in the Christian movement. This group would later supply many of the officers directed by Ortega during the Final Offensive. From Cuba, Ortega led them to Czechoslovakia for a first round of training. Subsequently, after being joined by the last of the students in Moscow, the combined group proceeded to North Korea for six months of military instruction. In 1973, the cadres infiltrated back into Nicaragua, while Ortega set up a secret command base in Costa Rica. Daniel joined him after his release from prison at the end of 1974.

By the end of 1976 Carlos Fonseca was dead, Tomas Borge was in prison, and the FSLN had divided, over strategic differences, into two "tendencies": the Prolonged Popular War Tendency (GPP), and the Proletarian Tendency (TP) led by Jaime Wheelock, who had been ideologically trained in East Berlin and Leipzig and believed in the concept of organizing the urban masses as a necessary precondition of revolution. Humberto Ortega, who had been commuting between Costa Rica and Cuba since his return from North Korea, began to redevelop the strategic concept of insurrectionalism to integrate the two tendencies.

Humberto Ortega was supported by his brother Daniel and Victor Tirado. The latter, a member of the Mexican Communist Party (PCM), had joined the FSLN through the Moscow-line PSN in the early 1960s and risen to a place on the National Directorate. (Today he is a Nicaraguan citizen and one of the nine Comandantes.) The insurrectional line was further endorsed by Castro, as evidenced by the presence at the Costa Rican command center of Renan Montero (*nom de guerre*), the Cuban DGI agent assigned by Fidel in the mid-1960s to monitor the development of FSLN strategy. As of 1983 Montero was a Nicaraguan citizen, one of the 32 Guerrilla Commanders (Subcomandantes) under the National Directorate, and foreign intelligence chief in Tomas Borge's Interior Ministry.[27]

The insurrectional line was mapped out in the 1977 Political-Military Platform, primarily authored by Humberto Ortega, which included the broad-front strategy later summarized in Ortega's *Granma* interview. The Platform called for strict adherence to Marxism-Leninism within a united vanguard, the solving of strategic differences through coordination of both guerrilla and urban organizational tactics, and the absolute maintenance of military hegemony during all phases of alliance with non-FSLN sectors. In order to effect such alliances, it emphasized the necessity of masking the real nature of the FSLN beneath the public emergence of a third, moderate, and seemingly dominant "tendency" led by Humberto, Daniel and Tirado.

The *Terceristas*, as they came to be known, wanted to project a social-democratic, as well as nationalist and Christian, image that would extend the *manto* and be the linchpin in a broad unity of all anti-Somoza forces led by the FSLN. Further, the broad alliance would serve to attract political and material support from the emergent social-democratic forces in Latin America, especially in

Costa Rica, Venezuela and Panama, thereby enhancing the international isolation of Somoza and obscuring the FSLN's ties with Cuba.

THE MANTO OF THE "GROUP OF TWELVE"

The first step in projecting the required democratic image was the creation in 1977 of the *"Grupo de los Doce"* or "Group of the Twelve," a dozen members — at least ostensibly — of the bourgeois opposition to Somoza who banded together to give political support to the proposed *Tercerista* military offensive and to form ultimately an FSLN-backed provisional government. However, the Twelve was actually a front group recruited and controlled by Sergio Ramirez, a secret noncombatant militant of the FSLN since at least 1975. Two others among the Twelve were Miguel D'Escoto and Fernando Cardenal, the Christian *manto* of the FSLN. The group also included Arturo Cruz, then with the Inter-American Development Bank in Washington, and UNAN Rector Carlos Tunnerman.[28]

The Twelve was the FSLN's axle of alliance with the Broad Opposition Front (FAO) of democratic political groups, trade unions and private sector organizations that was formed under the leadership of Alfonso Robelo in 1978. As spokesman and representative of the Twelve in the FAO, Ramirez was the FSLN's man-in-disguise who played a key role in negotiations within the alliance and later with the OAS and the United States. In coordination with the military insurrection engineered by Humberto Ortega, Ramirez' position was pivotal in sustaining FSLN leadership of the anti-Somoza forces throughout the revolution. Nonetheless, Fernando Cardenal was able to dissemble at the time: "This Group of Twelve is an unusual one. None of us is a politician. None of us has ever been involved in politics. None of us is interested in power."[29]

PASTORA AND THE SOCIAL-DEMOCRATIC MANTO

The creation of the Twelve represented the political aspect of the broad-front machination. The enlisting of armed social democrats added to the *manto* on the military side.

Eden Pastora had been involved in armed activities in Nicaragua beginning in the late 1950s, and then worked to support the FSLN's

Pancasan guerrilla insurgency in 1967, although he never became a member of the vanguard. Impatient with the slow pace of "prolonged popular war," he retired to Costa Rica in 1973 and went into the fishing business. His ideological beliefs, like those of the brothers Fernando "El Negro" and Edmundo Chamorro, who had engaged in sporadic anti-Somoza violence, were a vague mix of social and Christian democracy.

These three agreed to join the FSLN fighting forces in the summer of 1977 in exchange for an FSLN promise that the revolution would create a pluralist system in which social democrats could present their version of the revolution to the people.[30] By incorporating these men and their reputation into a Southern Front army, the FSLN was able to secure protection and logistical support from the Carazo Government in Costa Rica, and money and weapons from the Andres Perez Government in Venezuela and the Torrijos regime in Panama, key factors in the eventual military victory.

A year later, in the summer of 1978, with the FAO threatening to rob the initiative through a general strike, the FSLN preempted the spotlight and beamed its *manto* to the world when an Eden Pastora-led commando seized the National Palace. By holding the Nicaraguan Congress hostage, the FSLN was able to gain the release of Tomas Borge and 58 other prisoners, $500,000 and their passage to Panama. It was also able to present its manifesto to the global media. This was basically the same program, with social-democratic accents, that had been issued several months earlier and that now called on all Nicaraguans — workers, students, women, Christians — to rise up and replace Somoza with a "democratic-popular government" guided by the FSLN and the Twelve, with all guarantees of basic human freedoms, including those of capitalists and the bourgeoisie.[31]

While Pastora, as an international hero, projected the outward image of FSLN social democracy, Humberto Ortega and the National Directorate stayed in the background. The facade was enhanced when Pastora was publicly appointed chief of the Sandinista army two months later. All FSLN field commanders, however, were instructed to report directly to Ortega and the National Directorate.

THE PRELUDE TO THE FINAL OFFENSIVE

The Fall 1978 insurrection, although it failed to oust Somoza, was a preview of the final act and showed the FSLN in control. When the United States attempted to mediate a negotiated settlement between the Somoza regime and the FAO, the Twelve led by Ramirez walked out, taking half the coalition with it and leading to a breakdown in the talks. The end of the talks effectively foreclosed the possibility of any democratic option to Somoza. The Prolonged Popular War and Proletariat tendencies, previously hesitant over *Tercerista* insurrectionalism, perceived that the strategy of military initiative, combined with the selling of the new FSLN image, had incited the first stage of a national mutiny that the National Guard had been hard pressed to put down.

In December 1978 the three factional FSLN tendencies met in Mexico City. They affirmed their ideological unity within the FSLN vanguard and agreed that their tactical differences would be subsumed under a coordinated division of labor in the overall insurrectional plan. It was also agreed that all tendencies would promote the *manto*. At a news conference following the meeting, Tomas Borge declared:

> Somoza painted us as Marxists. We have some Marxists with us, but the Frente is much wider. The concept of prolonged popular war was not Marxist. It is a military concept.... We have to be realistic and realize that it is in our best interest to have normal relations with the United States, to forget the past.... We are neither Marxist nor liberal, we are Sandinistas.[32]

A month later and in less public circumstances — in fact, in a letter to one of his field commanders — Humberto Ortega summarized the results of the strategy of the 1977 Platform:

> Without slogans of "Marxist orthodoxy," without ultra-leftist phrases such as "power only for the workers," "toward the dictatorship of the Proletariat," etc., we have been able — without losing at any time our revolutionary Marxist-Leninist Sandinista identity — to rally all our people around the FSLN....[33]

The prelude to the final offensive was the formal unification in March 1979 of the FSLN tendencies and the announcement of a combined National Directorate with equal representation from each. The *Terceristas* were represented by the Ortega Brothers and Victor Tirado. Tomas Borge, Henry Ruiz and Bayardo Arce came from the GPP. Jaime Wheelock, Luis Carrion and Carlos Nunez represented the Proletariats. There were no armed social democrats from the Pastora–Chamorro camp and no civilians. The Directorate, as it remains today, was pure FSLN vanguard.

Fidel Castro, who had orchestrated the previous meeting in Mexico City, made unity a *quid pro quo* for a massive infusion of military aid through Costa Rica to fuel the final assault.[34] Furthermore, Fidel's supervisory hand on the FSLN through DGI agent Renan Montero had been reinforced by the presence in the Costa Rica command center of Julian Lopez, a DGI political specialist who would monitor the creation of the Junta of the Government of National Reconstruction that the FSLN would present to the OAS for recognition during the final offensive. Since 1979 Lopez has been the Cuban Ambassador to Nicaragua.[35]

THE MANTO OF THE JUNTA

As the fighting escalated in June 1979, few expected Somoza to survive. But in order to ensure the hegemony required to consolidate power and "progress through the democratic revolutionary phase toward socialism,"[36] the FSLN had to fashion a final broad-front deception: the Government Junta. On June 16, after meetings between leaders of the entire anti-Somoza alliance in Puntarenas, Costa Rica, the five-member Junta and Government Program were announced. The Junta appeared to be composed of two representatives of the democratic opposition in Alfonso Robelo and *La Prensa* publisher Violeta Chamorro, two ostensible ideological moderates in Sergio Ramirez of the Twelve and Daniel Ortega of the FSLN *Terceristas*, and only one professed Marxist, Moises Hassan, leader of a leftist coalition of pro-FSLN political groups and mass organizations. In actuality, Ramirez and Ortega, along with Hassan, were all committed to the 1977 Platform and members of the FSLN vanguard.

The Government Program called for political pluralism, universal suffrage, a mixed economy, an apolitical army that would gradually be dissolved, and press and religious freedoms. Yet, the program also stipulated that, until the formation of a co-legislative Council of State at some undetermined time, the Junta would be able to make "refinements" in the program and rule by decree based on a vote of its members.[37] Through ideological obfuscation, the FSLN had built in the hidden majority. The Junta was the *manto* through which the real power, the National Directorate, would seek to reshape Nicaragua in accordance with FSLN ideology.

When the FSLN rolled into Managua on July 19, 1979, the vanguard numbered less than 500 members. [38] The FSLN knew, by dint of their Marxist-Leninist ideology, that consolidation and expansion, even under the banners of nationalism, Christianity and democracy, would soon bring the revolution into conflict with the "forces of imperialism." Several months after victory Comandante Luis Carrion commented:

> The revolutionary process will continue to press forward and deeper, and the two will eventually become incompatible. Imperialism will then take up an openly aggressive stance. World experience is crystal-clear. We don't have to look far or wide to be convinced that this will happen. It is our duty to keep ourselves prepared.[39]

THE MANTO OF A DISJOINTED FSLN

In a telephone interview during the 1978 Palace seizure, Eden Pastora emphasized the distinction between the true *Sandinismo* of the *Terceristas* and the dogmatism of the GTP.[40] In 1979, the National Directorate understood that their unity of purpose must remain camouflaged, that friendly forces in the West could be retained, cultivated and ultimately confused by the continued projection of an FSLN divided between moderates and hardliners — and that "pragmatists" like Daniel Ortega and Jaime Wheelock could act as magnets of outside support for the benefit of the entire FSLN. More important, the apparent presence of social-democratic strains in the FSLN following the revolution could give pause to the "forces of imperialism," provide breathing space for consolidation, and lure direct assistance from such significant sources in the West as the Socialist International and its regional network.

One of the first tasks of the State Security Department set up within Tomas Borge's new Interior Ministry was to reinforce the image of division. State Security chief Lenin Cerna created a network of informants and agents to promote the scenario to whoever was willing to listen, and amplified it further through control of the newspapers *Barricada* and *El Nuevo Diario* and the television stations.[41] The effectiveness of the deception was particularly evident in 1984 when the Western press and observers debated the "pragmatic" qualities of the FSLN's presidential candidate, Daniel Ortega.[42]

In October 1979, in a National Directorate policy paper delivered to the first Assembly of Cadres, the FSLN made it clear that, because of geopolitical vulnerability to American reaction, it was necessary to continue operating on the two-tiered basis that had been central in the seizure of power. First, it was noted retrospectively that the alliance that took the form of the Government Junta "was designed to neutralize Yankee intervention policies in light of the imminent Sandinista military victory."[43] Second, it was explained that, despite its sweeping triumph, the FSLN would have to maintain the appearance of democratic legitimacy within the new government so that there would be no outside intervention during the consolidation of power. The statement to the Assembly of Cadres was explicit:

> *Sandinismo* has not made radical moves to transform all of this power once and for all into the power of workers and peasants. This is because our political tactics are to develop conditions more favorable to the revolution and because our most urgent task at present is to consolidate the revolution politically, economically and militarily so that we can then move on to greater revolutionary transformations.[44]

Finally, the two-tiered strategy on the international stage was clearly delineated. The FSLN would seek "to secure the support of friendly countries. . . to neutralize the reactionary sectors," while acting on "the principle of revolutionary internationalism...to strengthen the Central American, Latin American and worldwide revolution."[45]

THE SANDINISTA MODEL OF SUCCESSFUL LATIN REVOLUTION

Manuel Pineiro Losada is the head of the Americas Department of the Cuban Communist Party, and the former head of the General Directorate of Intelligence (DGI). The Americas Department emerged in 1974 to coordinate and centralize all operational control of Cuban support for revolutionary guerrilla movements. The operation brings together the expertise of the Cuban special forces and the DGI into a network of training camps, the covert movement of personnel and material between Cuba and abroad, while sponsoring propaganda support for the insurgencies.[46]

In April 1982 Pineiro addressed a conference in Havana, sponsored by the Communist Party of Cuba, on the current state and future of revolution in Latin America and the Caribbean.[47] The conference included delegations from revolutionary groups and communist parties from throughout the hemisphere. Pineiro stressed the need for a common strategic line:

> It follows that, in the strategic conception and tactics, the revolutionary processes of Latin America must adopt, as their principal line, unity in the effort to defeat the overall enemy. This point of view is shared by all revolutionary parties and organizations in the region.[48]

Pineiro then held up the sophisticated synthesis of guerrilla warfare and broad-front techniques that produced the FSLN conquest in Nicaragua as a hemispheric model. In the military sphere the Sandinistas "reaffirmed the validity of the road to power opened by Cuba and have enriched the heritage of the continent's revolutionary culture."[49] With respect to broad-front tactics, Pineiro invoked Lenin to emphasize how the FSLN's success came through "taking advantage of any, even the smallest, opportunity of winning a mass ally, even though this ally is temporary, vacillating, unstable, unreliable and unconditional."[50]

Pineiro identified "social democracy, Christian democracy, the Christian movement and progressive military sectors" as "the four fundamental forces with which revolutionary forces in Latin America and the Caribbean have to develop tactical or strategic alliances."[51] Finally, the strategy and the mechanism are held together by a Leninist vanguard: "The Sandinista triumph reaffirmed the crucial value of the unity of the vanguard as the nucleus providing cohesion and orientation to the antidictatorial, democratic, anti-imperialist and revolutionary forces as a whole."[52]

Thus, not only is the *manto* in place and functioning in Nicaragua, but, in its successful adaptation by the Sandinistas to regional circumstances and the broader interplay of international forces, it is being elevated as a model for hemispheric revolution.

NOTES

1. Training camps and their curricula are detailed by the Department of State in "Cuba's Renewed Support for Violence in Latin America," *Special Report*, No. 90, December 14, 1981, and in "Cuban and Nicaraguan Support for Salvadoran Insurgency," *Congressional Record—Senate*, May 6, 1982.

A review of Arab support for Central American revolutionaries is contained in "The PLO in Central America" by Shoshana Bryen, *Newsletter*, Jewish Institute for National Security Affairs, Vol. III, No. 21, June 1983. Libyan and Cuban cooperation in providing logistical support for revolutionaries and terrorists is discussed in John K. Cooley's account of the Libyan revolution in *Libyan Sandstorm* (New York: Holt Rinehart and Winston, 1982), p. 227 ff., and in Claire Sterling, *The Terror Network* (New York: Holt, Rinehart and Winston, 1981) p. 267 ff.

Regarding Sandinista political training in the Soviet Union, see Carlos Fonseca, *Un Nicaraguense en Moscu* (Managua: Publicaciones de Unidad No. 4, 1958) reprinted in Carlos Fonseca, *Bajo la Bandera del Sandinismo: Textos Politicos* (Managua: Editorial Nueva Nicaragua, 1981).

2. For a detailed analysis of Stalin's deception, see Stephen de Mowbray, "Soviet Deception and the Onset of the Cold War," *Encounter*, July–August 1984.

3. Gabrial Cabrera Infante, from the Foreword to *Family Portrait with Fidel* by Carlos Franqui (New York: Random House, 1984), p. xvi.

4. FSLN National Directorate, *Nicaragua: On the General Political-Military Platform of Struggle of the Sandinista Front for National Liberation for the Triumph of the Sandinista Revolution*, 1977. The author's copy was obtained from former Sandinistas. Emphasis supplied.

5. The interview, conducted by exiled Chilean journalist Marta Harnecker, originally appeared in *Granma* on January 27, 1980. The English translation appears under the title "Nicaragua—The Strategy of Victory," in *Sandinistas Speak* (New York: Pathfinder Press, 1982). The passage quoted here is from pp. 77–78.

6. Ibid., pp. 77–78

7. FSLN National Directorate, "Why the FSLN Struggles in Unity with the People," *Latin American Perspectives*, No. 6 (Winter 1979), pp. 108–113.

8. FSLN, *Political-Military Platform*, op. cit.

9. The early history of the FSLN presented here was assembled from numerous sources including David Nolan, *The Ideology of the Sandinistas and the Nicaraguan Revolution* (Coral Gables, FL: Institute of Interamerican Studies, University of Miami, 1984); John A. Booth, *The End and the Beginning: The Nicaraguan Revolution* (Boulder, CO: Westview Press, 1982); *Nicaragua: La estrategia de la victoria* (Mexico City: Editorial Nuestro Tiempo, S.A., 1983); *Carlos, the dawn is no longer beyond our reach: The prison journals of Tomas Borge* (Vancouver, Canada: New Star Books, 1984).

Additional material was obtained during the author's interviews with Antonio Ybarra-Rojas, who has been a member of the Social Christian Party of Nicaragua since 1964. During the years 1965–1975 he was a member of the FSLN. After resigning in 1975 he was a professor at the National Autonomous University of Nicaragua. From 1979 to 1980 he worked for the Interamerican Institute for Cooperation in Agriculture in Costa Rica. He is currently a doctoral candidate in sociology at Iowa State University.

10. Nolan, op. cit., p. 20.

11. Agustin Farabundo Marti, letter to Uruguayan poet Blanca Luz Brum, quoted in Thomas P. Anderson, *Matanza: El Salvador's* Communist Revolt of 1932 (Lincoln, NE: University of Nebraska Press, 1971), p. 38.

12. "Fidel Castro y los Cristianos Revolucionarios," *Folletos Monograficos*, No. 6 (Managua, Nicaragua: Instituto Historico Centroamericano), p. 3.

13. Ibid., p. 13. For Ernesto Cardenal's account of his trips to Cuba and his meetings with Fidel Castro, see Ernesto Cardenal, *In Cuba* (New York: New Directions, 1974).

14. Teofilo Cabestrero, *Ministers of God, Ministers of the People* (Maryknoll, NY: Orbis Books, 1983), p. 27.

15. Ibid., p. 60.

16. Ibid., p. 96.

17. Nolan, op. cit., p. 75.

18. Author's interview with former Sandinista Miguel Bolanos Hunter. Bolanos organized solidarity committees in the United States while a student at Louisiana State University in 1977–1978. He became a field commander in the FSLN military forces in 1978. After the revolution he received training in Cuba and held a position in the F-2 section of the Sandinista State Security system until defecting in 1982. Interviews with Bolanos have appeared in the *Washington Post,* June 19, 1983, and in *Briefing Paper No. 1* (Washington, DC: Institute on Religion and Democracy, 1983).

19. Nolan, op. cit., p. 142.

20. An account of this operation appeared in the FSLN newspaper, *Barricada,* December 17, 1984.

21. Cabestrero, op. cit., p. 62.

22. Biographical material on the Ortega brothers was obtained from Resistance International in Paris, from *Patria Libre,* the official publication of the Nicaraguan Ministry of Interior and during the author's interview with Ybarra-Rojas.

23. Sterling, op. cit., p. 232 ff.

24. Ibid., p. 232.

25. Regarding the Sandinista PLO relationship, see Shoshana Bryen, op. cit., and *PLO in Lebanon,* Raphaeli Israeli, Ed. (London: Weidenfeld and Nicolson, 1983). Other materials on FSLN training abroad were obtained during the author's interview with Ybarra-Rojas.

26. For a discussion of links maintained by the FSLN with these groups today, see "World's Leftists Find a Haven in Nicaragua," by Juan Tamayo, *Miami Herald,* March 3, 1985.

27. Author's interview with Miguel Bolanos Hunter.

28. For a complete list of the Twelve, see Nolan, op. cit., p. 72 ff.

29. *Nicaragua: Combate de un Pueblo, Presencia de los Cristianos* (Lima, Peru: Centro de Estudios y Publicaciones, 1978), p. 96. Also quoted in George Black, *Triumph of the People: The Sandinista Revolution in Nicaragua* (London: Zed Press, 1981), p. 104.

30. Nolan, op. cit., p. 73.

31. Ibid., p. 91.

32. Bernard Diederich, *Somoza: And the Legacy of U.S. Involvement in Central America* (New York: E.P. Dutton, 1981), p. 221.

33. Nolan, op. cit., p. 68.

34. Ibid., p. 97.

35. Author's interview with Miguel Bolanos Hunter.

36. FSLN, *Political-Military Platform,* op. cit.

37. Junta of the Government of National Reconstruction, "Programme of the Government of National Reconstruction," in Jon Karmali, et al., *Nicaraguan Dictatorship and Revolution* (London: Latin American Bureau, 1979).

38. Henri Weber, *Nicaragua: The Sandinist Revolution* (London: Verso Editions, 1981), p. 55.

39. Ibid., p. 69.

40. Nolan, op. cit., p. 92.

41. Author's interview with Miguel Bolanos Hunter.

42. Three examples are " 'Pragmatic' Daniel Ortega to be Sandinista candidate," by Dennis Volman, *Christian Science Monitor,* July 19, 1984, "As Nicaraguans Prepare to Vote Success Undercut," by George Black, *New York Times,* November 2, 1984, and "Hard Questions on Nicaragua," by Michael Massing, *The Nation,* April 6, 1985.

43. The document was entitled "Analysis of the Situation and Tasks of the Sandinista People's Revolution" and is also known as the "72-Hour Document." It was delivered by the FSLN National Directorate at the "Rigoberto Lopez Perez" Assembly of Cadres held in Managua, September 21–23, 1979, and printed by the FSLN on October 5, 1979. The quoted passage appears on p. 8 of an English translation obtained by the author from former Sandinistas.

44. Ibid., p. 9.

45. Ibid., p. 31.

46. R. Bruce McColm, "Central America and the Caribbean: The Larger Scenario," *Strategic Review,* Summer 1983, p. 36.

47. An English translation of Pineiro's presentation appears as "Imperialism and Revolution in Latin America and the Caribbean," in *New International: A Magazine of Marxist Politics and Theory* (New York), Vol. 1, No. 3, Spring-Summer 1984.

48. Ibid., p. 122.

49. Ibid., p. 112.

50. Ibid., p. 125.

51. Ibid., p. 125.

52. Ibid., p. 124.

4 The Sandinista Regime Past the Watershed

Arturo J. Cruz

EDITOR'S NOTE: Then an emergent leader of the democratic opposition to the Sandinista Regime, Arturo J. Cruz wrote the essay that follows in early 1984, at a time when he still harbored the hope that the regime would yield to popular aspirations and peaceably open doors to political pluralism in Nicaragua. Especially because of its nature as a personal credo and as an expression of hope, the essay is reprinted here entirely in its original form, along with a postscript by the author that reflects upon intervening changes in that hope. This chapter appeared as an article, entitled "Nicaragua: The Sandinista Regime at a Watershed," in the Spring 1984 issue of Strategic Review.

As Nicaragua's revolution approaches its fifth anniversary, the intense debate — both internal and external — over the definition of its political system is reaching a climactic phase.

It is now clear that the revolutionary process is somehow irreversible — that Nicaragua will not return to its former feudalistic status which prevailed prior to July 1979. Yet, it is at least equally evident that the establishment, in its place, of communist rule will not remain unchallenged. Therefore, the leadership of *Frente Sandinista de Liberacion Nacional* (FSLN) has a choice between social democracy, which would assure the viability of the regime, and Marxism-Leninism, which will provoke endless confrontation.

Revolutionary social transformation in Nicaragua is not questioned. Even the staunchest adversary of the Sandinistas — the *Frente Democratico Nicaraguense* (FDN) — pretends to justify its military stand on the ground that the revolution has been betrayed by the FSLN. The dissidents in arms constantly reaffirm their revolutionary vocation. This is true of *Alianza Revolucionaria Democratica* (ARDE). The array of dissident forces working inside Nicaragua through civic action — the Church hierarchy, business leaders, *La Prensa,* as well as other non-Sandinista media, independent political parties and labor unions — incessantly manifest their willingness for a democratic accommodation with the revolution.

What the dissidents (including elements within the Sandinista regime, who at this time cannot express their feelings publicly) adamantly oppose is the revolution's Sovietization. This writer acted as moderator at the meeting where ARDE's creation was decided. It was agreed that in order for any individual or group to be eligible for membership in the organization, two conditions had to be met — to be both revolutionary and democratic.

The concern is one that is openly shared by the Central American nations, and in various degrees by democratic governments in Latin America and Europe.

THE CRUX OF THE NICARAGUAN PROBLEM

Largely moved by security reasons and showing a resolve to check the Sandinistas, the United States invokes the right to thwart what it perceives as a threat emanating from Soviet expansionism. Addressing a Joint Session of the U.S. Congress in the spring of 1983, President Reagan evinced a somber view:

In 1979, when the new government took over in Nicaragua, after a revolution which overthrew the authoritarian rule of Somoza, everyone hoped for the growth of democracy. We in the United States did, too. By January of 1981, our emergency relief and recovery aid to Nicaragua totaled $118 million — more than provided by any other developed country. In fact, in the first two years of Sandinista rule, the United States directly or indirectly sent five times more aid to Nicaragua than it had in the two years prior to the revolution. Can anyone doubt the generosity and good faith of the American people?. . .

No sooner was victory achieved than a small clique ousted others who had been part of the revolution from having any voice in government. Humberto Ortega, the Minister of Defense, declared Marxism-Leninism would be their guide, and so it is. . . .

The Sandinista revolution in Nicaragua turned out to be just an exchange of one set of autocratic rulers for another, and the people still have no freedom, no democratic rights, and more poverty. Even worse than its predecessor, it is helping Cuba and the Soviets to destabilize our hemisphere.[1]

There is a great deal of discussion about the actual involvement of Cuba and the Soviet Union in Nicaragua and, in particular, about Sandinista backing of the Salvadoran rebels. FSLN supporters argue that the evidence presented by the United States is inconclusive — that no smoking gun has yet been produced.

In this writer's judgment, the real issue is not the number of guns from Cuba which Nicaragua has smuggled into El Salvador. The real issue, rather, is that in its present form the Sandinista regime is perceived as a source of political unrest and economic decline in Central America. Consequently, the crux of the matter lies in finding an effective and permanent solution — such as that being earnestly sought by the Contadora Group — which would prevent the meddling of one state in the internal affairs of another and assure the respect by governments for individual rights within their borders.

The definitive removal from Nicaragua of Cuban and other Soviet Bloc military advisors, as well as an end to the Sandinista military buildup and to Managua's support of insurgency in neighboring Central American countries, must be part of the solution. Notwithstanding how important these conditions may be, they would achieve very little as a contribution to lasting peace and stability if they are not accompanied by a genuine FSLN decision finally to honor its unfulfilled 1979 commitment before the Organization of American States (OAS) to guarantee pluralism in Nicaragua. Central in such a formal decision should be a total separation of the Sandinista political party apparatus from the state.

Given the Sandinistas' predisposition to totalitarianism, this proposition may sound like a platitude to skeptical critics. Such critics may point out that this is foolishly asking a clique of hard-line ideologues to accept the failure of their project to establish a Marxist totalitarian regime — a doctrine which they consider as their gospel and departure from it as sinful. Nevertheless, it must by now be evident even to members of the Sandinista regime that the experience of the last five years corroborates the unsuitability of that regime's orientation to the objective conditions of Nicaragua and its people, of Central America and of the hemisphere — that the obsession of the most radical leaders and cadres of the FSLN with communism has undermined not only Nicaragua as a nation-state but also their own viability as a government.[2] By now they must realize that they are in serious danger of being toppled from power.

The Managua regime's recent gestures of somewhat softening press censorship, granting partial amnesty to its adversaries and the announcement of elections in November 1984 may constitute signs of Sandinista intentions to explore the possibility of a tactical settlement with both the United States and the regime's domestic opponents. It is obvious that the FSLN wishes to cut short its losses in the two areas where its vulnerability has been demonstrated. On the one hand, the Sandinistas desire an agreement with the United States, hoping it will stem the hemorrhage inflicted on them by U.S.-supported guerrillas. On the other, in order to reactivate an economy which has been reduced to a state of virtual paralysis, they need an entente cordiale with the Nicaraguan private sector, as well as with the other political parties.

Having squandered their credibility, it is little wonder that the Sandinistas' overtures have been received, at home and abroad, with skepticism. Nevertheless, some "Sandinologists" suggest that a final judgment regarding the regime's ultimate intentions ought to be tempered somewhat by symptoms of pragmatism in its behavior. In fact, the FSLN has allowed more than a modicum of pluralism — albeit more formal than real — the remnants of which still linger in Nicaragua. Thus far, the Sandinistas have been testing the climate of geopolitical tolerance in order to determine how far they can go on the road to Marxism-Leninism. They must have learned by now that it is not an easy journey.

THE SEEDS OF THE NICARAGUAN REVOLUTION

The 1979 revolution was mainly the result of a pervasive disposition among young Nicaraguans for social change. This is a feeling that began to take root in the previous generation.

In the latter part of the 1940s, one of the early expressions of this revolutionary animus was manifested by a new movement led by Pedro Joaquin Chamorro-Cardenal and known as *Union Nacional de Accion Popular* (UNAP). The movement was dissolved in 1955, when several key Unapistas joined some of the traditional political parties. Had this not occurred, UNAP might have become the vanguard of the revolution — the Democratic Revolution. The Sandinistas would subsequently fill the vacuum left by the Unapistas, successfully forging the revolution according to their own Marxist-Leninist model.

Although Carlos Fonseca Amador, as a young student in the early fifties, gave some consideration to an invitation to join UNAP, he desisted. The youthful leftist radical, who was to become founder of the FSLN, probably thought that UNAP was dull and empty of ideological content. The Unapistas' basic principles called for the decentralization of public power and freedom of labor organization. They proclaimed their opposition to communist totalitarianism and defined the ultimate objective of the movement to be national reconstruction, not the conquest of public power.[3]

It would be dishonest to deny that in 1979 there prevailed in Nicaragua a horrendous state of social injustice which loudly cried out for a remedy. In the 1960s, Nicaragua had expanded its exports of cotton, coffee, beef, sugar, tobacco, sea products and sesame. All basic grains — except wheat — were produced in the country and in quantities sufficient to meet domestic demand. In the industrial sector, national production made strides in the output of pharmaceuticals, textiles, fertilizers, insecticides, food and beverages. Assisting the economic upsurge was a functional financial system.

Large cotton growers became solid producers, and wealth brought for them a will to invest in cotton gins and vegetable oil plants, as well as in flour mills, distilleries, banks and urban development companies. Their profits also gave them a new life-style: fine residences in town as well as on the beach, shopping trips to Miami and vacations in Europe. At the same time, laborers continued to sweat in Nicaragua's plantations and ranches, earning meager salaries as their children went undernourished.

It must be said that Nicaraguan entrepreneurs were hardly the epitome of the heartless exploiter. Many of them were naturally inclined to be paternalistic. Prosperous businessmen not only learned about fine French wines, Italian shoes and expensive German cars, but, in a way became aware of what some years ago were referred to as "the rising expectations of the masses." Along with their chambers of commerce, industry, cattlemen, etc., they established a development institute to provide financing to small producers' cooperatives, scholarships and sundry social services. Nevertheless, this social attitude could hardly provide a basis for a stable society.

By no means could these token gestures stop the tide. A dictatorial regime's repression contributed highly to social unrest. Furthermore, the condemnation by the Church and the international community of the atrocities committed by the National Guard against restless campesinos was sapping the effectiveness of the military, making upheaval inevitable in the long run.

The sons and daughters of the bourgeoisie, who through their education had become aware of the need for social change, did not find in the traditional political parties a satisfactory response to their anxiety. Thus, many of them joined the FSLN in the rural areas and the city slums, preparing themselves for the ultimate consequences of what they saw as a necessary liberation war.

It is therefore important to underline the role of young Nicaraguans in the revolution. One of the conditions for the onset of the revolutionary process was precisely that the Nicaraguan population is largely young.

Another key element in the revolutionary process is the role of the private sector. Business representatives who for decades had found room for an accommodation with the Somoza dynasty gradually distanced themselves from it during the 1970s. In early 1978, everyone became incensed by the assassination of Pedro Joaquin Chamorro-Cardenal, which plunged Somoza into further infamy and raised the prestige of his adversaries to lofty levels. In

a decisive movement, the entire business community went on strike
and, somewhat gingerly at first, supported the FSLN as the
vanguard in the liberation war.

THE PIVOTS FOR SANDINISTA VICTORY

Four factors were determinant in ensuring victory for the Sandinistas. In the first place, Somoza acted for them as their catalyst
of turmoil. Hence he was their most reliable "ally," and therefore
it was convenient that he remain in the presidential bunker until
he was ripe to fall — and along with him the Liberal Party and
the National Guard. Had Somoza resigned even as late as the spring
of 1979, the Sandinista rocket would have fizzled.

Next, as was indicated above, the widespread popular indignation over Pedro Joaquin Chamorro-Cardenal's assassination proved
a windfall for the Sandinistas. Third, by enlisting the young, the
FSLN assured a popular uprising. Finally, the business entrepreneurs were a source of financial support, and they along with labor
could stop production — an essential step to make the government
crumble. The Group of Twelve — which from its inception had
at least four FSLN members — current Junta member Sergio
Ramirez, Minister of Justice Ernesto Castillo, head of the
Alphabetization Campaign Fernando Cardenal and Foreign Minister
Miguel d'Escoto — acted in the final analysis only and actually
as a Sandinista lobbying force.

The FSLN's alliance with the youth and the business community took shape under circumstances which ecumenically warranted
the ignoring of ideological preferences. By and large, the young
have remained steadfast Sandinista supporters. Immediately after
victory-day, businessmen started to act as a restraining force.

It should be noted at this point that Carlos Fonseca Amador, the
Sandinistas' Mao, found in Marxism the answers he had eagerly
sought. In his youth, he joined *Partido Socialista Nicaraguense*
(PSN) — which had been formed in 1944 — and subsequently
traveled to the Soviet Union, where his enthrallment with communism was reinforced. Upon Batista's defeat by Castro in 1959,
he began to develop ties with Havana, remaining a devout Marxist-
Leninist until his death in 1976.

The FSLN was founded in 1961 by Fonseca Amador, together with Silvio Mayorga (now also dead) and Tomas Borge, adopting a much harder line than the PSN. In spite of abundant evidence that he was not a communist, the new organization was named after the legendary, anti-imperialist hero, Augusto Cesar Sandino. This was also a shrewd political move designed to express nationalism. In fact, the FSLN has a monopoly on the term "Sandinista," which it uses as a brand-name for all the organizations it controls — e.g., *Ejercito Popular Sandinista* (EPS), *Central Sandinista de Trabajadores* (CST), etc. Non-FSLN political groups are strictly barred from using the designation.

In addition, the FSLN adopted Rigoberto Lopez Perez as one of its heroes. Rigoberto, as he is popularly known, killed Anastasio Somoza Garcia five years prior to the appearance of the FSLN. His adoption for worship was also part of the Sandinistas' public relations strategy, with the objective of capitalizing on popular anti-Somocista feelings.

It is then quite clear that the hard core of the FSLN is Marxist from its origins. Their quest for power is a unique case in political history. Without gaining any status of consequence, the Sandinistas struggled for sixteen years with incredible tenacity and personal valor. They were merely an irritant for Somoza; the establishment looked upon them with apprehension but without immediate fear.

Coinciding with the heart ailments which afflicted Anastasio Somoza-Debayle, the turning point in the Sandinistas' political life began in 1977, when the *Tercerista* faction relaxed Marxist rigor and pressed for insurrection. The key element which really afforded the FSLN an historical opportunity was their foresightedness. Ironically, the other two FSLN factions — the *Proletarios* and the *Guerra Popular Prolongada* — vehemently criticized them for their adventurism and lack of ideological purity.[4]

Subsequently, a series of events took place in which there was an interplay of resolve, fate and opportunism: the initial, bold *Tercerista* attacks in October 1977 against National Guard outposts and the first public declaration of The Group of Twelve; mass protests against the killing of Pedro Joaquin Chamorro-Cardenal in early 1978; the Indians' uprising in Mobimbo; the daring seizure of the House of the Congress and the September insurrection; the unification of the three FSLN factions into a National Directorate; and the final onslaught in 1979.[5]

During the insurrectionary period, the FSLN showed its flair for mounting spectacular operations: outstanding among them was the assault against the National Palace, site of the legislature. It is common knowledge that this action provided the Sandinistas with newspaper headlines throughout the world. Less known is the fact that at the same time they began to give some first indications of their potential for absolutism, disquieting non-Marxists in the broad alliance, among them Alfonso Robelo. One example was their persistent opposition to any solution, labeled as "Somocismo without Somoza," which did not guarantee a position of paramountcy for the FSLN. It was for this reason that, as did Somoza, they strongly rejected U.S. Ambassador William Bowdler's proposal for a popular referendum. Neither did they rest until achieving the disruption of the *Frente Amplio Opositor* (FAO), which they had originally joined in order to secure for themselves a place in that pluralistic body formed by legitimate opposition groups. After wards, however, when their own *Movimiento Pueblo Unido* (MPU) and *Frente Patriotico Nacional* (FPN) were ready, they abandoned the FAO.

Nonetheless, with a great deal of political acumen — even if for cosmetic reasons — the FSLN's leaders organized their first government with the participation of non-Sandinistas, both on the Junta and in the Cabinet. Such a timely flexibility contributed to assuaging the misgivings of erstwhile non-Marxist opponents to Somoza and disposed them to collaborate with the Sandinistas. The difficulty for establishing effective and long-lasting credibility rested in the fact that the Sandinistas' tolerance has been ebb-and-flow all along. Eden Pastora's closest followers ascribe this lack of consistency to the composition of the FSLN's Directorate by representatives of the three factions in equal numbers. Thus, they claim, the *Terceristas'* pluralist attitude is neutralized by the more radical elements. Based on my personal experience, however, I do not totally share their views.

The assassination of Pedro Joaquin Chamorro-Cardenal is by far the most relevant of all the circumstances which led to the

Sandinistas' ascent to power. One year before his unfortunate death, I met with him in Managua. During our conversation, I became aware of the genuine friendship which existed between him and the President of Venezuela. Thus, upon learning of his tragedy and amid my personal grief, the thought came to my mind that it meant Somoza's end — regardless of whether or not he was directly responsible. I also knew that this would have an impact on Carlos Andres Perez. The sequel proved my premonition to be correct: the Venezuelan President was filled with indignation. From then onward, he defiantly supported Somoza's ouster from power as the only way to free the people of Nicaragua and as a first step toward the establishment of democracy.[6]

THE SOVIET BLOC CONNECTION

It is reasonable to assume that only those at the top of the Sandinista ladder of power know exactly the depth and substance of the relations between the Soviet Union and Nicaragua. Formal diplomatic relations were established three months after the Sandinista government took office.

Following the exchange of ambassadors, delegations from Nicaragua have visited the Soviet Union, with the participation of both the government and the FSLN. This composition indicates that the evolution of the relationship has been at state and party levels. Notable among visitors to Moscow have been Tomas Borge, Humberto Ortega, Carlos Nunez and Daniel Ortega, who is also Nicaragua's head-of-state. The Soviets have sent delegations to Managua to attend celebrations commemorating the revolution's anniversaries and several officials on other missions. More important, during his visits to the Soviet Union, Daniel Ortega held discussions with Brezhnev and Andropov.

The results of the rapprochement have been the strengthening of political and ideological ties between the FSLN and the Communist Party of the Soviet Union (CPSU), as well as military assistance in substantial amounts and economic cooperation from the USSR and other Warsaw Pact countries.

Cuban influence on the Nicaraguan revolution is notorious and to a certain extent understandable. Fidel Castro is, first of all, a Latin American charismatic leader widely admired by Sandinistas and not a few other Nicaraguans. During the hard days, Havana was a safe haven and training ground for the struggling FSLN. Sandinista revolutionary and guerrilla commanders, soldiers and political activists quite often try to imitate Fidel in their speech and way of dressing — to the extreme that they are ridiculed by the people for their phony Cuban accent. Cuba is reflected in Nicaragua not only in the presence of Cubans but also in the Sandinista party structure, defense committees, grass-root organizations, titles and slogans.

In 1980, on the occasion of the first anniversary of the revolution, Fidel Castro visited Managua. He was the center of attention, upstaging all other dignitaries, among them the late Maurice Bishop of Grenada, former Venezuelan President Carlos Andres Perez, Prime Minister Price of Belize, U.S. Ambassador to the United Nations McHenry, PLO leader Arafat and Colombian Nobel Prize novelist Garcia Marquez.

There is hardly a high government or party official in the Sandinista regime who has not visited Cuba since July 1979. Nicaraguan delegations attend celebrations commemorating the Cuban revolution's anniversaries, and visitors from Managua to Havana and vice-versa are a daily occurrence.

Nicaragua's already existing bonds with the Communist Bloc may grow to a degree of indissolubility if one takes into consideration the thousands of scholarships being granted, year in and year out, to young Nicaraguans. Along with being educated as doctors, nurses, teachers and engineers (whom Nicaragua badly needs), they are also trained as soldiers or warplane pilots (an absurdity for a small developing country). What is worse, they may be receiving ideological indoctrination.

If Nicaraguan–Soviet Bloc relations were examined only superficially, the Sandinista government could claim — as it does — that the Nicaraguan people is master of its own destiny. Yet, the question arises regarding the extent of those relations. If they were normal in their content and intentions — i.e., limited to economic and cultural exchange — the Sandinistas cannot be blamed: after all, this type of foreign policy is conducted by the world's free democratic countries, including the United States. However, if the aims are to obtain support for the imposition of a totalitarian system, they can be considered as betraying the Nicaraguan people.

THE EAST-WEST CONFRONTATION FACTOR

Similarly, the Sandinistas cannot be criticized if they are buying weapons from communist countries solely for defense purposes. It is obvious, nevertheless, that if their ties with the Soviet Bloc entail military agreements for East-West confrontation purposes, they pose a threat to the United States and Nicaragua's neighbors. The Sandinista regime must therefore be analyzed in that context.

The figures of 2,000 Cuban military advisors and 4,000 civilians stationed in Nicaragua are generally accepted as fairly accurate.[7] Washington views Cuba's influence in Nicaragua with alarm, regarding it as a Soviet proxy in the Third World which presents a challenge to U.S. vital interests. Of particular concern to the United States is the knowledge that the effectiveness of the Cuban Air Force for action in the region can be enhanced with bases on Central American soil.[8] The American press, as well as other international media, have extensively reported the swelling of the Nicaraguan Armed Forces to 70,000, with Cuban technical support. East Germans, Bulgarians and the PLO are among those who have helped the armed and security forces.[9]

There have been rumors that Nicaragua might have provoked Washington's anger by trying to blackmail the United States into a sort of "Khrushchev-Kennedy" understanding (following the Cuban Missile Crisis of 1962) in order to guarantee the sanctity of the Sandinista-Marxist regime's existence — thus giving rise in Washington to the image of another Cuba being created, this time right in the middle of the Western Hemisphere. In this connection, Brezhnev's statement concerning the possibility of placing Soviet nuclear missiles close to U.S. shores, in response to continued U.S. deployment of its own missiles in Europe, highlights the strategic importance of the Caribbean basin to the security of the United States.[10]

If such a folly has ever been contemplated by the FSLN, it may have hardened the Reagan Administration's determination to curb the Sandinistas' design, by maintaining financial and logistical assistance to Nicaraguan counterrevolutionary forces and converting Honduras into a bulwark against Nicaragua. If this were the case, the Sandinistas would have grossly miscalculated the United

States' level of tolerance, exposing Nicaragua to serious danger in a senseless adventure resulting from sheer ideological fanaticism. What is worse, the FSLN might have been duped as an expendable pawn in the East-West confrontation. Its leaders have excelled in the arts of subtlety, but to quote a popular Nicaraguan saying: *"hasta al mejor mono se le cae el zapote"* (even the shrewdest may goof).

On the other side of the coin, there are authoritative, cautious opinions advising that the crisis ought to be placed in its proper perspective: the East-West confrontation factor in Central America should not be magnified, and consequently neither should the Soviet-Cuban threat.

Some have argued that Washington has no real disposition to negotiate, giving preference to the military approach, and that the Contadora approach will be effective only if the United States is willing to employ this mechanism for settling disputes.[11] This does not mean that such a school of thought, including distinguished Latin Americans, ignores the danger for the hemisphere if Soviet-aligned communist regimes were to take footholds on the mainland, as Octavio Paz views it.[12] Carlos Fuentes, like Paz a Mexican intellectual of international stature, does not see a Soviet threat to or from Central America because he considers Soviet interests there to be peripheral. Furthermore, he warns that a "quick fix would turn out to be a prolonged agony." Fuentes prescribes for Central America a "Zimbabwe solution."[13]

CUBA AS A MODEL?

Notwithstanding an unmistakable Cuban trait in the genesis of Nicaragua's revolutionary process, it might be an exaggeration to regard the Nicaraguan revolution merely as an offshoot of the Cuban revolution.

If one takes the rhetoric alone, isolating it from the unfolding events which may contradict it, Cuba sounds like a prudent counselor to the Sandinistas. For this reason, it is worthwhile to examine the speeches of Cuba's "maximum leader" in Managua and Ciego de Avila in July 1980 and, previously, in Holguin in July 1979. The prevailing tone of these speeches was that of advising moderation for the Nicaraguan process, recognizing that conditions in that country indicated that pluralism and the mixed economy constitute positive elements. In fact, while addressing his own people at Ciego de Avila, Fidel Castro repeated some of the concepts he had expressed a few days earlier before a multitude of Nicaraguans. He referred to the Sandinista revolution as a new revolutionary project in Nicaragua, implemented by the Nicaraguans, adapted to international circumstances and to the objective conditions of Nicaragua, in which businessmen are stimulated to participate. Fidel underscored a distinction between the two revolutions, pointing out that each should apply its own formula.[14]

In their writings, several Sandinista defenders have contrasted Nicaragua with Cuba. They contend that polarized critics of the FSLN have eyes only for the similarities, while ignoring remarkable differences. Additionally, they often highlight the fact that the Sandinista model is not yet altogether Marxist-Leninist and that the internal debate concerning the speed required for reaching socialism still continues.[15] In an interview with Patricia J. Sethi on the occasion of the 25th anniversary of the Cuban revolution, Castro himself stated the following: "In the coming years, and possibly before the year 2000, Cuba will not be the only Latin American country to have chosen socialism as a system of government, even though others may not follow the erroneously called 'Cuban model' — which in no way do we intend to universalize."[16]

The United States Government dissents from the foregoing views. Washington sees in Nicaragua a repetition of the pattern set by Fidel Castro in Cuba. A State Department paper has depicted this pattern in the following short-hand fashion:

During the Insurrection:

- Unification of the extreme left, i.e., of the three Sandinista factions into a nine-man FSLN National Directorate.

- [Establishment of a] Broad National Opposition Front with participation by both the Sandinistas and all other parties and civic associations — progressive and conservative — so as to project an image of pluralism that would marshall support from the Western World.

Once in Power:

• Establishment of a Sandinista-controlled government with participation of non-Marxists, thereby obtaining the international funding required for the new regime's consolidation.

• The Party (FSLN) as the inner core to exercise the real power and to establish the Army, State Security and official media, as well as all the organizations necessary to dominate society and the nation.[17]

LOOMING PENALTIES OF SANDINISTA POLICIES

The Sandinistas' failure to define the revolution in pragmatic terms — categorically and in its earliest stage — could prove in the long run to be their own undoing. Worse still, coupled with the foregoing, their excesses of intolerance have filled dissidents, and by and large the nation, with unmitigated distrust. For much too long has the FSLN engaged in gamesmanship: stalling, scheming, it has emptied the bag of tricks. In order to survive, the Sandinistas must yield to reality and offer a forthright settlement proposal to both the United States and democratic opposition.

During their first four years in power, the Sandinistas have tried to act simultaneously on three separate stages — as in a three-ring circus performance — with distinctive behavior in each. A careful observer, however, detects contradictions among them. These contradictions, which have naturally impeded a smooth and well-coordinated performance, simply reflect the FSLN leaders' aims of achieving a revolution according to their own preconceptions, with little regard for other forces of society — except, of course, for tactical reasons. In more than one way, such a triple-staged approach is tantamount to the Sandinistas wanting the best of all worlds.

On the domestic stage, the FSLN has demonstrated its disposition to reflect solely a see-saw tolerance for dissidence, keeping the private sector's future under the revolution in a state of uncertainty. Thus far, the Sandinistas' rule has been authoritarian.

On the second stage, the FSLN has endeavored to preserve normal relations with the international financial community: Sandinista Nicaragua has renegotiated an inherited foreign debt while retaining membership at the Inter-American Development Bank, the International Monetary Fund, the International Bank for Reconstruction and Development, the Central American Bank for Economic Integration and other Central American Common Market (CACM) institutions. This policy — in which the Nicaraguan regime has shown a sign of statesmanship, in sharp contrast to its narrow-minded style in domestic and foreign policies — is intended to reassure international financing sources that they should not be alarmed by the revolution.

On the third stage, Nicaragua implements a foreign policy with a sales-label of "nonalignment," while in reality it is based on an antagonism toward the United States and identification with the Soviet Union, Cuba and the PLO. Concurrently, friendly lines of communication and trade with the European and Latin American countries are being preserved. Special emphasis is given to Nicaragua's solidarity with Third World countries and liberation movements.

In summary, the FSLN seems determined simultaneously to exert authoritarianism inside Nicaragua, conduct business "as usual" with Wall Street and be a team-player of the Communist Bloc.

A "point-and-counterpoint" approach to the study of the Nicaraguan revolution's Marxist-Leninist taint could prove to be a prolonged undertaking and possibly inconclusive. Instead, a more simplistic analysis, based on visible symptoms, leads one to conclude that the FSLN's political intolerance, together with its ties to the Soviet-Cuban Bloc and its embracing of Marxism-Leninism, may have several serious consequences — all of them costly to Nicaragua and the revolution. Among these are loss of popular support, weakening of economic growth in Nicaragua, apprehension of other Central American countries regarding the Nicaraguan revolutionary process, erosion of international solidarity with the revolutionary government and, finally, confrontation with the United States.

Marxist dogmatic intolerance has undercut the base of the moral strength expected of the revolution. Such a totalitarian attitude is a child of the ill-fated decision of the FSLN's founders — continued by their followers — to choose Marxism-Leninism as their ideology. First and foremost, it reveals a lack of sophistication and a propensity for rigidity. Consequently, their ignoring, or failing to grasp, their long-oppressed people's yearning for true freedom is staggering. Those who combat them are driven by a deep-seated feeling that they were betrayed.

Sandinismo's breeding grounds were the public institutes of secondary education (high school) and the National University. Influenced by a primitive anti-Americanism — largely fed by a U.S.-protege status of the Somoza dynasty — those milieus lacked sufficient access to information on democracy, much less exposure thereto. A proof that such anti-U.S. feelings are counterproductive is the absence of pragmatic efforts to capitalize on old grievances in a positive way.

Yet, even at this juncture, it is still not too late for the FSLN to find inspiration in the recent change which took place in Argentina as a result of Alfonsin's election — from military rule to effective pluralistic democracy. Likewise, the Spain of Felipe Gonzalez and his Socialist Party ought to present a good alternative for the Sandinistas in relation to the quasi-Cuban model which they actually have. If Fidel Castro's revolution has failed as an adequate example for Nicaragua, why not then change the bench-mark? It makes no sense to insist on imposing on the Nicaraguan people — who by nature are individualists and to a large extent small proprietors — a political doctrine which has been characterized as a zero-sum game.[18]

The democrats' frustration regarding the revolution's Sovietization is twofold: it signifies both limitations of individual freedoms and the emergence of a new lifetime dictatorship. Admittedly, some of the elite's members are selfless, though fanatical, revolutionaries. However, there exist those who, lusting for sheer power, embrace communism as an opportunity and a means for becoming — as long as they are part of the "in" few — commanders or ministers.

Emilio Alvarez Montalvan, of Nicaragua's Democratic Conservative Party, states that a Marxist system (like Managua's present regime) puts the people in the hands of a bureaucracy which cannot be removed from office and is not accountable for its errors.[19]

"So many times," writes Jean-Francois Revel, "we have seen, during the past 20 or 30 years, the leaders of a movement of national liberation —acting on behalf of the state they now control — submit the people they have just 'liberated' to their fixed ideas, appetite for power and the megalomaniacal dreams of their foreign policy."[20] For his part, Ronald Radosh has made the incisive observation that "despite the terrific ideological and political distances that separate them, the colonels and commissars of Central America have this in common — they are in the business of power, not in the business of justice."[21]

THE LARGER CENTRAL AMERICAN ARENA

Political tensions are so polarized and intertwined with Central America's economic and social reality that economic development and social progress cannot take place unless violence is first ended. We are witnessing the waging of an ideological war, politically and militarily. Depending on who the victors in this struggle are, they will either impose a totalitarian model for all of Central America or they will open the way for a pluralistic society.

The Sandinistas committed a serious miscalculation in their inability to remain aloof from the Salvadoran insurrection, which broke out shortly after their own takeover in Managua. Their misguided and untimely involvement is perhaps one of the principal prods behind the difficulties which presently beset Nicaragua and hinder regional political stability and economic advancement. The intrusion into El Salvador made Nicaragua a controversial actor on Central America's political stage, arousing suspicions in the United States of a newly emergent regional threat. Moreover, from the moment of that intrusion a correlation was established between the radicalization of the Sandinistas and the economic deterioration in Central America. Consequently, unlike what democrats throughout the world — and particularly in Central America — had originally hoped, Nicaragua today is far from being a leader to be emulated, but rather is looked upon as a hotbed for subversion. Additionally, as a political institution, the FSLN has become hostage to constant scrutiny by its neighbors. In fact, in an atmosphere of brinkmanship, the Sandinistas have placed on themselves the responsibility for their own decision: *change or confrontation*.

The magnitude and complexity of the current Central American economic crisis is so alarming that its exacerbation for ulterior political motives cannot be anything but a crime against the people of the region. The five small, underdeveloped republics, with a combined population of 21 million, will need $23 billion in foreign capital inflows to recover by 1990 the standard of living they enjoyed in 1980. That figure exceeds total regional exports of the last four-year period or the aggregate gross domestic product of 1982.

The real rate of GNP growth has fallen from 8.1 per cent in 1977 to minus 3.7 per cent in 1982. Trade within the Central American Common Market has decreased in terms of value and of intra-regional exports and imports as a share of total trade.

It is true that the largest countries with the strongest economic bases in Latin America, e.g., Mexico and Venezuela, have lately been in dire straits. Yet, Central America differs from them in that political uncertainty — during these years of turmoil — bears an important share of responsibility for reductions in investment and production levels. This is largely due to "the ghost of communism looming on the horizon." It is equally true that external factors of a purely economic nature have seriously affected Central America, but there is a coincidence of rising social and political unrest with dwindling economic growth.

With the 1978 outbreak of open civil war in Nicaragua, the real growth rate of the regional GNP began to falter. By 1981, when Nicaragua's drift to the Soviet Bloc became more evident, and the guerrillas in El Salvador continued with renewed strength after the failure of their January "final offensive," this economic indicator had dropped to 1 per cent.

One of the principal obstacles which the Sandinistas have encountered in the implementation of their Marxist-Leninist project in Nicaragua is the apprehension with which the other Central American countries have reacted. There is nothing strange about it. The capillary interlinking of the five republics renders it impossible for any one of them unilaterally to adopt an ideological model of society which is unacceptable and deemed a threat by the others.

Misgivings regarding Managua's regime are the more comprehensible in light of the Left's grandiose design for a unified Central America ruled by revolutionaries.[22] A statement by the Honduran Government before the Organization of American States (OAS) is more than candid in denouncing the Sandinista government for what Honduras views as, inter alia: Nicaragua's breach of security terms in the Central American isthmus; Nicaragua's indifference to the tremendous consequences which may arise for all Central America from the creation of an "enormous" army (which is larger than the combined armed forces of all the other republics); and Nicaragua's role as a supplier of arms for subversion and terrorism.[23]

The Regime's Paling Credibility

By now, the Sandinistas must know that the days when their international prestige was founded on the image of heroic and dashing guerilla commanders are gone. Nowadays their capacity to deserve international approval is proportionate to their respect for domestic pluralism and for human rights. For this reason, they attach great importance to public relations—and to all propaganda tools. Whenever they have applied restrictions on freedom of information or curbed the political activities of dissidents, they have faced international pressure. Subsequently, they relax their grip. Thus far, it has been akin to a trial-and-error period. However, they have gone through these political calisthenics so often that in the process their image in the Western World has been eroded, making Sandinismo appear as Somocismo revisited. Their disposition to assert their authoritarian rule is a reflection of their communist credo.

More recently, they have suffered two fiascos. One of them was the case of the Bishop of the Northern Zelaya Department. Managua publicly reported that the U.S.-born prelate had been kidnapped by Miskito counter-revolutionaries and that the government "feared for his life." A few days later the bishop appeared in Honduras at the head of more than a thousand Indians. He had voluntarily accompanied them there so as to give them spiritual comfort on their escape from Sandinista oppression.

The other case where the FSLN has seen its credibility impaired is the lack of seriousness in the decrees regarding both amnesty for dissidents and the electoral process. A close examination of those documents reveals that they are misleading, even devious. The exclusion of citizens responsible for committing acts against the state prior to December 1, 1981, leaves out the principals of the popular September 1980 Bluefields uprising against the Cuban presence in Nicaragua. Nor is it clear whether important heads of exiled political movements may return to Nicaragua to participate in the elections.

CHANCES FOR AN ACCOMMODATION?

Upon my appointment as Ambassador to the United States in the spring of 1981, I was advised by the Government in Managua that relations with Washington were the keynote of our foreign policy. That parameter should have been faithfully observed. Common sense dictated that Nicaragua broaden the base of its international relations in order to achieve the wide interdependence which was imperative for its own viability as a nation-state and as a safeguard for its self-determination. Naturally, this implied retaining the respect and support of socialist governments. Wisdom also called for seeking ways to strengthen economic ties with Canada and the Arab oil-producing nations. A part of that policy might have been an adequate level of rapport with Cuba, and, to a lesser degree, with other members of the Soviet Bloc.

Notwithstanding the relevance of those ties, however, the center of Nicaragua's foreign policy continues to be the United States. Nicaragua cannot reach an effective political and security settlement with its Central American neighbors — so essential to Nicaragua—without some kind of U.S. guarantee. Furthermore, the economic and security factors are so overwhelmingly strong that it is unnecessary to discuss them.

The overriding issue in diplomatic relations between Washington and Managua is whether or not there is room for accommodation of the respective ideological beliefs. Above all, however, the issue is whether, in light of strategic considerations, an agreement will bring the two countries closer or conflict will separate them even more. From the beginning — given the misgivings of Washington about the new revolution — it was clear that the degree of tolerance on the part of the United States would be positively influenced if the revolutionary leadership appeared to be fundamentally nationalist, and negatively so if it behaved from a provocative "internationalist" posture. Unfortunately, the FSLN leaders have overlooked geographical realities and attempted, much too soon, to alter the course of Central American contemporary history.

According to a press report, key U.S. policymakers view the concessions being offered by the Sandinistas solely as a tactical maneuver to free themselves from pressures, subsequently resuming their attempts to export revolution. These policymakers reportedly contend that, in order to promote long-term stability in Central America, it is necessary to replace the Sandinistas.[24] I still believe that an effort toward serious negotiations must be made. However, I also regard as insufficient the conclusion reached by a *New York Times* editorial: "The realistic American response, therefore, should be to encourage the Sandinistas' overtures while pressing for proof that they will now promote revolution only in their own country."[25]

The "Finlandization" of Nicaragua is hardly a solution. In order to obtain permanent stability in Central America, it is first necessary for the Sandinistas to restore domestic pluralism in Nicaragua. After all, if export of the revolution is to be stopped, it is communist ideology — expansionist by its own nature — that needs to be restrained. This holds true in the same manner that the insurrection problem in El Salvador should be resolved — through a settlement accepted by and binding upon all forces of the spectrum.

President Reagan's comments in his December 1983 interview in *U.S. News and World Report* seemed to clarify Washington's intentions vis-a-vis the Sandinistas, and spell out what it expects from them. The President stated: "We are not demanding the overthrow of the Sandinista Government. All the Sandinistas have to do is to go back to the 1979 democratic commitments they made to the OAS as a part of the political agreement leading to the end of the Somoza regime."[26] All the political parties, organizations and groups composing the Nicaraguan dissidence demand that any solution should initially start by resolving the internal situation.

Let us call a spade a spade: There is sufficient tangible evidence that the FSLN is dominated by Marxist-Leninist influences. The Sandinistas have abundantly corroborated this by words and deeds. The ideological commitments of the leadership have a determinant bearing on the revolution's conduct, causing distress among Nicaraguans and concern among neighboring nations. There is, similarly, enough evidence concerning the Sandinistas' ties with the Communist Bloc, which are construed by the United States as a threat to regional security. Central American countries, on their part, have denounced Nicaragua for sponsoring subversion against them.

All this has boomeranged on the Sandinista regime, which is also subjected to insurgency supported by the United States, ostensibly to offset FMLN guerrilla actions against the Salvadoran reformist government, and by Honduras, which claims that it is so doing mostly as a "preventive" measure. More recently Washington justifies its backing of counter-insurgency as a pressure to bring the Sandinistas to the negotiating table. It is obvious that fear of communism's spread has reduced Central American economic activity to a state of near-paralysis. In Nicaragua, political uncertainty has divided the nation and constrained the national economy, thereby subjecting the people to deprivation.

At the present time, the FSLN is making gestures, expressing — at least formally — an intention to talk things over with its adversaries. The dissidents have manifested their willingness to hold a dialogue, in spite of their justified distrust of the Sandinistas. It seems only fair that they demand international guarantees.

Accommodation requires that both sides be willing to make some tradeoffs. It would be an illusory perception of reality for the FSLN to expect the legitimate opposition to agree on unchallenged and permanent FSLN rule in exchange for some concessions. As a matter of fact, the entire initiative would be destined to fail if it is ideated solely on the basis of Sandinista "concessions." The key to the matter lies in the Sandinistas' recognition of the rights of others. The FSLN cannot hope to reach an agreement unless it is willing to accept that the perpetuation of a Marxist-Leninist system poses intolerable implications for Nicaragua as a nation and for Central America as a whole.

POSTSCRIPT

The consolidation of totalitarianism in Nicaragua has continued apace since the spring of 1984, when the above was written.

In the intervening period popular support for the Sandinistas has shrunken to the extent that they have become, in clear fact, a dictatorial minority retaining public power by the force of arms. Political repression and deprivation are the regime's "credentials." The military buildup provided by the Soviet Bloc has reached the highest levels in the entire history of Central America. Church leaders are persecuted, and *La Prensa* has been closed. In response, the resistance forces are committed with even greater resolve to liberate Nicaragua. The United States is backing their struggle. My country endures a state of civil war, where the East-West confrontation has been brought in deliberately by the incumbent regime. Therefore, its ideology has been and will be a stumbling block to peace.

In the process, the Sandinista Front adamantly rejects any real solution to the conflict. Its refusal to renounce or even reduce its arbitrary hegemony was demonstrated by lack of freedom and fairness in the 1984 elections, and by the failure of Contadora. Now the Central American democracies are trying to persuade the Sandinistas to accept democracy — with little hope of success. The opposition made a peace proposal in February 1986, which was arrogantly rebuffed by the government. It is quite clear that the Sandinista leadership does not want to admit change and chooses confrontation.

I feel entitled to claim that Sandinista intransigence, as well as the national and regional problems resulting from it, corroborate my previous assertion that the imposition of a Marxist-Leninist system poses intolerable consequences not only for Nicaragua, but also for all of Central America. That is the key issue.

NOTES

1. President Reagan's address before a Joint Session of Congress, "Central America: Defending our Vital Interests," Bureau of Public Affairs, U.S. Department of State, April 27, 1983.

2. See Arturo J. Cruz, "Nicaragua's Imperiled Revolution," *Foreign Affairs*, Summer 1983.

3. "Documentos de la Historia: El Manifiesto de UNAP," *La Prensa* (Literaria), Managua, December 10, 1983.

4. John A. Booth, *The End and the Beginning — The Nicaraguan Revolution* (Boulder, CO: Westview Press, Inc., 1982), pp. 143–144.

5. Ibid., pp. 155–181.

6. Confirmed to this writer by Carlos Andres Perez.

7. Bureau of Public Affairs, U.S. Department of State, "Cuban Armed Forces and the Soviet Military Presence," April 1982.

8. Ibid.

9. See Max Singer, *Nicaragua, The Stolen Revolution*, U.S. Information Agency (no date), p. 15.

10. See Jaime Suchlicki, "Why the Russians might—or might not—be tempted by Nicaragua," *Christian Science Monitor*, November 2, 1982.

11. See James Chace, "The Endless War," *The New York Review of Books*, December 8, 1983, pp. 46–52.

12. Ibid.

13. Carlos Fuentes, "An Open Letter to Dr. Henry A. Kissinger, National Bipartisan Commission on Central America," *Harper's*, January 1984.

14. I was present at both Managua and Ciego de Avila when Fidel Castro delivered these speeches. There are official texts published by the Cuban Government, from which I took my notes for a symposium, "The United States and Cuba: Prospects for a Dialogue," September 1981.

15. See Marlise Simons, "Inside and Out, Pressures on Nicaragua Are Rising," *New York Times,* July 17, 1983.

16. *Newsweek*, January 9, 1984.

17. U.S. Department of State and Department of Defense, background paper, *Central America*, May 27, 1983.

18. See Michael Novak, *The Spirit of Democratic Capitalism* (New York: Simon and Schuster, 1982), p. 123.

19. Emilio Alvarez Montalvan, *Sintesis Critica del Marxismo* (Managua: Partido Conservador Democrata de Nicaragua, 1982).

20. Jean Francois Revel, *La Tentacion Totalitaria* (from the French original, La Tentation Totalitaire) (Buenos Aires: Emece Editores, 1976), p. 20.

21. Ronald Radosh, "Darkening Nicaragua," *The New Republic,* special issue, October 24, 1983.

22. Stephen Kinzer, "Of Latin America's Political Volcanoes," *Boston Globe,* December 12, 1982.

23. Government of Honduras, *Exposicion del Gobierno de Honduras ante el Consejo Permanente de la OEA sobre las amenazas a la paz y a la seguridad centroamericanas,* July 1983.

24. See Robert S. Greenberger, "Latin Quandary," *Wall Street Journal,* December 30, 1983.

25. "What's Negotiable with Nicaragua," *New York Times,* November 25, 1983.

26. *Washington Times* reproduced the *U.S. News and World Report* interview with President Reagan in its December 30, 1983, edition.

5 Revolutionary Change and the Nicaraguan People

Nestor D. Sanchez

The policy of the United States does not subscribe to the notion that the social and economic problems of Central America are susceptible to a "military solution." This view is not shared by all of the parties involved in the region, some of whom are actively trying to promote such a solution — one favorable, of course, to their interests — while at the same time picturing the United States as the aggressor. Humberto Ortega, Nicaragua's Defense Minister, tersely described his concept of the utility of the military solution as follows: "We took power by arms, and it should be clear who has the power in Nicaragua today."

In fact, it is not entirely clear who has the power in Nicaragua today. The Nicaraguan Directorate has ceded a portion of its power to its Cuban advisers, who themselves are party to the furthering of the interests of the Soviet Union.

A Superstructure of "Internationalism"

In a sense, this East-West dimension comprises a superstructure built upon social conflicts deeply rooted in Central American history. It represents an injection of Soviet strategy, adapted by a client state — Cuba — to Hispanic culture and history. It is designed to divert the energies of reform and revolution from their natural courses and channel them to wider internationalist goals — to goals

This chapter appeared as an article in the Summer 1984 issue of Strategic Review.

which have little to do with the basic problems faced by the peoples of Central America. Designed for these wider purposes, this strategy impacts not only upon the societies of the region, but also upon the security interests of the United States, other countries of this hemisphere, and even nations seemingly distant and unaware of the stakes of the contest. To ignore this in the face of the accumulated evidence is to display what theologians call culpable ignorance.

Another grave error is to forget that the countries of Central America vary considerably in their social, economic and political circumstances, despite their common Hispanic heritage. The Central American crisis, seen only in its broad outlines, looks like a single event, one typical of the developing world. However, when the situation is studied in detail, this apparent homogeneity breaks down. Despite similarities, El Salvador is not Nicaragua. In key aspects, each of the countries of the region is unique. This is not always recognized, even by the principal actors, and that is a serious mistake.

When Nicaraguan Foreign Minister Miguel D'Escoto said in 1980, "You may look at us as five countries, six now with Panama, but we regard ourselves as six different states of a single nation, in the process of reunification," he was expressing a wish rather than describing reality.[1] The statement represents one pole of the ambivalence felt in Central America toward unification. Yet, D'Escoto's revolutionary regionalism has more to do with Marxist-Leninist internationalism than with the ideal of regional unification as it has been expressed since the breakup of the Federation of Central America in 1837.[2]

This Marxist-Leninist internationalism finds frequent expression among Nicaraguan leaders. In a speech in Managua on the second anniversary of the Sandinista victory, Tomas Borge, Minister of the Interior and Assistant Commander in Chief of the Sandinista People's Army, asserted: "This revolution goes beyond our borders. Our revolution was always internationalist from the moment Sandino fought in La Segovia." The Sandinista Coordinator General for Foreign Affairs, Bayardo Arce, averred: "We will never give up supporting our brothers in El Salvador." The Minister of Defense and Commander in Chief of the Sandinista People's Army,

Humberto Ortega, has stated: "Of course, we are not ashamed of helping El Salvador. We would like to help all revolutions."[3]

THE PERCEPTIONS BY NICARAGUA'S NEIGHBORS

The conditions leading to the Sandinista victory in Nicaragua were unique in important ways in today's Central America. The Sandinistas and their allies carried out an applauded and broadly based struggle to bring down a detested ruler. The promise of that struggle was democracy and freedom, as it usually is in revolutions. Rare today is the revolutionary leader who will talk openly of fighting to establish a dictatorship, but the credentials of these leaders usually do not support their statements of support for democracy. Given their records once they attain power, it is surprising that their claims continue to be accepted.

Nicaragua's neighbors cannot be accused of culpable ignorance. Thus, the Honduran Minister to the President, Carlos Flores Cacusse, gave the following perspective: "Nicaragua represents a threat to our internal order and our democracy. We have a regime on our border that does not respect our self–determination and that is armed to the teeth and pledges to continue arming itself. Must we sit back with our arms folded?"[4]

The question was somewhat rhetorical. From August to October 1983, the Honduran Armed Forces annihilated a 96-member guerrilla group infiltrated from Nicaragua and led by Jose Maria Reyes. The group planned to establish a base in the Department of Olancho and become the advance element of a larger force that was to conduct operations throughout the country. Members of the group received guerrilla instruction at Camp P-30 operated by the Cuban Department of Special Operations in the Cuban province of Pinar del Rio.

Fernando Volio, former Foreign Minister of Costa Rica, offered this assessment:

Every communist regime is expansionist, because to fulfill its objectives, international communism should and must extend communist domination everywhere. Not even the communists themselves deny this. Hence, this kind of heavily armed regime — armed beyond its needs for national defense — represents a threat to our peoples and to Costa Rica. The international community must, therefore, wake up from its lethargy and come to the defense of countries like Panama and Costa Rica, which want to live in freedom.[5]

THE SUPPLYING OF THE SALVADORAN GUERRILLAS

Whether the international community will "wake up" is uncertain. As an example, there is the matter of Nicaraguan logistical, command and communications support for the Salvadoran guerrillas. Although the Sandinista Directorate professes solidarity with the guerrillas in El Salvador, the Directorate usually denies that Nicaragua is supplying them. This denial is understandable, but less easy to understand is that the denial is still believed.

The 10,000 guerrillas fielded in El Salvador today comprise a loose confederation of separate groups which together represents the second largest insurgent force in Central America.[6] Their logistical support system has been traced through Nicaragua, where its operation is closely supervised by the Sandinista Government in coordination with Cuba, the Soviet Bloc and other parties, including the PLO and Libya. The evidence of arms movement is anecdotal rather than statistical, and relatively little appears in the media. However, information has accumulated steadily since the end of 1979, and on May 13, 1983, the Boland Committee was able to make the following categorical statement:

> The success of the insurgents in El Salvador has not been matched by political victories. It is not popular support that sustains the insurgents. . . .This insurgency depends for its lifeblood — arms, ammunition, financing, logistics and command-and-control facilities — upon outside assistance from Nicaragua and Cuba. This Nicaraguan and Cuban contribution to the Salvadoran insurgency. . . began shortly after the overthrow of Somoza in July 1979. It has provided — by land, sea and air — the great bulk of the military equipment and support received by the insurgents. . . .Neither El Salvador nor its close neighbors possess the capability to interdict arms supplies reaching the insurgents.[7]

These supplies are delivered across the Gulf of Fonseca by small craft, infiltrated through Honduras or occasionally dropped by air.[8] Guerrilla offensive capability is conditioned by this more or less constant trickle, which enforces a pattern of politically timed "offensives" followed by periods of recovery and resupply, punctuated by ambushes and terrorist actions. Logistics, as much as any factor, determine guerrilla activity.

SALVADORAN GUERRILLA TRAINING IN NICARAGUA

The international movement and training of personnel are at least as important as this infiltration of materiel. Much of the guerrilla fighting force in El Salvador is composed of youths of uncertain reliability, some of them even kidnapped,[9] but many of the leaders have received training in Cuba or Eastern Europe and maintain ties with international terrorist organizations. These are highly motivated "internationalist" professionals, adequately educated and financed, supported from abroad and hardened by experience.

At least three camps in Nicaragua have been identified as training sites for Salvadoran guerrillas: Ostinal in the province of Rivas, a converted National Guard camp near the Rio Tamarindo, and Tamaga, 20 kilometers from Managua. They reportedly were operated by Cuban military personnel serving as instructors, supervisors and administrators. The Tamaga camp was run by the Cuban major who trained the Farabundo Marti National Liberation Front (FMLN) group which assaulted the Salvadoran Air Force base of Ilopango in January 1982. The Salvadoran who led that attack, Alejandro Montenegro, later left the guerrillas and gave the details of the training he and his sapper team had received at Tamaga and in Cuba.

Again and again we witness activities like the following: Refugees testify to Sandinista army and secret police atrocities. The Nicaraguan Council of State limits civil guarantees and imposes censorship. Mobs are organized to attack labor and religious representatives. Nicaraguan television broadcasts confessions of "subversives."[10] Daniel Ortega "fraternally" and "enthusiastically" congratulates Konstantin Chernenko for his election as USSR Supreme Soviet Presidium Chairman.[11] Construction begins at Punta Huete on the largest military airfield in Central America.[12] Another Bulgarian ship arrives at El Bluff to deliver more tanks to form additional tank battalions and more armored personnel carriers to form additional motorized infantry units.

A Revolution Betrayed

In 1979 many Nicaraguans and foreign observers expected that the Sandinista leaders would not take the path of Marxist-Leninist internationalism, that they would respond to the evident wishes of the people of Nicaragua, and that they would follow through on the promises they made to the OAS, consolidate a responsive and pragmatic government and address the country's daunting economic and social problems — in short, deal with the needs of Nicaragua. Daniel Ortega restated his government's ostensible commitment in May 1983: "Our first obligation is to meet the needs of our own country and consolidate our own revolution. This means not giving any pretexts to governments like Mr. Reagan's to attack our revolution."[13]

Yet, after an encouraging start, especially in the promotion of public health and basic literacy, the National Directorate seems to be behaving exactly contrary to its declared obligation. The regime has called upon East Germany to help build its police apparatus. It keeps its prisoners in conditions reportedly equalling those experienced under Somoza. It has imported some 3,000 Cuban military advisers, together with 7,000 Cuban teachers, technicians and doctors, most of whom have military training.

Bulgarian and Soviet ships regularly unload war materiel at Bluefields and Corinto, and the Nicaraguan Army steadily grows, in a buildup impressive in comparison with the mini-armies normal to the region and in relation to the population base. This is supposedly in response to a foreign threat; yet, the buildup began before any threat appeared on the Sandinista horizon.

International considerations compete with national needs for the dogmatists of the Directorate, who see the process within one country — in this case, their country — as part of a worldwide struggle. Given this view, it follows that the struggle must be extended as swiftly as prudence permits. "Consolidation of the revolution" means cementing the power base more than it means addressing the problems of the nation. In consolidating this base, the new leaders "defend the revolution" — which is to say, their own power. They put the absolutist "I am the state" into a modern idiom: "I am the revolution."

After the revolution prevailed, idealists who continued to believe that they had been fighting for a democratic government which guarantees respect for human rights, freedom and justice — and who thought that it was now time to make good on those promises — found themselves shunted aside by the Marxist-Leninist professionals. We see embarrassing side-effects for the Sandinistas in the number of veterans of the fight against Somoza driven to oppose the current National Directorate.

Carried to its extreme, revolution implies the destruction of opponents as "counterrevolutionaries," or at least their silencing. The National Directorate terms the armed opposition "Contras" or counterrevolutionaries.[14] More than propaganda, the term accurately reflects the Directorate's view of its opponents and suggests a fundamental reason why it excoriates them and finds dialogue or negotiation so unacceptable.

The irony, at least to the non-Marxist, is that the same dogmatic regime which will not admit to dialogue with its opponents works to marshal international opinion to force the Duarte Government of El Salvador to negotiate with *its* Marxist-Leninist opponents who, for reasons associated with their worldview, see negotiation only as a weapon in their struggle. What appears to the non-Marxist as an absurdity is entirely reasonable in the eye of the world revolutionary who, certain in his understanding of objective reality, makes a fundamental distinction between those who by nature are allies and those by nature enemies.

Having chosen their path — or, more accurately, having had their path determined for them by their ideology — the Sandinista leaders found it natural to void the promises of democracy, pluralism and individual rights they made in 1979 to the OAS and to the people of Nicaragua. To keep these promises, to admit that they were anything more than the tactics of the united front, would be to admit to the weakness or uncertainty that compromise must signify to the absolutist. Compromise is only to be used as a tactic, for it implies the sharing of power and hence the risk of its loss to counter-revolutionary elements.

On any issue, be it internal freedom or the export of the means of revolution, the Sandinista directorate has shown impressive Marxist-Leninist tenacity, giving ground only where absolutely necessary. Opposition, any opposition, is demonized. Thus, Eden Pastora "should be treated in a psychiatric hospital."[15] The Miskito Indians are "confused." The Catholic Church is led by "false prophets."[16]

The ironies of the situation abound. In 1979 the Sandinistas came into power on a crest of worldwide goodwill. Nicaragua was bankrupt and ruined, but other nations and international institutions stood ready to help.[17] Energized by a dynamic leadership, free of a corrupt dictatorship, for a brief time Nicaragua held the promise of lighting a path for the peoples of Central America, of showing what a revolution could be.

Eden Pastora testifies eloquently to the betrayal of revolution and of opportunity:

> This is what we resent in these nine comandantes. . . . We made our revolution in the 20th century supported in the first two years by $1.2 billion in aid from around the world. We got help from everyone — from the gringos, Germans, Russians, French, Spanish, Swedes, Norwegians — from all of Europe, Latin America and the Arab world. . . . We lost the chance that no other people in the world had: the chance to make a true revolution, genuine, the prototype of a Latin American revolution.[18]

And the poet Pablo Antonio Cuadra adds the following poignant personal testimony:

> I am excluded and marginalized just as is anyone who suggests an independent point of view or who defends the independence of the writer in the face of the power of the state. . . . I am against the perversion of the revolution they have engineered. . . . My obligation as a poet is to hold up the banner of resistance against the tremendous damage which is being done to Nicaraguan culture.[19]

WHICH ROAD FOR NICARAGUA?

Toughened by their struggle, certain of their virtue, betrayed by their ideology and increasingly beholden to Cuba and its patron, the Soviet Union, the Sandinista leaders have driven themselves into a corner. They have alienated supporters, abused their people and frightened their neighbors. They have built the most powerful armed force in Central America, and they keep adding to that force.

When their army was small, the Sandinistas confronted no enemies. Today they face, in the Nicaraguan Democratic Force (FDN), the Revolutionary Democratic Alliance (ARDE), the Misura and the Misurasata, the largest aggregation of insurgents in Central America. In contrast to the guerrillas in El Salvador, who appear constrained more by shortage of recruits than by lack of materiel, the Nicaraguan insurgents seem to have more than enough volunteers. Yet, lacking the scale of political and material support enjoyed by the Salvadoran guerrillas, the Nicaraguan insurgents have been unable effectively to arm and employ this willing manpower.

The Sandinistas have heavily supported the guerrillas in El Salvador, and in a sense have mortgaged their own reputation — and perhaps even their own future — to guerrilla success there. El Salvador has experienced three honest elections since the Sandinistas came to power. The latest round of voting resulted in the election of President Jose Napoleon Duarte. The future remains unclear, but President Duarte seems to have at least as good a chance of achieving his goals as the Sandinista leaders have of accomplishing theirs. Perhaps El Salvador, and not Nicaragua, will light the path.

Nicaragua need not accept the road of Marxism-Leninism. The present National Directorate chose that road — perhaps without truly realizing where it would lead — long before success in the fight against Somoza was assured. What has been done cannot easily be undone, but it is possible. The critics of the Directorate are not the Somocistas and traitors they are painted to be. As much as the Directorate, they were makers of the revolution and they do not want it to fail, fossilized into a police state, a danger to its neighbors and to its people. They do not want a return to a feudal past, and they do not want Nicaragua to become a client of the Soviet Union, garrisoned by another client, Cuba. The people of Nicaragua have a right to freedom from the repression they have endured under both the dictatorship of the Somozas and the Directorate of the Sandinistas.

POSTSCRIPT

In the two years since the above was drafted, the force of democracy has made substantial headway throughout Central America, with the glaring exception of Nicaragua. Over the past two years, the Sandinistas have gone beyond the betrayal of their revolutionary promises in an attempt to consolidate their power. In characteristic Marxist-Leninist style, they have proceeded to build an imposing military to guarantee a monopoly of power.

The consolidation of a Marxist-Leninist regime in Nicaragua would present a significant security threat to all of its neighbors on the isthmus. Since June 1984, there have been numerous documented border incidents initiated by the Sandinistas against Honduras and Costa Rica. The United States has continued to follow a policy in support of development, democracy, defense and diplomacy. Specifically, the United States has responded to Sandinista intransigence with its two-track policy of dialogue and pressure.

The United States has consistently supported a negotiated settlement to the Central American conflict. Through active diplomacy and extensive consultations, the United States has expressed a willingness to abide by a Contadora Agreement that implements the twenty-one points of the September 1983 Document of Objectives in a comprehensive, verifiable and simultaneous manner. Specifically, the United States supports an agreement that achieves those basic objectives included in the twenty-one points, especially those relating to: implementing democratization, ending Sandinista support for regional subversion, removing Soviet and Cuban military presence, and reducing the excessive Sandinista military forces. Honduras, El Salvador, Costa Rica and Guatemala similarly insist upon the inclusion of these conditions as a necessary safeguard against continuing Sandinista aggression. As of this writing, there has been no agreement primarily because of Sandinista refusal to accept the provisions for democratization and national reconciliation.

With the exception of efforts aimed at influencing U.S. Congressional votes on aid for the resistance, the Sandinistas have continued their consolidation of a totalitarian state, while opting for military operations against, rather than dialogue with, the resistance. Experience shows that the Sandinistas enter into negotiations only when they are forced to do so.

From June 1984 to September 1986, the United States Government provided no arms or war-fighting assistance to the Democratic Resistance Forces (DRF) in Nicaragua. Opponents of assistance argued that the Sandinista intransigence with respect to meaningful negotiations, their military buildup, and the suspension of civil rights for the Nicaraguan populace were reactions to the external pressures presented by U.S. assistance to the DRF. On the basis of this premise, one would have reasonably expected a positive sign or response by the Sandinistas during the two-year respite from U.S. military support to the resistance.

Instead, Sandinista activities have demonstrated their true objectives of manipulation, consolidation and intimidation. The military has grown from a force of 5,000 men in 1979 to one now totalling 75,000 active duty forces with another 45,000 reserves and militia. The growth of the military forces dates back to 1981, prior to the emergence of an armed opposition. The Sandinista inventory of equipment includes 46 helicopters, 45 fixed-wing aircraft, and 350 armored tanks and armored vehicles. The recent Soviet and Soviet Bloc deliveries have improved Sandinista mobility and strength, dwarfing the military capabilities of the other countries of the region.

During the two-year period, the Sandinistas have expanded their appalling record in human rights. They have repressed the Church, the Indians in Nicaragua, the press, and the political opposition. They have attacked churches, banned *Radio Catolica,* conscripted seminarians, barred the reentry into the country of Monsignor Bismarck Carballo, and expelled Bishop Pablo Antonio Vega. Between March and April of 1986, at least 10,000 Nicaraguan Indians were forced to flee to Honduras after their villages were attacked by Sandinista forces; many of them were part of the 10,000 to 12,000 who had been allowed to return to their homelands after being forcibly relocated to government camps in the interior in 1981–1982. On October 15, 1985, Daniel Ortega announced a new State of Emergency which suspended virtually all civil liberties, denying freedom of the press, assembly, expression and from arbitrary imprisonment.

The Sandinistas will continue on their present internal and external courses until they are compelled to the realization that the forces of opposition confronting them are too strong to be ignored or successfully repressed. The $100 million voted by the U.S. Congress for aid to the DRF will enable them to apply that needed pressure on the Sandinistas. The resistance need not achieve a military victory; rather they can galvanize the democratic opposition within the populace in order to force the Sandinistas to negotiate with the true representatives of the Nicaraguan people. At some point, the Sandinistas will have to accommodate the popular discontent represented by the opposition forces or face being overwhelmed by it. Then and only then can the true Nicaraguan revolution, one steeped in freedom and development, flourish and prosper.

NOTES

1. "Nicaragua and the World," *Christianity and Crisis,* May 12, 1980, p. 141.

2. In the early 1840s, Nicaragua took the lead in the first serious, but unsuccessful, effort to reunite Central America. A federation of Nicaragua, Honduras and El Salvador did endure until 1845, but in reality each state operated independently.

3. Michael Kramer, "The Not-Quite War," *New York Magazine,* September 12, 1983.

4. *New York Times,* April 26, 1984.

5. RPC Television, Panama, July 30, 1983.

6. As one example of the abundance and quality of materiel supplied to the guerrillas, the Salvadoran Armed Forces recently furnished the serial numbers of 155 weapons, principally M-16, AR-15 and FAL rifles, captured from guerrillas by Army units during the first quarter of 1984. Since

units often retain captured weapons for use and do not report them, the 155 figure represents a partial list of weapons captured. In February, the Army captured guerrilla documents giving the serial numbers of 109 other rifles, principally M-16, AR-15, G-3 and FAL.

7. *Report of the Permanent Select Committee on Intelligence,* House of Representatives, 98th Cong., 1st sess., May 13, 1983.

8. Chinandega Peninsula at the southern end of the Gulf of Fonseca is one of the embarkation areas for materiel infiltrated into El Salvador over water. On September 14, 1983, an FDN raiding party blew up a warehouse and three boats on the island of La Concha, claimed to be an embarkation point for arms shipments to the Salvadoran guerrillas. *Barricada,* the Sandinista newspaper, called the attack a "criminal irrationality," and the Nicaraguan Defense Ministry denied that any military facility existed on the island. However, investigation by reporters confirmed that the site was the loading point for a 14-boat arms smuggling fleet. *Washington Post,* September 21, 1983.

9. Kidnapping to fill guerrilla ranks in El Salvador is reported frequently and has been thoroughly documented. In Nicaragua, the Sandinista People's Army (EPS) has resorted to the method of the press gang to fulfill the universal conscription law. Reports of "disciplinary" incidents and desertions are common.

10. One recent example was the May 17 Nicaraguan television showing of a "confession" of subversive activities by jailed *La Prensa* reporter Jose Luis Mora.

11. As reported by FBIS, April 17, 1984.

12. The 4,000 meter concrete runway at Punta Huete will accommodate any aircraft in the Soviet inventory.

13. Daniel Ortega Saavedra, interview, *Time,* June 6, 1983.

14. The Bishop regime in Grenada called its opponents—real and suspected—"Counters."

15. Tomas Borge Martinez, Minister of Interior, interview in *Playboy,* July 25, 1983.

16. Daniel Ortega Saavedra, interview, Managua Domestic Radio, April 27, 1984.

17. The United States alone supplied $118 million in direct aid to Nicaragua between July 1979 and April 1981. By the end of the Carter Administration, it became clear that Nicaragua was channelling increasing support to the Salvadoran guerrillas, but disbursement continued through the first three months of the Reagan Administration. The Sandinistas did not turn to Moscow because we, or the other nations of the

West, cut off aid. U.S. funds dried up only after the Sandinistas were fully implementing their policies and had made their aims clear.

18. Eden Pastora, interview, *El Tiempo,* San Pedro Sula, October 25, 1983.

19. Pablo Antonio Cuadra, interview, *La Nacion Internacional,* October 5, 1983.

PART III

The Broader Regional Arena

6 The Dying War in El Salvador

H. JOACHIM MAITRE

The war is winding down in El Salvador. After seven years of armed insurrection, the rebel forces of the Frente Farabundo Marti para la Liberacion Nacional (FMLN) and Frente Democratico Revolucionario (FDR) are farther from victory than ever before in the face of El Salvador's Armed Forces that are now more professional, more efficient, better equipped, better led and better motivated after a crash program of U.S. training.

The war is thus fading, with the insurgents regressing from open warfare to small-scale harassment and terrorist-style assassinations and destruction of economic targets. It is clear by now that the succession of the insurgents' "revolutionary campaigns" since 1979 represents a chain of severe miscalculations. The key to those miscalculations is that — contrary to the picture that has been painstakingly painted by American media — the insurgency never could rely on popular support. At the height of their military offensive in 1983, Archbishop Arturo Rivas y Damas summed up the insurgents' central failure: "If the Salvadoran guerillas had popular support, they would have won by now."[1]

Indeed, the insurgents' military strategy has amounted to a war of attrition against the Salvadoran economy, against the political structures and against the Armed Forces. The strategy's minimal objective has been to increase — within the context of a prolonged military stalemate — the political, economic and military costs of

This chapter appeared as an article, entitled "The Subsiding War in El Salvador," in the Winter 1985 issue of Strategic Review.

the war to an intolerable degree and to force the government into negotiations, resulting in the rebels' victory through "power-sharing."

By the end of 1984, however, the insurgents had failed decisively on the political as well as military fronts. Both El Salvador's new constitution and its modernized Armed Forces have passed severe tests, and there are no indications that the Fuerza Armada might contemplate future action against any democratically elected government loyal to the constitution, or that the Duarte Government might plan unconstitutional "power-sharing" with the FMLN/FDR after mere "negotiations."

Yet, if in 1981 the word "negotiations" could not even be found in the dictionary of the insurgents seeking total victory, it now harbors their final hope for gaining power. "When you speak of negotiations, you speak of power-sharing," the FDR's spokesman Ruben Zamora stated in October of 1984, admitting that "we thought before that total triumph was possible, but we have come to terms with reality."[2] The reality in El Salvador, however, embraces the present political correlation of constitutional forces, with the Government's opposition holding a solid majority in the National Assembly, dead-set against any deal with the insurgents, and with the Armed Forces — mirabile dictu — guarding the constitution. As President Duarte stated on June 1, 1984, with justified pride: "Our Army has grown considerably, has received better training and is imbued with a deep patriotic sentiment to defend the country and prevent our fall into the hands of Marxist subversives that try to implant a totalitarian dictatorship in El Salvador."[3]

Socio-Economic Reforms

In the heady atmosphere following the Sandinista takeover in neighboring Nicaragua in July of 1979, a group of Salvadoran Army officers led the October 1979 coup that deposed the regime of General Carlos Humberto Romero and the old ruling class, including large segments of the Army officer corps. Colonel Jaime Abdul Gutierrez, the coup's mastermind, was determined from the start to initiate major economic reforms, to clean up the security forces and to establish a government of law based on free elections.

El Salvador — then exposed to a wave of kidnappings, assassinations and bombings, and reacting with harsh anti-terrorist measures — had been one of the first countries in the world selected, criticized and ostracized by the Carter Administration in 1977 for "human rights violations." A result of these strictures was that El Salvador rejected further U.S. military aid. During 1978 and 1979, the country thus received no such assistance.

The picture changed in 1979, primarily from the U.S. vantage-point. According to a U.S. State Department assessment, "October 15, 1979, was a watershed date for El Salvador's five million people, who for decades had suffered under the rule of a tiny oligarchy that monopolized land, credit and trade, and manipulated the armed forces to repress opposition. On October 15, in a bloodless military coup, young military officers joined with moderate civilian leaders to undertake a peaceful and democratic revolution."[4]

The Carter Administration's new ambassador to El Salvador, Robert E. White — who during his confirmation hearings had described himself as a supporter of the "passionate left" — declared that "no Salvadoran government can stay in power unless it embarks on a broad program of reforms."[5]

Washington's pressure for "reform" was heeded by El Salvador's new "Revolutionary Governing Junta," which on March 7, 1980, nationalized all banks, savings and loan associations, and loan companies. With that step completed, the Government commanded the heights of the economy, placing business and citizens at the mercy of the state. At the same time, El Salvador's "land reform," planned entirely by U.S. "experts," commenced on March 6, 1980, with the security forces confiscating at gunpoint the large farms. In sum, "the United States, the supposed bastion of private enterprise, had imposed on a client state a reform that effected the wholesale seizure of private property. The United States, the supposed bastion of free enterprise, had imposed on that client state financial reforms that meant the seizure of the basic catalyst of free enterprise — the banking and credit system."[6]

The myth of land reform as the engine of Salvadoran socio-economic advancement lives on. Thus, while admitting that many who had lost land under the reform were not wealthy and "that there is some evidence [that] the most violence and illegal evictions come from the former owners of the smallest, not largest farms," Secretary of State George Shultz — under no obligation to honor, continue or defend the activism of the Carter Administration's State Department — maintained four years later that "promotion of land reform stands at the very heart of El Salvador's effort to encourage social equity, political stability and economic development."[7]

The assessment and its optimism are dangerously miscast. El Salvador's land reform has in no way encouraged social equity, political stability or economic development. On the contrary: the redistribution of wealth through expropriation is destroying what little wealth, confidence and private sector initiative are left in the country. Land reform in an overpopulated country where there is not enough land to go around has perpetuated the frustrations of the landless majority and has led the nation into an irreversible state of sub-subsistence "flowerpot farmers." Furthermore, much of what is described in the United States as "death squad" activities in El Salvador originates with farmers and other property owners lashing out against their deprivation.

The myth about Salvadoran land reform is the child of a larger one. Underlying U.S. activism in the promotion of "social equity" is the hard notion that revolutions are caused by poverty. Consequently, El Salvador, under U.S. pressure, is still trying to solve its internal problems with a gamut of political cure-alls that have the effect of transforming the country into a dependent welfare state.

It can be argued, of course, that El Salvador's radical economic reforms befit the emergency under which the country is laboring. The present U.S. Ambassador to El Salvador, Thomas R. Pickering, has argued: "The reforms were a last-ditch effort by Salvadorans to save their society and prevent a takeover from the extreme left."[8] He is seconded by the former commander of the U.S. Military Group in El Salvador, Colonel John D. Waghelstein: "Without those reforms this discussion would be in the 'what might have been' category, with the FMLN guerrillas in control in El Salvador."[9] There exists no proof for the truth of these assertions. Yet, they document again that a pure "military solution" has never been part of U.S. and Salvadoran counterinsurgency strategy.

THE GOVERNMENT'S CIVIC ACTION PROGRAM

Indeed, contemporary concepts of counterinsurgency are never limited to purely military analysis and campaign planning. The stakes and objectives involved in an insurgency are always "political" in the broadest sense of that word. This proposition may seem self-evident, but it has escaped those critics in the United States who are constantly hammering the charge that the United States Government is reaching for a "military" rather than a political solution in El Salvador. There can be no such thing as a "military solution."

The Salvadoran Government's strategy since June 1983 has centered on a National Campaign Plan, which was initially applied in two departments, San Vicente and Usulutan. The primary objectives in the National Campaign Plan have been to dislodge the insurgents from their strongholds, to disrupt their logistics networks, to secure formerly rebel-held areas and to conduct, in coordination with nonmilitary agencies, civic action programs with the aim of rebuilding the country's social and economic infrastructure.

The civic action programs consist of reopening schools and clinics, roads and bridges, establishing health and social programs, distributing food, conducting amnesty programs toward the rebels, and training local civil defense forces to protect the area following the military's departure. Eventually, all static defense of key targets such as bridges, railroads, production facilities and power stations is to be taken over by civil defense units, freeing the military to engage in offensive operations.

El Salvador's National Campaign runs counter to one of the insurgents' key objectives, which is to destroy the country's remaining wealth through relentless attacks against property and infrastructure. Thus, increasingly the insurgents' military operations have been aimed at those targets, at shattering the growing confidence of the Salvadoran citizen in his government — and also at fueling antiwar sentiment in the United States.

THE MYTH OF U.S. MILITARY INTERVENTION

From the start, U.S. military involvement in the war has been limited. At no time has there been a need for direct U.S. military intervention. U.S. military assistance in the form of arms deliveries and training proved sufficient for enabling El Salvador's Armed Forces to go it alone. The positive result of U.S. military restraint carries constructive lessons for probable future U.S. involvement in low-intensity conflicts elsewhere.

In January 1981, during the rebels' "final offensive," 19 U.S. military trainers were stationed in El Salvador. Their role was to encourage training in unconventional warfighting methods and modernization of the Armed Forces' antiquated equipment, as well as to monitor the urgent, general expansion of the Armed Forces. According to an assessment by the Pentagon in February 1981, the military outlook for the Salvadoran Government was bleak, inasmuch as the Salvadoran Army was "not organized to fight a counterinsurgency now engulfing the entire country."[10]

Early in 1981, the number of U.S. military trainers was increased to 55 — 15 of them Special Forces experts in counterinsurgency assigned to train El Salvador's first "immediate reaction" battalion, the "Atlacatl." The formation of the battalion highlighted a drive to correct the infantry's major operational deficiencies, such as a lack of mobility and alertness. Over the next four years, El Salvador's Armed Forces — while growing from an overall numerical strength of 9,028 in 1980 to 30,000 by December 1984 — were transformed into a modern, aggressive fighting machine.

In August of 1982, General Wallace H. Nutting, then heading the U.S. Army's Southern Command in Panama, testified before the Senate Foreign Relations Committee: In the functional areas of military operations, the Salvadoran Army "faced deficiencies in command and control, tactical intelligence, tactical mobility and logistics."[11]

In the preceding months, the Army had demonstrated its ability to defend the country's urban centers, but also its inability to dislodge the rebels from their strongholds in the northern and eastern mountains. Even the newly trained elite units proved ineffective when used in conventional large-scale sweeps rather than in counterinsurgency-style small-unit operations. All operations near the Honduran border were hampered by the still-unresolved dispute over the "bolsones," demilitarized border pockets used fully by the guerrilla forces as sanctuary, but respected by Salvadoran troops.

Throughout 1982–1983 the war remained essentially deadlocked, with the insurgents determining the time and place of action, and the Army tied up in the defense of static, non-military targets. During 1982, the Army assigned 70 per cent of its combat troops to guard just eight of such installations.

The State Department, in its January 16, 1984, report on the situation in El Salvador, concluded that "the overall result on the battlefield has been a continued stalemate" — meaning that Government forces, while able to deploy anywhere in the country, had been unable to deal a decisive blow to the guerrilla forces. On their part, the guerrillas had shown no ability to hold territory in the face of a concerted Government effort. The National Bipartisan Commission on Central America (or so-called Kissinger Commission), in its final report to President Reagan in January 1984, agreed that the war was "at a stalemate." Citing the Pentagon's evaluation "that it would take approximately $400 million in U.S. military assistance in 1984 and 1985 to break the military stalemate," the report concluded somewhat melodramatically: "A collapse is not inconceivable."[12]

THE ARMY'S SETBACKS IN LATE 1983

In the closing months of 1983, weak combat performance by several individual units of El Salvador's Army had revived old doubts about the Armed Forces' fighting capabilities and overall morale. On November 15, the "Fonseca" battalion was eliminated in an unexpected encounter with ERP rebel forces near the village of El Tablon in Morazan. Offering little resistance, the battalion was overrun, and the majority of its conscripts were taken prisoner. On December 13, the "Tecana" battalion was decimated at Cacahuatique, also in Morazan, when rebel forces assaulted Tecana's position at night with mortar and machinegun fire.

On December 30, insurgents attacked, took and destroyed the Fourth Infantry Brigade headquarters at El Paraiso in Chalatenango, defended by 300 men. The following day, rebel sappers took Cuscatlan Bridge on the Panamerican Highway, a vital link in the country's infrastructure, and dynamited it in the early morning hours of New Year's Day, 1984.

To the observer in the United States and elsewhere, the sudden flow of bad news from the front in El Salvador seemed a confirmation of the pessimistic analysis that had been published by *Newsweek* even before the Army's defeats: The Salvadoran Army "was losing ground fast.... If the rebels are not likely to triumph immediately, they do seem to have time and momentum on their side." Backing this unrealistic assessment with a quote from the usual anonymous "highly placed Administration official," *Newsweek* concluded on December 12: "There is a fear that the Army could be swept out. It could all be over by Christmas."[13]

Taken as a whole, the defeats at El Tablon, Cacahuatique, El Paraiso and Cuscatlan Bridge represented primarily psychological setbacks for the Government and its fledgling strategy of counterinsurgency: Entire units had demonstrated grave negligence in conducting basic tactical duties such as constant reconnaissance and patrolling. For the insurgents, however, four tactical victories in a row amounted to a major propaganda triumph at a time of mounting problems within their own ranks and operations.

The Salvadoran Government's embarrassment extended to the Pentagon and its role in El Salvador. The expansion and training of the Fuerza Armada had taken place under U.S. auspices. What had gone wrong?

The ill-fated "Fonseca" battalion, vanquished at El Tablon, provided one part of the answer. Its leader, Major Miguel Borja, was relieved of his command and placed under house arrest. Yet, poor leadership alone could hardly be blamed for the unit's dismal performance on the battlefield. Rather, the adversary had radically changed the terms of warfare for which "Fonseca" and all of its 35 sister CS battalions (CS for "Counter-Subversion") had been trained: During their fall 1983 offensive, circumstances permitting, the rebels opted for open conventional warfare, attacking with large, regiment-sized formations. The CS battalions — the brainchildren of the Pentagon — contained a maximum of 280 troops each. At El Tablon, "Fonseca" was attacked by roughly 900 guerillas. It was not only outmaneuvered: it was also outnumbered and outgunned. Similarly, at El Paraiso the guerrillas' attacking force numbered 800 men, at Cacahuatique 650.

Yet, the setbacks of late 1983 were symptomatic also of other problems in the Salvadoran Army. Throughout 1982 and 1983, the Army's command and control system had exhibited coordination breakdowns and lack of detailed planning and timely responsiveness at the general staff and departmental level. Other shortcomings had been visible in the areas of mobility and transport, medical evacuation and care, and operational and logistic planning.

THE TURNING POINT IN 1984

An essential (and overdue) change in the military was the reorganization in November of 1983 of the High Command, ordered by General Carlos Eugenio Vides Casanova, Minister for Defense and Public Security Forces. Until then, 26 separate commands had reported to the Defense Minister. With the appointment of six brigade commanders, the number of subordinate commands was sharply reduced. Simultaneously, Colonel Adolfo Onecifero Blandon, highly respected as an aggressive field commander, was appointed Chief of Staff of the Armed Forces.

Under Blandon's direction, a shakeup of U.S.-designed organization and tactics in key combat units was implemented within weeks, and an increase of overall troop strength by 20 per cent during 1984 was announced. Other measures aimed at retaking the military initiative from the guerrillas, included the bolstering of manpower through the introduction of a general draft, enforcement of the draft — amounting to mobilization — and the lengthening of enlistment terms.

Key command and staff changes, and improved command and control by the General Staff began to facilitate more vigorous operations under new and aggressive commanders early in 1984. Still, in addition to force expansion and training, enhanced mobility and communications were needed — as well as a radical review of strategic and tactical doctrine.

In the past, rebel-held territories — primarily those lining the Honduran border in northern Chalatenango, San Miguel and Morazan — had been declared unofficially "non-strategic" and were in fact conceded temporarily to the rebels. Similarly, the country's roads had been abandoned to the insurgents at night. Rebel units were known to travel the length of the country under the cover of darkness without being molested by Army patrols investigating traffic at roadblocks.

Recognizing that in counterinsurgency wars there can be neither "non-strategic" areas nor open communications facilities for the insurgents, an active policy of "denial of sanctuary, denial of movement, and denial of supplies" was implemented in 1984. The Army's new offensive doctrine was communicated to the insurgents on February 19, 1984. In the early hours of that day, a Sunday, a company-sized immediate-reaction unit brought a helicopter assault against the field headquarters of Joaquin Villalobos, commander of the rebels' Ejercito Revolucionario del Pueblo (ERP), near the town of San Gerardo in northern San Miguel, inflicting heavy losses on the ERP's elite unit and capturing large amounts of communications gear and intelligence documents. The attack marked a turning point in the war: it not only dislodged the ERP from its traditional stronghold, but also demonstrated that the Salvadoran Armed Forces had finally shed the image of primarily fighting a "nine-to-five war."

PROBLEMS IN U.S. EQUIPMENT ASSISTANCE

Backing the Salvadorans' new aggressiveness, and enhancing their tactical mobility, the Pentagon in 1984 brought the Air Force's helicopter fleet from 24 in April to 49 in December. The 1984 U.S. military assistance package reflected the recognition and correction of past follies in U.S. assistance policies.

In the late 1970s, following an initiative by Senator Edward Kennedy, President Carter had suspended the sale and shipment of all U.S.-made antipersonnel bombs and rockets to countries suspected of human rights violations. In the Reagan Administration's first year, El Salvador remained on the embargo list. As a consequence of this early gap in U.S. aid, Salvadoran pilots flying ground attacks still tend to launch armor-piercing missiles after rebels fleeing on foot.

Until early 1984, equipment delivered by the Pentagon to the Salvadoran Air Force was always used, often very old and sometimes nearly useless. By May of 1984, the Air Force had taken delivery of 23 UH-1H "Huey" tactical transport helicopters for employment in a wide variety of roles, including air assault, close-air support, medical evacuation and administrative duties (due to the largescale destruction of bridges and roads in the countryside). The heavy use of the helicopters results in constant and major repair work. With four to six Hueys constantly assigned in the field, the Salvadoran Air Force was left with only ten to twelve helicopters for quick reaction; the remainder were grounded due to malfunctions. The ratio amounted to reacting with only 100 soldiers at a time to counter an enemy who might outnumber the Army's conscripts five-to-one.

The problem of aging equipment can be illustrated with specific examples. Huey 66-16620/270 is a typical helicopter delivered to El Salvador under the Pentagon's military assistance program. It was built in 1966 and shipped to South Vietnam. Having suffered crash damage there in 1970, it was rebuilt in the United States, used heavily for pilot training at Fort Rucker, Alabama, and then shipped to a U.S. Army unit in West Germany. After undergoing superficial overhaul in Corpus Christi, Texas, in 1983, it was handed over to the Salvadoran Air Force. The price tag for this overused item was $650,000; a fair market price would have been $150,000.

Another Huey (Number 66-16037/268) arrived in El Salvador in 1983, also costing $650,000, with 8,796 flying hours on the airframe. Since 1966 it had gone through three transmission overhauls, the last immediately before delivery to El Salvador, where it broke down after only three weeks of heavy use.

To provide fire support to infantry units in the field, El Salvador's Air Force by 1984 had six A-37 "Dragonfly" light attack jets. Most of them were more than ten years old and required excessive, unscheduled maintenance time. The result was a maximum of only three A-37s on the line, and a limited ability to respond to simultaneous requests from different areas of the country.

The Fuerza Aerea's oldest A-37 aircraft (Number 70-1294) was built in 1970 and had flown numerous combat missions over Vietnam. It then saw service with U.S. Air National Guard units in Barksdale, Louisiana, and Battle Creek, Michigan. With roughly 7,500 hours on the airframe, this venerable museum piece was sold to El Salvador in 1982 for $800,000.

Salvadorans, who do not actually "pay" for military hardware and training received from the United States (an account is set up in the Pentagon, and all items delivered are then held against the account), do not complain aloud about the occasional poor quality or frequent old age of many of the items arriving from the United States. Nor do they claim a right to demand better quality or greater quantities of acceptable hardware. But the Pentagon's military assistance program, as applied to El Salvador and linked to continous squabbling in the U.S. Congress, is viewed as a strange way of supporting an ally under attack.

U.S. TRAINING POLICIES

Much has been argued about the number of U.S. military "advisers" active in El Salvador. Allegedly, there are "too few" of them. Given the refusal by the U.S. Congress to increase their number (and the Salvadoran Armed Forces' reluctance to accept more of them, based on documented dissatisfaction), the alternative seems obvious: namely, to select for the task highly qualified volunteers who are specialized in counterinsurgency warfare, and to extend their tour-of-duty from the present one year to two years.

U.S. Army Special Forces Colonel Joseph Stringham exemplified the rotation problem. He arrived in El Salvador in mid-summer 1983. As head of the U.S. Military Group he was widely respected by Salvadorans for his expertise and solid grasp of local military affairs, acquired through on-the-job training. In accordance with the Pentagon's traditional rotation routine, Colonel Stringham left El Salvador after just one year, and a new Military Group commander entered his on-the-job training program in the summer of 1984.

Similar waste of manpower, expertise and general resources has hampered the long-term success of U.S. combat training for Salvadoran crack units. All of the Salvadoran Army's six "Immediate Reaction" (IR) battalions are American-trained. As the majority of the troops are relatively low-paid conscripts who serve for up to two years only, the resulting turnover and dropout rate in the ranks has negatively affected the units' stipulated combat professionalism. For instance, in the "Atlacatl" battalion, trained in 1981, less then 10 per cent American-trained soldiers remained by December 1984; in the "Ramon Beloso" battalion, trained in 1982 in the United States, 30 per cent of the original trainees remained by the end of 1984.

Conscription still lies at the core of the Army's problems. While it is capable of producing conventional forces to counter conventional military challenges, conscription does not, as a rule, generate the kind of fighting force that can successfully cope with insurgency war: the history of such conflicts has proven conclusively that an all-volunteer, professional army—supported by competent civil defense and militia forces — is better equipped for the task. Counterinsurgency requires the constant availability of highly mobile rapid deployment forces in tandem with countrywide static defenses provided by paramilitary units. The requirement was met in El Salvador during 1985 as announced in early January by the Armed Forces' Chief-of-Staff, General Blandon: emphasis was now placed on rebuilding a civil defense system and upgrading rapid reaction capabilities.

THE LONGER-RANGE VARIABLES

All wars of insurgency, "small wars," are long and slogging conflicts, often inconclusive. Such wars do not end suddenly with one side declaring "victory." Insurgencies can simply fade away — and then reappear when new strategic realities promise greater success.

Such is the case now with El Salvador's insurgency. The five factions that make up the FMLN cannot hope to win power by military means. Similarly, a "political solution" — that is, "power-sharing" — seems remote in light of the Salvadoran Armed Forces' growing strength and the insurgents' demonstrated weakness in the field. The FMLN/FDR's sole present hope rests elsewhere — namely, with the media and political forces in the United States that still favor and stubbornly advocate a "political solution" for El Salvador notwithstanding the changed strategic realities in the Central American region.

These new realities — along with the reality of a second Reagan Presidency — run counter to an accommodation with Marxist-Leninist forces anywhere in the region. If El Salvador has been defined repeatedly by President Reagan as the main battlefield between democracy and communism in the Western Hemisphere — and if El Salvador's success in combatting its insurgency could not have been achieved without determined assistance from the United States — the defeat of El Salvador's insurgency is the direct outcome of the U.S. Congress' commitment, signed into law in 1962 by President J. F. Kennedy: "to prevent by whatever means may be necessary, including the use of arms, the Marxist-Leninist regime in Cuba from extending, by force or the threat of force, its aggressive or subversive activities to any part of the hemisphere."

Ever since Castro's advent to power in Cuba in 1959, the Western Hemisphere has been subjected to probing attacks by the Soviet Union and Cuba through surrogate force. This strategy reached an apex in 1979 with the Sandinista capture of Nicaragua. It has been rolled back in 1983 in Grenada, and in El Salvador since 1984.

The international left has proclaimed publicly (in 1982) that "the defense of Cuba, the protection and deepening of the gains made in Nicaragua, and the expansion of the newly unified guerrilla movement in Guatemala have all become part of a single movement that depends vitally upon a popular victory in El Salvador."[14] With the vision of such "popular victory" turning into an illusion in El Salvador, the "single movement" is suffering setbacks elsewhere in Central America.

At the center of the Central American equation stands the resolve of the U.S. Administration "to stay the course." Already the clear trend of recent political and military developments in the region has prompted even members of the political-academic opposition in the United States to pay grudging acknowledgement to the Administration's "major foreign policy accomplishment in Central America, thanks to both policy design and good luck."[15]

A steadfast continuation of this policy is required if the subsiding insurgency in El Salvador is to be extinguished. Even though the insurgency has been gravely weakened in the face of a determined Salvadoran Government and U.S. assistance, it will be fully defeated only when its roots are severed: Nicaragua's militant "Sandinismo" and the Cuban connection.

NOTES

1. *La Nacion Internacional* (San Jose, Costa Rica) September 22–28, 1983.

2. Clifford Krauss, "Leftists Lose Optimism About Soon Prevailing in Central America," *Wall Street Journal,* October 15, 1984.

3. Inaugural Speech, San Salvador, June 1, 1984.

4. John A. Bushnell, Deputy Assistant Secretary for Inter-American Affairs, before House Appropriation Committee's Subcommittee on Foreign Operations, March 25, 1980.

5. Robert E. White, Senate Confirmation Hearing, February 21, 1980.

6. James R. Whelan and Patricia B. Bozell, *Catastrophe in the Caribbean* (Ottawa, IL: Jameson Books, 1984), p. 78.

7. "Salvador's Fibrillating 'Heart'"," *Wall Street Journal,* February 21, 1984.

8. Letter to the Editor, *Policy Review* (Washington), Winter 1985, p. 7.

9. Ibid, p. 8.

10. *New York Times,* February 21, 1981.

11. Ibid, August 4, 1982.

12. *The Report of the President's National Bipartisan Commission on Central America* (New York: Macmillan, 1984), p. 120.

13. *Newsweek,* December 12, 1983.

14. James Dunkerley, *The Long War — Dictatorship and Revolution in El Salvador* (London: Junction Books, 1982), p. 163.

15. Jorge I. Dominguez, "Luck Lends a Hand in Central America," *Boston Globe,* June 25, 1984.

7 The U.S. Action in Grenada: Its Context and Its Meaning

Jeane J. Kirkpatrick

EDITOR'S NOTE: On November 2, 1983, the U.N. General Assembly took up the question of Grenada in a resolution sponsored by Nicaragua, Zimbabwe and Guyana, which called for the immediate cessation of fighting on the island and withdrawal of all troops, characterizing the intervention as a "flagrant violation of international law." Debate on the resolution was preempted by a cloture motion introduced by the People's Democratic Republic of Yemen and carried by 60 votes to 54, with 24 abstentions. The Nicaraguan resolution was adopted 108 to 9, with 27 abstentions. The only countries voting with the United States were the Eastern Caribbean states that had requested the intervention, plus El Salvador and Israel.

Ambassador Kirkpatrick later described that day as the "lowest point" in her three years at the U.N. She expressed indignation at spurious comparisons between Grenada and Afghanistan, and bitterness at allied nations which seemed to have forgotten their own armed liberation from oppressors. She scored the curtailment of debate in a body that was created expressly for the full airing of international issues.

There was additional irony in the circumstance that the cloture motion came from South Yemen, a Soviet-controlled state that in 1978 experienced the assassination of its pro-Soviet president and his replacement by an even more staunchly pro-Soviet leader — in other words, experienced a pattern remarkably similar to that which unfolded in Grenada in 1983.

What follows is the speech that Ambassador Kirkpatrick prepared for the debate on November 2, but was prevented from delivering. This chapter appeared as an article, entitled "The U.N. and Grenada: A Speech Never Delivered," in the Winter 1984 issue of Strategic Review.

Mr. President: The United States did not oppose the inscription of "The Situation in Grenada" under Rule 15 as an additional item for consideration by the General Assembly during the current session. The United States does not object to debate of this issue. To the contrary, we welcome a full, judicious consideration of all the facts pertaining to the situation in Grenada, convinced that an understanding of the situation will support the actions of the Organization of Eastern Caribbean States and its associates, including the United States; that the use of force by the task force was lawful under international law and the U.N. Charter because it was undertaken to protect U.S. nationals from a clear and present danger, because it was a legitimate exercise of regional collective security, and because it was carried out with due concern for lawful procedures in the service of the values of the Charter — including the restoration of the rule of law, self-determination, sovereignty, democracy and respect for the human rights of the people of Grenada.

We did object to giving special priority to the consideration of this item, not because we do not deem it important — obviously we do — but because the situation that now prevails in Grenada is not *more* urgent than other matters still to be considered by the Assembly — matters that involve the same basic values of the Charter and even more human lives, such as the situation in Lebanon, Southern Africa, Central America, Afghanistan, the war between Iran and Iraq — or other issues that will not come before the Assembly at all, such as the aggression against Chad, or the repression of the Polish people, or the persecution of Andrei Sakharov, Anatoly Shcharansky, Jose Pujals, Ricardo Bofil, Eloy Gutierrez Menoyo and other beleaguered defenders of human rights. Moreover, we deemed it hypocritical and politically tendentious to turn the Assembly's urgent attention to the situation in Grenada only after the real emergency in that country had passed — which is to say, only after Grenada had been rescued from the murderous elements that had taken over the country, threatening the people of that country and the neighboring states as well.

"Application of Universal Norms"

But now the issue is before us, so let us consider it in all its aspects. Let us consider all the issues raised in this resolution. Let us consider the situation that prevailed in Grenada before the intervention of October 25th. Let us consider whether that situation was such as to warrant the use of force in a manner consistent with the Charter of the United Nations. Let us consider whether the principle of self-determination was violated or upheld. Let us consider whether the sovereignty of Grenada was destroyed or restored. Let us consider whether the people of Grenada were victimized or liberated. Let us consider whether the cause of peace was damaged or served.

These may appear to be difficult questions, but the difficulties disappear when they are addressed not in the abstract, but in the context of the concrete circumstances that led small, peaceful, democratic island states of the Caribbean not merely to sanction the intervention but to request and to participate in it. The test of law lies not in the assertion of abstract principles, but in the application of universal norms to specific situations. A court that cannot distinguish between lawful and criminal use of force, between force used to protect the innocent and force used to victimize them, is not worthy to sit in judgment. The failure to draw such distinctions will not preserve law as an instrument of justice and peace, but will erode the moral and legal — and ultimately political — foundations of civilized existence.

"An Authentic Reign of Terror"

First there is the question of force. The intrusion of force into the public life of Grenada did not begin with the intervention of October 25th. From 1979 Grenada had been ruled by a government that came to power by coup, overthrowing a corrupt, though elected, predecessor. The government of Maurice Bishop was initially welcomed by Grenadians. Initially it promised to hold elections and respect basic human rights. These promises were honored in the breach, as the government attempted to impose a Castro-style dictatorship with Cuban and Soviet aid. Eventually, when Bishop sought to free himself from the Cuban-Soviet grip, he was arrested by his Cuban-trained deputy, Bernard Coard, and shot in cold blood on October 19th along with other members of his cabinet and political leaders. At least 18 deaths were confirmed and many more were reported, including those of women and children. There was no court, no trial, no judgment, only murder. Expressing "horror at these brutal and vicious murders," Prime Minister Tom Adams of Barbados said that the division in the Caribbean now went "far beyond ideological pluralism" and "is the difference between barbarians and human beings."

In the wake of these murders, the People's Revolutionary Army announced the dissolution of the government and the formation of a 16-member Revolutionary Military Council with General Hudson Austin as the nominal head. This group was not a government — it indicated that it would subsequently announce a government — but literally a gang of murderers who imposed an authentic reign of terror upon the Grenadian people. It decreed a 24-hour curfew, warning that violators would be shot on sight, and closed the airport, thereby entrapping nearly 1,000 U.S. citizens — each and every one a potential hostage. Although the Military Council gave assurances that the airport would be opened on October 24th and foreigners allowed to depart, it failed to fulfill that assurance. The threat of violence against these American citizens, and against the people of Grenada, was real and imminent.

"INFRASTRUCTURE FOR HOSTILITY AGAINST NEIGHBORING STATES"

Grenada's neighbors also feared for their security. During the period of his rule, Bishop had permitted Grenada to be transformed into a base for the projection of Soviet and Cuban military power in the Western Hemisphere. The instruments of violence and deception assembled during Bishop's tenure now fell into the hands of Bishop's murderous successors, presumably even more pliant tools of Soviet and Cuban designs. Here is how this new threat was viewed by Prime Minister Edward Seaga of Jamaica, one of Grenada's Caribbean neighbors. The danger, he told the Jamaican Parliament on October 25th, arose "from the capacity of the leadership which seized power to use the armed capabilities and military infrastructure of Grenada for acts of hostility against neighboring states." He went on:

The size and sophistication of the armed force of Grenada can be measured by a comparison with those of Jamaica. Grenada, having only one-twentieth of the population of Jamaica, had mobilized an army that was one and a half times as large as the Jamaica Defense Force. Some of Grenada's neighbors have no army at all; others have armies of less than 200 men.

The new airstrip, in the final stages of completion by Cubans, added another capability which in the hands of sane men would have offered no threat, but against the background of the insanity of the past two weeks would be a logical staging area for countries whose interests are similar, and who have ambitions for using Grenada as a center for subversion, sabotage and infiltration within the area and against member states of the Organization of Eastern Caribbean States.

Again, the powerful broadcasting station in Grenada, standing on its own, although capable of reaching from one end of the Caribbean to the other and far exceeding the power of any station in Jamaica, would in itself not necessarily be a threat, but in the hands of extremists of a military or ideological nature, both of whom exist in Grenada, constitutes a potent weapon for subverting neighboring states.

While Maurice Bishop was alive, there was some indication that these capabilities could and would be used in this subversive manner against neighboring states, as there were complaints regarding training of a paramilitary nature taking place in Grenada among citizens of neighboring countries known for their own subversive interests.

However, whatever may have been the threat, it was minimal in the hands of Maurice Bishop, who was a moderate in comparison with the military and political leaders of the regime which overthrew him. A totally different picture emerges when this array of military and subversive capability came to be at the disposal of one of the most extremist groups of men to assume control of any country in recent times. Few countries can have claimed the experience of having its entire cabinet wiped out in the manner in which that of Grenada was exterminated. Who then can blame the Eastern Caribbean states for perceiving this combination of awesome might and brutal men, who apparently had no

concept of where to stop in taking human life, as a prelude to
hostile action being taken beyond their own borders by those in
power in Grenada?

"WAREHOUSES PACKED WITH ARMS"

Prime Minister Seaga made these comments on the basis of the
perceived threat emanating from Grenada but *before* the full scope
of the Soviet and Cuban military capability on the island had been
uncovered. These fears, as he subsequently said, were amply confirmed by what was found on the island, including "thousands of
crates filled with millions of rounds of ammunition and a large
number of other crates of Russian AK-47 submachine guns. Heavy
artillery capable of firing 2,000 rounds per minute, anti-tank
weapons and anti-aircraft installations...embedded in the hillside
around Point Salines have been uncovered...." He went on:

> There is no longer any mystery, therefore, about what was going
> on at the Cuban-built airport at Point Salines. The airport has
> turned out to be nothing less than a sophisticated military camp.
> All the signs and directions are in Spanish, none in English.
> Facilities are present throughout for the storage of arms, and there
> is no evidence of provision being made for any normal commer-
> cial or civilian traffic. The installation is filled with places to
> hang rifles — even in the sanitary conveniences. The six
> warehouses packed with arms and other discoveries speak more
> eloquently than any words could of a Grenada that was being
> converted into a fortress and a base camp for hostile activities
> against its neighbors and within the region.

The Prime Minister does not speak of the weapons found in the
small island of Carriacou adjoining Grenada, where only yesterday were uncovered 700 rifles and 38 Soviet-made AK-47s, rocket-
propelled grenades, 150 cases of ammunition, two jeeps, a truck,
a generator, radio equipment and a dozen cases of TNT. Less than
a mile from Grenada's "tourist" airport, six warehouses were found
which contained materiel of a similar variety, but in far larger
numbers — enough to outfit two brigades, or 8,000 men, according to U.S. military officials.

"Secret Treaties for Covert Supply of Arms"

Mr. President, these discoveries revealed only what had already been emplaced in Grenada. They do not speak of the buildup that was envisioned through 1985 and agreed to in five secret treaties, three with the Soviet Union, one with Cuba and one with North Korea, which alone had agreed to supply $12 million worth of arms. These secret treaties provide for the covert supply of arms to Grenada from the Soviet Union, to be transshipped through Cuba — a pattern that is also being followed in Central America. The arms included millions of rounds of ammunition, sniper rifles, armored vehicles, naval patrol craft from North Korea, anti-aircraft guns, anti-tank guns, mortars, thousands of automatic rifles, hand grenades and land-mines, and 18,000 military uniforms — 18,000 military uniforms for a country with a population of only 100,000. In addition, the treaties provided for assistance in the creation of a force run by the Ministry of Interior and for surveillance equipment and other items used by the KGB. They also provided for training Grenadians in the Soviet Union.

Mr. President, the United Nations was established to beat swords into plowshares. In Grenada, the Soviet Union and its proxies beat plowshares into AK-47s, machine guns and heavy artillery.

"Direct Appeal to the OECS"

Is there any reasonable basis for concluding that the fears of Grenada's neighbors were unfounded? Can any prudent judgment question the urgent appeal from the Organization of Eastern Caribbean States for assistance in meeting this threat to their security?

The OECS, a subregional body established to promote regional cooperation and collective security, determined that the collapse of government and the disintegration of public order in Grenada posed a threat to the security and stability of the region. As a consequence, the OECS members decided to take necessary measures in response to this threat, in accordance with Article 8 of the OECS Treaty. They sought the assistance of friendly foreign states to participate in a collective security force. The United States, together with Barbados and Jamaica, agreed with the OECS assessment of the gravity of the situation and offered to contribute forces to a collective action in support of this regional measure. The Governor General of Grenada made a confidential, direct appeal to the OECS to take action to restore order on the island. As the sole remaining authoritative representative of government in Grenada, his appeal for action carried exceptional moral and legal weight.

Listen to the Governor General's description of his request and his thoughts about it, as expressed in a BBC interview:

Q : Does it not seem a little strange that the Governor General of a Commonwealth country should ask America to intervene rather than Britain?

A : Well, I thought the Americans would do it much faster and more decisively. At first, I was against invasion of the country. But things deteriorated very rapidly. You see, when the military took over, they quickly came to me and acknowledged my authority as representative of the Queen, in the same way as the People's Revolutionary Government did when they overthrew the elected government. And at first I thought they were the right people. I was impressed. But within a very short time I thought things deteriorated rapidly. For example, I still need to know what became of the bodies of people who were killed on that day, including the bodies of Prime Minister Bishop and three Cabinet Ministers. I know that these bodies have never been handed over to relatives, and I am advised that these bodies were never taken to the hospital or any of the two undertakers in town.

Q : What was the moment you decided that an invasion was necessary?

A : I think I decided so on Sunday the 23rd, late Sunday evening.

Q : But the British say that on that day you told them you still didn't want one; that was early in the day, was it?

A : I did see somebody earlier in the day, and during that time I did see somebody and they said you know invasion was the last thing they wanted, and I said it in my speech. But if it came to that, I would give every support; and later on, as things deteriorated, I thought, because people were scared, you know, I had several calls from responsible people in Grenada that something should be done. "Mr. Governor General, we are depending on you [that] something be done. People in Grenada cannot do it, you must get help from outside." What I did ask for was not an invasion, but help from outside.

Q : Do you regret that the British were not associated with America in coming in?

A : I would not like to comment on this. I'm afraid in my position I would not like to blame any country for anything or to express such regrets. But what I can say is that we were very, very grateful that these other countries came to our rescue and they came just on time.

Q : Did you invite Britain to take part?

A : No, I did not invite Britain to take part, and I asked for help from the OECS countries. I also asked the OECS to ask America whether they can help. And then I confirmed this in writing myself to the President of the USA.

Q : How long, sir, do you think the Americans should remain here?

A : I would like — and I speak for the people who have to live and work in Grenada — I would like them to remain here as long as it is necesary. This I cannot say at the moment. I cannot say two weeks or three weeks or two months. I don't know.

And Governor General Scoon said, further, in his radio speech to the people:

Innocent men, women and children were also killed or injured. To say the least, I was deeply saddened, and I shall like to extend heartfelt sympathy to the bereaved families. The killing of Prime Minister Bishop and the subsequent control of our country by the People's Revolutionary Army so horrified not only Grenadians but the entire Caribbean, the Commonwealth and beyond that certain Caribbean states with the support of the United States of America decided to come to our aid in the restoration of peace and order. Of course, intervention by foreign troops is the last thing one would want for one's country. But in our case, it has happened in deteriorating circumstances, repugnant to the vast majority.

"Consistent with the Charter of the U.N. and of the OAS"

Mr. President, collective action in response to the kind of dangerous situation that existed in Grenada is consistent with the Charter of the United Nations and with the Charter of the Organization of American States. Both Charters expressly recognize the competence of regional security bodies in ensuring peace and stability. The OECS states are not parties to the Rio Treaty, and the OECS Treaty, which concerns itself in part with matters of collective security, is their regional security arrangement.

Article 22 of the OAS Charter states that measures taken pursuant to collective security agreements do not violate the OAS Charter provisions prohibiting intervention and the use of force. Similarly, Article 52 of the U.N. Charter expressly permits regional arrangements for the maintenance of peace and security consistent with the purposes and principles of the United Nations. The actions and objectives of the collective security force, in the circumstances I have described, are consistent with those purposes and principles.

The OECS states, in taking lawful collective action, were free to call upon other concerned states, including the United States, for assistance in their effort to maintain the peace and security of the Caribbean. Assistance given in response to their request is itself lawful. Moreover, U.S. cooperation with the collective security force permitted the safe evacuation of endangered U.S. citizens. Such humanitarian action is justified by well-established principles of international law.

Mr. President, the extent of the danger faced by U.S. citizens in Grenada was vividly illustrated by the numerous photographs of American students kissing the ground after deplaning in the United States. "We thought we could be potential hostages," said one. "We just wanted to get out if we could." Said another, who talked to Grenadians about leaving: "They said they were afraid and they would leave if they could. If they feel that way about their own government, I don't see how I could trust it." Let me also quote, if I may, from a letter that was sent to President Reagan by 65 students last Thursday:

> We the students of St. George's University School of Medicine at Kingstown Medical College, St. Vincent, would like to express our appreciation of your concern for the safety of our fellow students in Grenada.... Having spent the past two years in Grenada and being in almost daily contact with American students there during the recent unrest, we support your decision....

"AN INTERVENTION POPULAR THROUGHOUT THE REGION"

There is no question, Mr. President, that the intervention in Grenada was immensely popular throughout the Caribbean region. The Prime Minister of Barbados, Tom Adams, said: "There has seldom been in these islands such virtual unanimous support in the media and at political and popular levels for an action so potentially divisive." The Jamaican columnist and opinion analyst, Dr. Carl Stone, wrote that the intervention in Grenada "is both popular here in Jamaica and in the rest of the Caribbean because of the feelings about the murderous butchers of St. George's." James Nelson Goodsell, the Latin American correspondent for the *Christian Science Monitor*, reported: "At the recent Inter-American Press Association meeting in Lima, Peru, there was virtually unanimous backing by Caribbean editors for the combined U.S.-Caribbean invasion of Grenada."

Mr. Goodsell's finding was amply confirmed by reactions in the region to the intervention. Mark A. Conyers, the Managing Editor of the *Trinidad Guardian*, said: "I thoroughly agree with the forces' landing. You have to protect Caribbean democracy. There must be an elected government in Grenada, and this landing should help bring that about." An editorial in the *Bridgetown Advocate* noted: "If we are really serious about the concept of sovereignty, what has been done has given the Grenadians a real chance to recapture their true sovereignty as a people." This point was echoed in *El Universal* of Caracas, which said that the action in Grenada was "taken to end totalitarian intervention in the Republic of Grenada, and it will guarantee that island's people the right to freedom and to elect their governments democratically." An editorial on October 27th in Colombia's leading daily, *Il Tiempo*, noted that the Cubans in Grenada were not simply workers and teachers "but a group armed to the teeth, capable of direct combat in a direct and efficient manner. . . . Now Fidel orders the Cubans dug in on the island to resist until the end, by which he virtually admits that they had already invaded the island by other means and that now they refuse to allow themselves to be pushed away."

"THE VIEWS OF THE PEOPLE OF GRENADA"

I could go on citing regional opinion, but the views that count most are the views of the people of Grenada. Let me quote from Alister Hughes, the Agence France Presse and CANA correspondent and the sole independent news link between Grenada and the outside world until his arrest on October 19th: "I don't regard it as an invasion, but a rescue operation. I haven't met any Grenadian who had expressed any other view." He added: "Thank God they came. If someone had not come in and done something, I hesitate to say what the situation in Grenada would be now."

TV interviews conducted by the Canadian Broadcasting Corporation found the people in the streets of St. George's uniformly favorable to the intervention, a reaction also found by *Washington Post* reporter Ed Cody. The Governor General himself, Paul Scoon, said: "The people of Grenada, the people who live and work here, . . . I am well advised have welcomed the presence of these troops as a positive step forward in the restoration not only of peace and order but also of full sovereignty that's enabling our democratic institutions to function according to the expressed wishes of the Grenadian people at the earliest possible time."

"SELF-DETERMINATION INVOLVES RESPECT FOR FUNDAMENTAL FREEDOMS"

The Governor General has, of course, raised here the central issue, the issue of democracy, the issue that is at the heart of the principle of self-government and self-determination. It is the Governor

General's intention, which we fully support, that the people of Grenada will exercise their right of self-government and self-determination through the instrumentalities of free elections and free institutions. How, then, has their right of self-determination been violated, as some claim?

The states which make this claim presumably believe that the Grenadian people enjoyed self-determination before October 25th, which is to say, when they were subjected to a brutal reign of terror. The fact that these states include the Soviet Union, Cuba, and Nicaragua and others of their imperial vocation should not be at all surprising, since they do not, in fact, see any contradiction between self-determination and totalitarianism, between self-determination and the seizure of power by armed minorities, between self-determination and the subversion of democratic neighbors, between self-determination and absorption into the Soviet Empire.

Self-determination involves respect for "human rights and fundamental freedoms," as stated in Article 55 of the Charter, and it is expressed through "self-government" that takes due account, as Article 76 states, of "the freely expressed wishes of the peoples concerned." Is there anyone here who can reasonably believe and credibly assert that the prospect for the full enjoyment of this right by the Grenadian people was not immensely better after October 25th than it was before that date? The Grenadian people do not take that view, nor do their neighbors who are closest to their situation.

Life is already returning to usual in Grenada. People are moving freely on the streets after having been confined for ten days.

The Governor General and the people of Grenada know precisely what it plans and how it proposes to achieve its goals. The Governor General is planning for a nonpolitical interim administration to prepare elections and return to democracy.

In the same broadcast quoted earlier, the Governor General announced that 400 soldiers and national policemen from the Eastern Caribbean countries that took part in the landing would be formed into a security force. The Governor General has ordered remaining members of the People's Revolutionary Army and the militia to stop fighting and has officially disbanded the armed forces.

The proof of the pudding, of course, is finally in the eating. It is one thing to rescue people from murderers and another for those same people to hold free elections. The latter does not necessarily follow from the former, although surely free elections and democratic life can hardly exist under conditions of terror. But let there be no question that it is the profound hope of the people of the United States that the Grenadian people shall soon enjoy freedom, democracy and stability. We trust that this hope is shared by those who invoke the principle of self-determination in their objection to the means used to rescue the Grenadian people.

"Force Used to Liberate and Force Used to Impose Terror"

There are those who say — let us be blunt — that the use of force by the United States in Grenada is equivalent to the use of force by the Soviet Union in Afghanistan or Eastern Europe. Let me just pose the following questions in response: Is there no distinction to be drawn between force used to liberate captive people from terror and force used to impose terror on captive people? Is Solidarnosc in Poland to be equated with the Revolutionary Military Council in Grenada? Is "socialism with a human face" in Czechoslovakia of the Prague Spring the same as communism armed to the teeth in the Grenada of Bishop's killers?

There is, let me say, a parallel to be drawn between Grenada and Afghanistan — a very meaningful parallel. Just as Maurice Bishop was murdered in Grenada because he tried to free himself from the Soviet stranglehold, so, too, was Mohammed Daoud murdered in Afghanistan and after him Hafizollah Amin. Let me here also remind the representative of South Yemen that on June 26, 1978, the President of South Yemen, Selim Rubai Ali, and two of his followers were executed for precisely the same reason. They, too, discovered that the only thing more dangerous than embracing the Soviet bear is trying to break loose from its deadly grip. They, too, learned that the price of trying to reverse the course of history — the inexorable course of history, in the Soviet view — is violent death. This, and this alone, is the parallel between Grenada and Afghanistan. The difference is that the people of Grenada have now been spared the cruel fate of the people of Afghanistan.

Speaking before the OAS, the representative of St. Lucia said that the United States is only "guilty of responding positively to a formal request for assistance from some of the Eastern Caribbean states who wish only to maintain their security and protect their people from the totalitarian grip which seeks to place a stranglehold on the Caribbean." There are others in this world who, if not now similarly threatened by the totalitarian grip of the Soviet Union and its proxies — who specialize in gaining power through subversion and terror and then consolidating totalitarian control — may well be so threatened in the future. In voting on this resolution, we ask them to consider what they would do were they to be in the position of the Eastern Caribbean states? What would they want done were their country subjected to the kind of terror that prevailed in Grenada? Would they, too, want assistance? And would they, too, appeal for rescue? And if they would — which would be entirely consistent with a desire to preserve and defend one's nation — we ask just one more question: How can they reconcile that position with a vote in favor of the resolution now before us?

"END OF THE DREAMS AND HOPES OF THE U.N.?"

Has it come to this: That this organization, founded in the wake of a great war against tyrants, comprising from the moment of its birth nations liberated by force from the troops and quisling governments of tyrants, should meet here to deplore the rescue of the people of Grenada from the grip of a small band of murderous men whose clear intention was to secure the permanent subjugation of Grenada and its people and put this small but strategically located island at the disposal of foreign tyrants?

If yesterday's victims of yesterday's tyrants should join today in "deploring" the liberation of today's victim from today's tyrants — and should do so in an organization founded precisely to ensure that there be no more victims, no more tyrants — it would surely mark the end of the dreams and hopes of the United Nations.

8   Cuba and the U.S.:
Constants and Variables

JAIME SUCHLICKI

The past several years have witnessed a variety of hints from the Castro regime in Havana of a willingness to enter into serious negotiations with the United States over the outstanding issues dividing the two countries. In a speech at Cienfuegos on July 26, 1984, Fidel Castro even expanded the possible purview of such negotiations beyond the Western Hemisphere:

> Our country can be approached through peaceful efforts. Talks can be held with our country. We will not turn down any effort. In other words, any effort that might alleviate tensions in our area and international tensions will be worthy of our most serious consideration, any effort tending to decrease the dangers of the madness of war. We are even willing to cooperate with any effort in the search for a political solution to the independence of Namibia, which is an important problem in South Africa, on the basis of U.N. Resolution 435. . . .[1]

Statements such as this one have prompted all sorts of optimistic expectations in the United States. The expectations merge with the more general hope that, somehow, a negotiated settlement can be found in order to contain the accelerating currents of instability and conflict in the Central American region, and to relieve the difficult choices that the United States confronts in responding to these developments. Clearly, Cuba would have to be a party to such a settlement.

This chapter appeared as an article, entitled "Is Castro Ready to Accommodate?" in the Fall 1984 issue of Strategic Review.

There is a certain irony to these expectations after two and a half decades of entrenchment of Castro's revolution in Cuba and the export of that revolution not only into the Western Hemisphere, but also to far-flung corners of the globe. In those years, Castro has periodically extended ostensible olive branches to the United States, only to retract them. In those years, also, the complex diplomatic avenues between Washington and Havana have never been completely barricaded. Negotiations have proceeded and *ad hoc* agreements have been struck — e.g., with respect to the treatment of skyjackers.

The question, therefore, is not whether Castro is willing to negotiate. The question, rather, is whether he stands ready today to render the kinds of meaningful concessions that he has barred in the past — concessions concerning Cuba's relationship with the Soviet Union, the Soviet military arsenals and presence on the island, Cuba's fomenting of revolutionary and terrorist insurgencies in the Western Hemisphere, and the direct involvement of Cuba's military forces in Africa and elsewhere.

In this context, it is interesting to note that Castro followed his above-cited offer of negotiations with the by-now standard qualifier: "Since certain things are sacred — independence, the country's sovereignty, its revolutionary principles — its political and social systems cannot be renounced. Whoever seeks to destroy them will have to fight us."[2] The expanded meaning of those words can be found in the "Resolution on International Policy" adopted by the Second Congress of the Communist Party of Cuba in Havana on December 17, 1980:

> The Cuban revolution's foreign policy is based on Marxist-Leninist principles: proletarian internationalism, friendship and cooperation with the Soviet Union and the other countries of the socialist community; close bonds of solidarity with the communist, workers' and revolutionary movements everywhere; and militant support of the national liberation movements and all peoples that are struggling to develop and defend their vital historic interests.

The basis of our party's foreign policy is its historic, lasting alliance with the Soviet Union, based on our common ideology and goals.

The Second Congress reaffirms that Cuba is and will continue to be an internationalist country that practices militant solidarity with the peoples struggling for liberation and national independence, and that this principle of our international conduct is not negotiable under any circumstances.

THE POWER STRUCTURE IN HAVANA

Fidel Castro's statement also came at a time when the more pro-Soviet, anti-American and "internationalist" elements within the Cuban government achieved ever greater power. Members of the Council of State and ministers, especially those associated with Raul Castro, can be expected to oppose any rapprochement with the United States that could undermine revolutionary commitments abroad and ideological purity at home.

This is not to say that Fidel Castro's authority has been weakened. On the contrary: despite the significant institutionalization of the power structure in Cuba over the past decade, Castro's hold on the reins is unchallenged. Yet, the very fact that he has surrounded himself progressively with the more hard-line elements in the party is certainly indicative of Castro's predilections. Starting in December 1979 the ranks of the "technocrats" in the regime, led by Vice President Carlos Rafael Rodriguez and Minister of Trade Marcelo Fernandez, were decimated by purges that victimized Fernandez and 22 other ministers, presidents of state committees and other high officials, removing them from the Council of Ministers and, in nine cases, from the new Central Committee that was installed in December 1980.

The current political elite's values, policy goals and organizational interests reinforce Castro's political inclinations and policy preferences. The hard foreign policy objectives of this group are: 1) maintaining Cuba's independence from and opposition to the United States; 2) actively supporting revolutionary movements in Latin America; 3) promoting national liberation and socialism in the Third World; 4) acquiring influence and supportive allies among the Third World states; and (5) securing maximum military, economic and political commitments from the Soviet Union.

The two Castro brothers and their respective followers are also in full control of the pivotal Executive Committee of the Council of Ministers, which was assigned enlarged powers under the governmental reorganization in the early 1980s. The old guard of civilian guerrilla veterans — *fidelistas* and *raulistas* — along with the Cuban Armed Forces now occupy the top posts of the party and the government to an extent unparalleled since the 1960s. The current profile of the regime indicates that it will be no more amenable to moderation or to U.S. conciliatory policies than it was two decades ago.

ECONOMIC INCENTIVES?

Optimistic appraisals of Castro's apparent overture have been encouraged to a large extent by the spectacle of Cuba's deepening economic straits. Indeed, there is little question that the Cuban Revolution has reached a critical stage in its development. Persistent structural and managerial problems in the economy, low prices for Cuba's export products and the inability to break away from economic dependence on the Soviet Bloc are forcing a reexamination in Havana of basic goals. Since production in most key sectors has fallen short of expected targets, emphasis is being placed on increased planning with more modest goals. The regime has adopted Soviet economic methods, has reduced emphasis on moral incentives, and is attempting more efficient economic organization. For the foreseeable future the Cuban people can expect more austerity with greater rationing of food and consumer goods, and therefore harder times.

The establishment of a Soviet-type centrally planned economy has burdened Cuba with a vast and cumbersome bureaucracy that stifles innovation, productivity and efficiency. Popular expectations for rapid economic improvement have been replaced by pessimism. There is dwindling enthusiasm among Cuba's labor force and increasing signs of weariness with the constant revolutionary exhortations. Underemployment is rampant, and labor productivity is at a low point.

Meanwhile, Cuba's per capita debt has grown into the largest in Latin America, four times that of Brazil and three times that of Mexico. The debt is approximately $10 billion, or more than two-hundred times that of 1959. Cuba's loans are short-term, floating-rate types and must be refinanced constantly at interest rates that have risen sharply since the debt was incurred.[3] Cuba's interest payments are increasing at a staggering rate, while Western commercial banks are reluctant to provide new hard-currency loans.

The island continues its heavy reliance on sugar for development of the domestic economy and for foreign trade, with little progress being registered in agricultural diversification or industrialization. Dependence on sugar will ensure the continuation of erratic swings in hard currency earnings. At the same time, Cuba must rely on the Soviets for massive infusions of aid to meet minimal investment and consumption needs, while depending almost entirely on imports of Soviet oil to meet its energy requirements. This supply will become ever more precarious, according to expert projections, as the Soviet Union is increasingly forced to curtail oil exports.

This dark picture from Havana's vantagepoint portends some agonizing choices in the immediate future. In the words of one analyst:

> Cuba has probably exhausted the gains as perceived by the population from the installation of socialist egalitarianism and has become more and more deeply involved in and dependent on trade with and subsidies from distant economies. Havana therefore faces crucial economic decisions in the next half decade which will set development prospects long into the future, including probably the post-Castro period.[4]

Yet, this is only one side of the picture. It is in the nature of totalitarian regimes that the key question relates not to economics per se, but rather to the impingements of economic factors upon the levers of political and social control. In an effort to boost productivity and forestall any further decline in revolutionary momentum, the Havana regime tightened the militarization and regimentation of society and institutionalized its rule by expanding the role and influence of the party throughout society. This progressive institutionalization has contributed to the further stabilization of the system, reducing its vulnerability to threats of external subversion and internal revolt. From an institutional standpoint, therefore, the regime appears equipped to withstand the difficult years ahead.

THE PERSONAL FACTOR

Indeed, it is a measure of the strange and pervasive economic determinism in the American outlook that we still tend to assign priority to economic analysis in trying to divine the motivations of revolutionary Marxist regimes like the one in Havana. The history of the past two decades offers clear proof that economic considerations have never dominated Castro's policies. On the contrary: many of the initiatives and actions that the Cuban leadership has undertaken abroad, such as intervention in Angola, Ethiopia, Grenada and Nicaragua, as well as constant mass mobilizations at home, have been costly, disruptive and detrimental to orderly economic development. If the economic welfare of the Cuban people had been the *leitmotif* of Castro's policies, we would be confronting a totally different Cuba today.

By the same token, American analysts generally neglect the personal factor as a key to the behavior of a revolutionary society dominated by the charisma and philosophy of a single personality. Notwithstanding the prominent attention that has been given to Castro the leader, there is still inadequate appreciation of Castro the man, and of the integral roles that violent revolution and "internationalism" exert in his personal makeup.

Thus, we tend to forget that revolutionary violence has been Castro's preoccupation ever since, as a 22-year-old university student, he received military training and enrolled in a subsequently aborted expedition against Dominican dictator Rafael L. Trujillo. One year later, in 1948, he participated in the"Bogotazo" — a series of riots in Bogota following the assassination of Liberal Party leader Jorge E. Gaitan. In Bogota to attend an anti-American student meeting, Castro was caught up in the violence that rocked Colombian society: he joined the mobs and roamed the streets distributing anti-U.S. propaganda and inciting the populace to revolt. Pursued by Colombian police, he sought asylum in the Cuban Embassy and was later flown back to Havana.

For Castro, violence represented the only road of opposing Battista's 1952 military coup. By then a seasoned revolutionary, Castro organized a group of followers and, on July 26, 1953, attacked the Moncada Barracks in western Cuba. He was captured, tried and sentenced to years in prison. While in jail he wrote to friends, urging them to create a movement "where ideology, discipline and leadership would be indispensable, especially the latter." "Be friendly to everyone," he emphasized, "there will be time enough later to crush all the roaches together."[5]

After being released by an amnesty in 1955, Castro traveled to Mexico to organize an expedition against Batista. In 1956 he and 81 men landed in Orient province to form the nucleus of the guerrilla operation which seized power after the crumbling of the Batista regime and the collapse of the Cuban Armed Forces on January 1, 1959. "Guerrilla war," emphasized Castro "came to be fundamental in the armed struggle."[6]

And armed struggle, in turn, has remained fundamental to Castro's mystique, as well as to the image that he has projected onto the larger world stage on which he is determined to play. Other revolutionary leaders may shed, in time, doctrinaire excesses in favor of the pragmatic pursuit of comfortable rule. Yet, there is truly nothing in Castro's personal makeup to suggest that he could foresake the global floodlights and resign himself to the role of just another authoritarian-paternalistic *caudillo* on an insignificant tropical island.

It should be noted, moreover, that "Castroism" is a good deal more than merely the phenomenon of a leader who has placed his ideological and charismatic imprint upon a movement and a nation. What Castro and his retinue have managed in the past twenty-five years is to harness the latent force of a romantic Latin nationalism to foreign adventurism and to a would-be great power role. Mark Falcoff describes this blend and its implications as follows:

> The nationalist component dictates not merely a proud rejection of the United States, which in itself would be understandable enough. It also informs an unconfessed desire for self-immolation, on one hand, and a messianic urge to project itself

throughout Latin America and the world, on the other. If Marxism-Leninism were the *only* feature of the Cuban regime, its inclination to export revolution would be seriously curtailed by the tasks of constructing "socialism in one island," striving, as it were, to become a sort of tropical Bulgaria.[7]

Evolution of Cuban-Soviet Bonds

Optimistic assumptions regarding Castro's willingness to strike a modus vivendi with the United States have fastened also on what some observers perceive as cracks, real or impending, in the Moscow-Havana axis. The Cuban-Soviet relationship is a complex subject, which calls for some necessarily compressed history.

Prior to 1968 Castro had been the foremost proponent in the Soviet Bloc of the principle of violent revolution. Latin American revolutionaries received training in Cuba and were reinserted into their native countries to organize and lead insurgencies. Cuba was channeling funds, arms and propaganda to rebel groups in various Latin American nations. Even areas where conditions hardly seemed propitious for violent upheavals were considered targets. Castro advocated reliance on the intrumentality of guerrilla fighters rather than on mass popular movements, believing that guerrilla campaigns could create the necessary preconditions for revolution.

The implementation of this strategy brought Castro into early conflict with Moscow and the communist parties of Latin America. In the 1960s, the Soviets called for the formation of popular fronts and mass movements. They criticized Castro's emphasis on armed struggle as "left-wing opportunism which leads the masses to adventuristic actions." Behind those strictures lay the obvious fear in the Kremlin that Castro's tactics could jeopardize the Soviet economic offensive in Latin America as well as their attempts to broaden political influence in the area. Another likely apprehension in Moscow was that Castro's gambits might draw the Soviets into unwanted involvements and confrontations with the United States — particularly at a time when their power position relative to the region, following the Cuban Missile Crisis, was demonstrably weak.

Most of the traditional communist parties in Latin America readily followed the Soviet lead. They chafed under Castro's claim to supremacy over the revolutionary movement and his branding of all communists who opposed armed struggle as "traitorous, rightist and deviationist."[8] Most of them having achieved relatively secure and comfortable positions in their respective countries, the communist parties and their aging leaders feared that a call to violence would invite failure, persecution and exile. They were devoted to the less hazardous path of creating "the necessary conditions for revolution" through propaganda, infiltration, popular fronts and even elections, and showed little inclination to plunge into armed struggle.

By the late 1960s, perhaps in response to Soviet pressures but also in the face of resounding setbacks to his strategy — particularly in the Bolivian debacle in 1967 — Castro was modifying his tactics and acknowledging that there were "different roads to power." While not completely renouncing his original goal of exporting his own brand of revolution, he became more selective in meting out Cuban support to guerrilla operations in the region.

Yet, beginning in 1968, Cuban-Soviet relations reentered a period of amity and close collaboration. The turning point came in August 1968, when Castro supported the Soviet invasion of Czechoslovakia, a response dictated primarily by political and economic considerations. First, he reached the basic conclusion that Cuba would reap greater security by solidifying its membership in the Soviet Bloc rather than by espousing the principle of sovereignty for small countries. Second, poor sugar harvests in 1967 and 1968 heightened the need for more Soviet economic aid and highlighted more generally the extent to which Cuba's future development was dependent on outside assistance. Third, as has been noted, the failures of Castro's guerrilla strategy removed a pointed irritant in the Soviet-Cuban relationship. Finally, Castro's ideas contrasted markedly with those of the Dubcek group in Czechoslovakia. Considering himself to the left of both the Soviets and the Czech leadership, the Cuban leader could not favor the liberalization taking place in Prague. For domestic reasons as well, he could not logically support liberalization abroad while sustaining orthodoxy and regimentation at home.

In numerous ways the Cubans went out of their way to demonstrate the new spirit of collaboration with the Soviets. In June 1969 Castro reversed one of the rare collective decisions by the

Central Committee of Cuba's Communist Party: namely, that Cuba would not participate in the World Conference of Communist parties convened by the Soviet Union. According to the new line, he sent as an "observer" to the Moscow conference Carlos Rafael Rodriguez, the most steadfast theoretician of the former Partido Socialista Popular and a member of the Politburo of the ruling Communist Party of Cuba. Rodriguez delivered a speech unstinted in its praise of the Soviet Union, which closed with the pledge: "We declare from this tribune that in any decisive confrontation, whether it be an act by the Soviet Union to avert the threat of dislocation or provocation to the socialist system, or an act of aggression by anyone against the Soviet people, Cuba will stand unflinchingly by the USSR."[19]

This show of solidarity had wide implications. Several other ruling communist parties, including those of China, Vietnam and Korea, had refused to attend the conference precisely because its main objective was to enlist support for a crusade against Beijing. Cuba's attendance and Rodriguez's statement showed support for the Soviet position: Castro was casting his lot with the USSR. This was followed by calls of the Soviet Navy at Cuban ports and the visits of prominent Soviet officials. In turn, Fidel and Raul Castro toured Eastern Europe and the Soviet Union for extended periods of time.

In the 1970s Soviet military and economic aid to Cuba rose substantially. In 1972 Cuba became a member of the Bloc's Council for Mutual Economic Assistance (CMEA); the consequence was an inflow of direct Soviet influence in the island. Soviet technicians became extensively involved in managerial and planning activities at the national level, and the total number of Soviet military and technical advisers multiplied. They were particularly prominent in the Ministry of the Sugar Industry and the Ministry of the Armed Forces, where a joint Soviet-Cuban advisory commission was organized. The Cuban Armed Forces were further modernized with Soviet weapons in the early 1980s. Of special significance were long-term agreements between Cuba and the USSR which geared the Cuban economy into the Soviet Economic Plans. A new Inter-Governmental Coordinating Committee was also established, giving the Kremlin considerable leverage on Cuban developments.

The renewed Soviet-Cuban entente was, of course, demonstrated most dramatically in the Cuban intervention in Africa, featuring the deployment of more than 40,000 Cuban troops and Soviet equipment to bring and maintain in power communist regimes in Angola and Ethiopia. Little needs to be said here about this massive enterprise beyond the obvious fact that it enhanced Castro's international prestige and influence, directly assisted the creation of Marxist regimes friendly to Cuba, honed the combat readiness of Cuban troops and gave full rein to Castro's ambitions for a global role. In the process, not only did Cuba vaunt its solidarity with the Soviet Union, but it also vastly increased its bargaining leverage in Moscow.

NICARAGUA AND CUBAN-SOVIET UNITY OF ACTION

If Castro modified his firebrand approach to revolution in Latin America in the late 1960s, events in the following decade prompted yet another reassessment of Cuba's hemispheric strategy. Those principal events were the electoral failure of the Popular Front in Uruguay and, more importantly, the overthrow of the Allende regime in Chile in 1974. The Cuban leadership now reverted to the conclusion that the path to Marxism lay not over electoral victories, nor could revolution await the spontaneous emergence of mass movements. Beginning in the mid-1970s, Castro intensified his support to select insurgent groups, particularly in Central America, providing them with propaganda material, training, advisers, financial help and ultimately weapons. An acceleration of armed struggle in the area followed apace.

Emboldened by Cuba-Soviet victories in Angola and Ethiopia, the Castro regime focused on the rapidly deteriorating situation in Nicaragua, where archaic and unjust social, political and economic structures, dominated by an oppressive, corrupt and inefficient dynasty, began to crumble in the face of mounting popular discontent. Cuba, jointly with Panama and Venezuela, increased support to the *Frente Sandinista de Liberacion Nacional,* the principal guerrilla group opposing the Somoza regime and led, among others, by Castro's longtime friend and Marxist leader Tomas Borge. In

July 1979, Somoza fled to the United States and the *Frente* rode victorious into Managua.

There is neither the space nor the need here to detail the tides of developments in the region since 1979 — particularly the insurgency in El Salvador — or the Cuban role in these developments. The main point to be made is that the Sandinista victory in Nicaragua stands as an imposing monument to Cuban strategy and ambitions in the hemisphere. Although the overthrow of the Somoza regime in Nicaragua was as much the work of internal forces as of external aid, Castro can lay claim to a major part in bringing down the Somoza dynasty. He can also claim vindication of the *fidelismo* tenet which stresses violence and guerrilla warfare as the roads to Marxist takeovers in Latin America. As Jesus Montane Oropesa, member of Cuba's Communist Party Central Committee, exulted on October 21, 1980: "the triumph in Nicaragua verified the effectiveness of armed struggle as a decisive means of taking power."[10]

The Nicaraguan episode also sealed what Bruce McColm has characterized as the triumph of Cuban-Soviet unity of action over unity of doctrine. He elaborates as follows:

> The Soviet view changed sharply in the late 1970s with the Sandinista's success in Nicaragua. Soviet theoreticians who previously had heaped scorn on Cuban concepts of revolution now indulged in revisionist payments of respect to Guevara's theory of guerrilla warfare and declared that armed struggle was the only option in the hemisphere. Local pro-Moscow communist parties from Uruguay to Guatemala ritualistically endorsed such a strategy and formed alliances with Castroite guerrilla movements and the broad political fronts opposing the standing governments in the region. The formula of a diverse political front combined with factional guerrilla forces now was considered capable of substituting as the "revolutionary vanguard" for communist parties.[11]

Finally, the strategic and political investments that Cuba has made in Nicaragua are strikingly demonstrated in the following statement by Fidel Castro in the Sandinista newspaper, *Barricada,* on

July 2, 1980: "The key thing in a people's revolution is to have the peoples and guns on your side. What happened in Chile cannot recur in Nicaragua in any form. Since the people have the power, since it has the weapons, the revolution is guaranteed and will follow its course as a function of the objective conditions of the country." In other words, there is little room in possible U.S.-Cuban negotiations with respect to a key U.S. demand: namely, the democratization of Nicaragua and the de facto withdrawal of Cuban props for the Sandinista regime.

CASTRO'S OPTIONS

At a time of a new leadership in Moscow and some indistinctness of the policy lines from Moscow to its international network, there may well be new frictions between Cuba and the Soviet Union. The economic trends noted above can accentuate these frictions.

Yet, countervailing these prospects are a Soviet influence and presence in Cuba far more extensive than ever before. At the same time, solidarity with the Soviet Union remains a vital element of Cuba's policy and of Castro's *raison d'etre*. To an American journalist who visited the island early this year and questioned Cuba's loyalty to the Soviets, Castro replied: "I am no Sadat." For the foreseeable future Cuba's policies and actions in the international arena will continue to operate in the larger framework of Soviet objectives. Castro will continue to pursue his own policies only so long as they do not clash with those of the Soviets.

Uncomfortable as he may feel in the embrace of the Russian bear, Castro's options are limited. Although relations with China have improved from their nadir in 1967, the Chinese seem unable or unwilling to take on Cuba as an expensive client. Castro's support of Moscow's policies are decried by Beijing as "revisionist," and his denunciations of Mao in the late 1960s are still remembered with bitterness by the Chinese.

Strengthened commercial ties with Western Europe and Japan may beckon as a healthy development from Cuba's standpoint. Yet, the ability of these countries to absorb the island's sugar exports is limited, and Havana has scant cash reserves with which to purchase European and Japanese goods. Cuba's heavy economic commitment to the Soviet Union and the East European countries is an additional deterrent to a broadening of trading partners, while U.S. pressures on Western allies tend to limit their willingness to trade with Cuba.

To be sure, all this might logically tempt the Castro regime to reduce its reliance on the Soviet Union and find some sort of accommodation with the United States. Rapprochement with the United States could lead to a loosening of the embargo and even access to an important and proximate market for Cuba's goods. It could bolster Cuba's immediate security position and provide Castro with greater leverage in his dealings with the Soviet Union. Recognition by the United States might also translate into an important psychological victory for Castro. In Latin America it would be interpreted as a defeat for "Yankee imperialism" and as an enforced acceptance of the Castro regime as a permanent, albeit irritating, neighbor in the Caribbean.

Yet, an accommodation with the United States would be fraught with uncertainties and dangers for the Cuban leadership. It would entail a loosening of Cuba's military ties with the Soviet Union, the curtailment of support for violent revolutions in Latin America, and the withdrawal of Cuban troops from Africa and other parts of the world. These are conditions that Castro is not willing to accept: he perceives them as an attempt by the United States to deny Cuba its claim to a great power role, to isolate the revolution and to strengthen anti-Castro forces within the island, thus posing a threat to the stability of the regime. Moreover, the economic embargo engenders in Cuba a sort of siege mentality which facilitates the mobilization of the population and justifies the government's constant demands for more work and sacrifices, while at the same time providing a ready-made excuse for economic failures. The close ties of the Cuban economy to the Soviet Union would prevent a rapid reorientation toward the United States, even if this were politically feasible.

Notwithstanding his tactically motivated statements, therefore, Castro appears neither willing nor really able to offer those meaningful concessions which would be indispensable to a U.S.-Cuban accommodation. Castro's political style and ideology and his apprehensions of U.S. motivations make him more prone to deviate to the left than to the right of the Soviet line. His awareness of his regime's vulnerability is reinforced by the activities of Cuban refugees in the United States. Commitment to violent revolution and solidarity with the Soviet Bloc remain the cornerstones of his foreign policy. He cannot modify, let alone abandon, these cornerstones without risking his power and obscuring his personal place in history — a consideration that is perhaps uppermost in Castro's outlook.

NOTES

1. FBIS, *Latin America*, July 30, 1984, p. Q16.

2. Ibid., p. Q18.

3. Ernesto Betancourt and Wilson Dizard, III, "Castro and the Bankers — The Mortgaging of a Revolution," Cuban–American National Foundation, 1982.

4. *Cuba Faces the Economic Realities of the 1980s*, a study prepared for the Joint Economic Committee, U.S. Congress, March 22, 1982, by Lawrence H. Theriot, Office of East-West Policy and Planning, International Trade Administration, U.S. Department of Commerce.

5. Luis Conte Aguero, *Cartas del Presidio* (La Habana: Editorial Lex, 1959).

6. Fidel Castro, *La experiencia cubana* (Barcelona: Editorial Blume, 1976).

7. From Mark Falcoff, "How to Think about Cuban–American Relations," in Irving Louis Horowitz, ed., *Cuban Communism* (New Brunswick, NJ: Transaction Books, 1984), p. 543.

8. *Granma* , March 18, 19, 1967; Radio Moscow, August 10, 11, 1967.

9. Havana Domestic Radio, June 23, 1969.

10. *Granma*, November 2, 1980.

11. R. Bruce McColm, "Central America and the Caribbean: the Larger Scenario," *Strategic Review*, Summer 1983, p. 35.

9 Castro's Ambitions Amid New Winds from Moscow

R. BRUCE MCCOLM

The Third Congress of Cuba's Communist Party (PCC), held in Havana in February of this year, provided the stage for another vintage performance by Fidel Castro. The *lider maximo* demonstrated that he was still in complete command of the affairs of his country — even though those are increasingly troubled affairs.

Before the 196 revolutionary movements and communist parties represented at the Congress, Fidel gave renewed testimony to Cuba as the leading, faithful ally and advocate of the Soviet Union and its interests. He claimed that Cuba never had been stronger militarily and would fulfill "its sacred internationalist duties in accordance with our abilities."[1] The Cuban Communist Party's platform paper, entitled "Principles and Objectives of Foreign Policy," pledged the PCC's abiding support to revolutionary movements around the world by helping to achieve unity and the consolidation of diverse forces that are part of the revolutionary process: "Our party and people will continue to fulfill honorably their internationalist duties, exercising solidarity with the peoples who are struggling for their independence and national liberation."[2] On February 8, 1986, Radio Rebelde reported Castro's warning that, should the United States increase its aid to the Nicaraguan Contras, Cuba would raise its assistance to Nicaragua accordingly — and that, by the same token, Cuba is ready to remain in Angola for another 10, 15 or even 30 years, if necessary.[3]

This chapter appeared as an article in the Summer 1986 issue of Strategic Review.

Still, this rhetorical litany could not obscure the fact that the horizons of *fidelisto* revolutionary visions are clouded — that the personal monument Castro intends to leave to history is being eroded by some adverse gales in the international environment and undermined by economic and social problems at home. Castro faces a situation in which his military is enmired in two protracted wars, in Angola and Nicaragua. He confronts a resurgence of American power that has already been invoked against two of his allies — Grenada and Libya — and by an American Administration which he has not been able to manipulate with the standard bait of accommodation. Against this somber background, and the knowledge that Cuba remains the most exposed salient in the Soviet Union's extended empire, Castro faces sharp uncertainties in his relations with a new Soviet leadership — relations that also spell vital lifelines for Cuba's listing economy and profoundly affect the administrative apparatus at Castro's command.

New Accents in the Kremlin

Most disturbing from Castro's vantagepoint must be the pronounced emphasis by the Gorbachev regime on domestic economic priorities, combined with the demand for stronger and more efficient economic performance from the Soviet Union's clients. Recent events have evidenced the Soviet Union's intent to seek a consolidation of its gains in Afghanistan, Angola and Nicaragua. Yet, Gorbachev's keynote address to the Twenty-Seventh Congress of the CPSU in February 1986 was notable for the absence of traditional Kremlin pledges to support "wars of national liberation" — the first such omission in over thirty years. It is precisely in these Third World arenas where Castro has been able to fulfill his ambitions.

It is not surprising, therefore, that Castro, in his brief but fervent address to the Soviet Party Congress, lobbied for greater support for Third World struggles. He reminded his audience that Third World issues demanded attention, and that national liberation struggles in "Vietnam, Nicaragua, El Salvador, Angola, Namibia, South Africa, Western Sahara, Palestine, Afghanistan and Kampuchea" demanded sacrifices. He pleaded that "the fruit of the blood and lives of many of the best sons of our peoples" not be reduced to "so-called low-level conflicts." And he exhorted: ". . .The Third World countries expect and are sure they will receive maximum solidarity from the Socialist Community in their struggle for just economic gains."[4]

The clear concern expressed by Castro in February followed palpable Cuban anxieties during the Andropov and Chernenko regimes, reflected in severe policy disputes between Havana and Moscow over Grenada and Nicaragua. In the tougher and less familiar Soviet leadership under Gorbachev Castro now faces the possibility of new tides that could wrest the Soviet-Cuban relationship from its previous ideological, political and strategic moorings in a direction with twofold implications: away from joint (or sanctioned) revolutionary ventures in the Third World and toward "socialist consolidation" — meaning in Cuba's case the imperative to grapple with an overwhelming array of economic, social and administrative tasks at home.

Virtually all those — including former intimates — who have observed Fidel Castro over the years have imparted a profile of the revolutionary megalo-missionary with overtones of *caudillo* flamboyance. His yearning for a personal place in history is sharpened with the dwindling of the time available for monument-building. He has occasionally affected the role of revolutionary elder statesman — e.g., in his recent bid for leadership of the debtor nations — but this is integral to neither his style nor his ambition. In the past, his ambition has been gratified largely through various forms of violence. Violence — conventional or guerrilla — has been the fuel of Castro's power and prestige, and it supplies the livid colors of his self-image.

The self-image merges, of course, with his view of his country's needs. Support for revolutionary movements and radical regimes is seen by him as inseparable from Cuba's role and weight on the international scales. The external mission is, moreover, imperative for sustaining an equilibrium within and among the country's institutions. As Jorge Dominguez has succinctly summarized:

> Support for revolution is a constitutive ideological dimension of the Cuban revolution. It defines a central concern of that

government. It legitimizes Cuba's own regime with a feeling of being on the side of history's march toward the future. It projects Cuba's influence internationally. It creates leverage in Cuban relations with the Soviet Union. It is a powerful weapon to combat the historical enemy.[5]

Ultimately, as Cuba's domestic and international policy courses reach a crisis point, it will be Castro and his worldview that will determine the political and military responses to the crisis. In a recent Rand Corporation study, Edward Gonzalez and David Ronfeldt see Castro as combining behavior patterns of Hubris and Nemesis. In their analysis, Castro continues to be driven by the same ambitions and to exhibit the behavioral patterns that have characterized his revolutionary rule for the past quarter-century. At times he adopts a more pragmatic posture for tactical reasons, only to return to militant confrontation as soon as the opportunity emerges. In the context of the endemic crises facing Cuba, Gonzales and Ronfeldt discern a latent *Goetterdaemmerung* tendency in Castro's personality:

> He arrogates to himself virtually all power in Cuba, pursues grandiose ambitions as a global and regional actor, and seeks immortality by combatting a far more powerful adversary. He may thus seem ripe for doing something that will lead to his downfall.[6]

CHANGES IN THE APPARAT

Meanwhile, Castro has had to adjust to the new winds from Moscow. He has done so primarily on that stage in communist societies that traditionally is used to signal "change," whether symbolic or real: namely, the hierarchy.

While Fidel dominated the opening and closing of the Third Cuban Party Congress, the spotlight was on dramatic personnel shifts in the Cuban Communist Party's governing bodies. The changes were surprising for a regime long noted for its slow turnover and the stability of its ruling inner circles. Castro retired three *fidelista* guerrilla veterans — the so-called *historicos* — from the 1986 Political Bureau for reasons of incompetence and ill health. These purges came on top of the removal in 1985 of at least 11 top

Cuban officials, most of them involved in economic management. At the same time, the position of Fidel's hardline, pro-Soviet brother Raul was strengthened with the elevation of two prominent *raulistas:* Vilma Espin, Raul's wife and the head of the Cuban Confederation of Women, and Division General Abeldardo Colome, head of Cuba's Expeditionary Force in Angola in 1975-1976 and the current First Vice Minister in the Ministry of the Revolutionary Armed Forces (MINFAR).[7]

After nearly two years of bitter negotiations, Castro was finally forced to render concessions to Moscow and to the voices within his regime that agitated for administrative reforms, the appointment of more competent leaders and a generally more efficient management of the economy. As if to reassert his prerogatives, Castro in July 1985 dismissed Humberto Perez, the Vice President in the Council of Ministers and head of JUCEPLAN, the planning board which coordinates economic policy with the Soviet's GOSPLAN. Perez, a Moscow-trained technocrat, was fired, according to recent defector Manuel Antonio Sanchez Perez (himself a former Vice President of JUCEPLAN but no relation to Humberto) "because he was not permitted to continue with the [Soviet-style] policy changes which might have represented a relatively greater increase in efficiency within the Cuban economy."[8]

Castro's personnel moves came after he had gambled that Moscow would take a more relaxed view of Cuba's grave economic problems. In several speeches before the changes, Fidel lamented the decay in the economy — complaining to the National Assembly of the drain of foreign exchange, scarcity of supplies, inefficiency of the bureaucracy and urgent need for further constraints on the bureaucracy. Before his defection, Manuel Sanchez Perez roundly denounced the regime's economic policies in the mass magazine *Bohemia* in March 1985, and called for an "economic revolution."

One theory has it that, after 15 years of close cooperation between GOSPLAN and Cuba's JUCEPLAN, Castro's intended gambit was to shift the blame for mistakes and mismanagement onto the Soviet technical advisers. Shortly after Sanchez Perez' officially sanctioned broadside, however, Gorbachev succeeded in the Kremlin, and Castro had to give up the hope for Soviet leniency toward Cuba's growing problems.[9]

While the changes crafted by Castro mirror the general thrust of Gorbachev's administrative "reforms" in the Soviet Union — the downgrading of ministries and elevation of regional party leaders — it is important to bear in mind that Fidel himself engineered them and that he has his own agenda. Within the top echelons of Cuba's elite, Castro must maintain a balance between the older generation of *fidelisto* guerrilla veterans and the younger technocrats and military elites whose energy and expertise are needed to run the government and carry out Cuba's "internationalist mission." Castro has attempted to defuse mounting generational tensions within the regime by fashioning a new Central Committee half of whose members are 45 or younger. Moreover, he has to fine-tune these gradual changes in the power base with an eye toward shielding it against total Soviet dominance.[10]

No matter how adroitly Castro has managed this intricate balancing act within the regime, however, the general outlook in the domestic arena is bleak, as are the prospects for any dramatic achievements in this arena. It seems likely, in fact, that Castro views Cuba's internal situation as a matter more for administration than for leadership. For that reason, he may be turning the day-to-day administration of the government and economy over to brother Raul, an orthodox communist considered trustworthy by the Soviets. Still, Fidel will not give his brother a free rein: although the latter's hand has been strengthened by the removal of the old-guard *fidelistas* from high- level posts in both the government and party, Fidel retains faithful supporters in both the Political Bureau and Cabinet. For example, the dismissal of Ramiro Valdes from the Interior Ministry was followed by the appointment to that post of General Jose Abrantes Fernandez, also known to be "fanatically loyal to Fidel."[11]

While placating the Soviets and their urgings for more efficient administration, Castro has thus made the most of the changes within the Havana hierarchy. They allow for an orderly succession in the event of his death or incapacitation. Although he seems to have delegated downward some of the major, day-to-day administrative burdens, the presence of trusted supporters in key positions ensures him abiding control over the apparatus, including ultimate veto-

power over the policymaking process. At the same time, he is freer
to give his personal attention to his favorite arena: foreign affairs.

CUBA'S ECONOMIC MORASS

But Castro has had to bow to pressures from Moscow — and from
his own elite — not only with respect to changes in the regime.
At the Third Party Congress in February, he also signalled his final
alignment with the economic policies of the Soviet Union.

In his Main Report to the Congress — which was attended by
Yegor Ligachev, the second-ranking member of the Soviet Politburo — Castro indulged in the most exhaustive attack since the late
1970s on poor economic planning and bureaucratic inefficiency in
Cuba. Parroting Gorbachev's report to the 27th Party Congress of
the CPSU, Castro sounded the themes of modernization and
economic self-discipline, especially as they pertain to Cuba's peren-
nial failure to meet its export commitments to the COMECON
countries.[12]

For the past year-and-a-half, the Soviet Union has evinced rising impatience with Cuba's poor economic performance. Since the
mid-1970s, like all smaller COMECON countries, Cuba has
registered huge deficits in its trade transactions with the Soviet
Union, while failing to meet production levels. Its debt to the Soviet
Union and the other East Bloc allies exceeds $22 billion — a figure
whose magnitude is demonstrated by the fact that it represents nearly
half of the Soviet Union's total indebtedness to the West of some
$50 billion. In addition, Havana owes Western banks and govern-
ments about $3.42 billion in hard currency, together with $85 million
in commercial credits. In recent months, Havana has been sug-
gesting in its Paris Club talks with representatives from France,
Great Britain, Italy, Spain, Canada and Japan that it would default
or pay only a small percentage of the outstanding interest.[13]

As the recipient of approximately 51 per cent of all Soviet foreign
assistance to communist and non-communist countries, Cuba can
ill afford to jeopardize its status as a privileged Soviet client. The
$4 to 5 billion annually pumped into Cuba give Moscow a heavy
bludgeon for compelling Havana to toe the new, stringent line of
economic reforms emanating from the Kremlin. Castro has

responded to this bludgeon: his peroration at the Cuban Party Congress was in keeping with "the economic war of the whole people" declared by him in 1984.

In April 1986, Soviet First Deputy Premier Ivan Artkhipov signed four trade and economic agreements with Cuba totalling approximately $3 billion in new credits. Representing a 50 per cent increase in Soviet economic and trade assistance to Cuba for the five-year 1986–1990 period, the pact was seen as a sign of Gorbachev's apparent satisfaction with Castro's reform initiatives, along with a strong recommitment of the new Soviet leadership to Cuba.[14]

Nevertheless, the Castro regime confronts tall obstacles to its economic priorities, and probably will soon redraft its five-year plan.[15] The plunge in oil prices will substantially exacerbate the island's trade deficit during 1986, according to a report by Banco Nacional de Cuba. Cuba is heavily dependent on the re-export of Soviet oil as a source of foreign exchange. During 1984 and 1985, Moscow allowed two-thirds of its oil supply to Havana to be resold on the spot market, and Cuban economists calculate that the country thereby gained about $1.41 billion, or nearly 40 per cent of its total export earnings. The drop in oil prices is expected to cost Cuba approximately $300 million.[16]

Compounding the picture is the damage wrought by drought and Hurricane Kate on Cuba's sugar crop. Not only will this entail a further drop in earnings, but it also means that, given its trade commitments to the Soviet Bloc, Havana cannot hope to capitalize on rising sugar prices by expanding its exports to the West. At the same time, such rising prices will prevent a repetition of the option exercised in 1984, when Cuba spent an estimated $200 million buying cheap sugar on the world market to sell to COMECON (at nearly ten times the price paid).[17]

In the past, the short-term solution to the problem would have been to borrow from Western banks. But the word circulating in the banking world is that Castro's diatribes against Western banks have prompted some of Cuba's credit banks to retract their trade credit lines, in effect closing that share of some 20 per cent of Cuba's economy that is dependent on the West. According to defector Sanchez Perez, it is virtually impossible for Cuba to generate any productive headway without these Western credits and trade. In all, the Cuban economy and, in particular, the industrial plant and organization of the island are ill-equipped to attain the goal of $1 billion in non-sugar exports to market economies by 1990 that are necessary to keep the island's economy afloat.[18]

Social Reverberations

These unbroken economic clouds cast a darkening shadow on Cuba's internal life. Should the island become nearly totally dependent on East Bloc subsidies, Soviet-imposed austerity programs will lead to a further, drastic decline in the Cuban standard of living, roiling popular discontent.

The demographic pressure of the "Revolutionary Baby Boom" — with 1.3 million in the 15–19 age group entering the labor market between now and 1990 — is well nigh insurmountable. Meanwhile, dissatisfaction and apathy in the labor force are manifest in a job-absentee rate of some 40 per cent. At the same time, joblessness has tripled over the last five years, increasing from 40,000 to more than 100,000 in mid-1985 — an official rate of 4 to 5 per cent. Those are official statistics: the real figures are believed to be considerably higher.[19]

The stresses generated by living conditions in the revolutionary society have taken a mounting toll on the Cuban people. Street crime has risen sharply. A staggering suicide rate of 21.1 per 100,000 places Cuba above Sweden (with a 17.5 rate) and at levels five times that of Costa Rica (with a 4.3 rate).

Natural disasters, such as Hurricane Kate in 1985 and periods of drought, have exacerbated the chronic failures of the Cuban system. Nearly 4 per cent of the total housing stock of the island was either wiped out or seriously damaged by the storm; official announcements estimated that 5,000 homes were destroyed and 80,000 damaged. The disaster only compounded the natural housing shortages created by the regime's economic policies; current production figures show that only 60 per cent of the housing needs of the island are being met. In total, Cuba's problems of inadequate housing are demonstrated by a housing deficit of 1.6 million units for a total population of over 9 million inhabitants.

Food, water and energy shortages will plague Cuba for the foreseeable future. Since 1980 the whole water system of the island has deteriorated badly, leaving entire sections of the population without water and other urban sectors with strictly rationed supplies. In 1985 water deliveries were cut to nearly 60 per cent of the previous year. The Cuban Government also has repeatedly failed to reach the goals of food self-sufficiency. Despite a brief and productive experiment in private farming, food supplies, especially meat, remain rationed and at levels lower than even in Arab states.[20]

And there is the particular phenomenon of the "generation of disenchantment," a label applied to the returning veterans of African wars. Cuban reservists with several tours of duty in Angola behind them are refusing to be sent again. Havana has reneged on its promises to some 200,000 returning veterans of housing and university education: there are simply too many of them to be accommodated.

The increasing reluctance of Cubans to serve as "internationalists" abroad and the burden placed on an already tautly stretched system by returning veterans clashes with the needs of the government to export services. Castro now confronts in a massive surplus of Cuban teachers and doctors the consequences of a totally unrealistic policy of national priorities undertaken in behest of the "internationalist" mission in the Third World. Since December 1984, when he announced the necessary curtailment of social expenditures, the only logical outlet for Cuba's surplus of educated manpower is the export of doctors and teachers for overseas duty, precisely the government activity which is now being resisted by the populace.[21]

THE MILITARY BURDEN

Cuba's economic woes feed directly into Castro's predicament in dealing with the Soviets in other realms, particularly the military arena. A recent analysis in the *Latin American Times* put it succinctly: "As the Soviet Union's financial, military and economic investment in the Cuban system has escalated, Moscow's demands on the Cuban system have escalated. Moscow's demands on the Cuban military have become intolerable."[22] The same article goes on to report a remarkable rebuff to Moscow in the following statement attributed to a Cuban Foreign Ministry official:

> The Cuban military forces are not intervening in the internal affairs of Angola. They are not there to fight the rebel UNITA, but only to furnish strategic defense against foreign aggression. They have fought UNITA guerrillas only to repel their attacks on Cuban positions or patrols. If we had decided to fight they would have been crushed by this time. This is the same policy as we have adopted in Ethiopia. Once the danger point was overcome, and the threat of a Somalian invasion had disappeared, we withdrew part of our troops and refused to participate in the Eritrean Liberation Movement.[23]

Today there are still an estimated 36,000–40,000 Cuban troops serving in more than 30 countries in the Middle East, Africa and Latin America. This marks the eleventh year of Cuba's involvement in the Angolan conflict. While the African expeditions provided the Cuban military with frontline battle experience and honed a highly professional officer corps, they have not been without cost. The war in Angola has settled into a stalemate and promises to become even more costly as Jonas Savimbi's UNITA forces receive the promised American assistance.

Manuel Sanchez Perez has reported on the growing unpopularity of the Angolan war in Cuba: "The first thing they [Cubans in Angola] notice is that Angolans are the first not to want us there. The situation has become so unpleasant that contact between Cubans and Angolans has been banned because of the consequences this might have."[24] These experiences obviously filter back to Cuba. There is mounting evidence that Cuban youths are increasingly persuaded that a two-year tour of duty in Angola is not preferable to the alternative of three years in fulfilling the general military service obligations in Cuba itself.

Resistance to serving overseas and the discontent of draftees are exacerbated by the practice of excusing the sons of the Party and Government elites from military duty. According to the Madrid-based Comite Pro Derechos Humanos en Cuba, over 30,000 Cuban youths have been imprisoned for avoiding obligatory military service. Refusal to serve in Angola has reached a point where, in some cases, members of the Union of Young Communists have given up their membership rather than go to Angola. A 1984 Communist Party Central Committee Study reported that the rate of desertions was "unacceptable" and confirmed that Cubans view the military as "a dumping ground of deviates" or an "instrument to punish anti-social or criminal activity."[25]

The weight of the abiding military commitments abroad apparently has grated on the relations between Cuba's managerial and military elites, generating a competition for trained manpower. Economic managers in Cuba have resisted giving up experienced personnel to "internationalist duties" — to such an extent that Castro himself has commented on the "exaggerated" criteria employed to defer civilian workers from overseas duty. In fact, there is a debate between military professionals and political leaders over the issue of whether, how and when mobilization of military reserves is disruptive to national economic production.

IMPLICATIONS FOR THE CUBAN MILITARY

There are indications of growing tensions within the military itself. With the conflict in Angola stalemated and in the wake of the devastating setback in Grenada in 1983, evidence has emerged of a possible rift between "nationalist" officers — the "*Maceistas*" trained at the Antonio Maceo Inter-Arms School in Cuba — and those officers who have developed strong ties with the Soviets through professional training and/or contacts with Soviet military advisers.

At issue appear to be the purpose and goals of the African Expeditionary Forces — whether those campaigns serve primarily Cuban or Soviet interests. Evidence of such a division is furnished by the defection in January 1985 of Lieutenant Colonel Mourino Perez, coordinator of African operations, who pronounced himself as "tired of burying Cuban soldiers in Africa." It is also encouraged by (unconfirmed) reports that Soviet officers have been placed in positions of authority over Cuban officers in the Western, Central and Eastern Army sectors in Cuba, as well as on air force bases and the naval installation at Cienfuegos.[26]

The defeat in Grenada undoubtedly impacted on these tensions in ways beyond shaking the morale of troops and officers, particularly those involved in overseas duties. "The Cuban government," Manuel Sanchez Perez claims, "viewed developments there as the first clash between Cuban and U.S. forces. During top-level meetings the conclusion was reached that the Cuban Armed Forces had failed totally."[27] In the aftermath, General Joaquin Mendez Cominches, the head of Cuban intelligence services, was removed, and Colonel Pedro Tortolo Comas was personally stripped of his officer's rank by Raul Castro. He and other military officers were then detailed to Angola to "rehabilitate" themselves as common soldiers. There are allegations that a videotape of this debasement was shown to all military units in Cuba. It has also been reported that 30 members of the Cuban security team on Grenada were executed for treason.[28]

Cuba's military, the Revolutionary Armed Forces (FAR), is still unique among contemporary communist countries in commanding the center of political power in Cuba, even though it has had to cede some of that power of late to the civilian elements of the Communist Party. Along with the Ministry of Interior, it is the core institution of political mobilization and state control. In addition to the active and ready reserve forces under its authority, it also has formal command of the Youth Labor Army, the Territorial Militia troops and the organized Civil Defense forces. Over the years, a relatively high proportion of active military and former military officers have come to occupy positions within the government. Indeed, the FAR has become a major source of managerial expertise for the various ministries and state-controlled economic sectors.

Although the FAR's proportion of seats in the PCC's Central Committee has declined over the years, military officers still make up almost one-fifth of the membership of that body. Moreover, its influence cannot be measured strictly by that proportion, given the key positions occupied by FAR members in various state agencies.

Over the years, the Cuban military has swollen to 125,000 active personnel, along with another 200,000 battle-seasoned reserves. In combination with the Ministry of Interior, the FAR commands, or can mobilize, anywhere from 225,000 to nearly 2 million citizens for national defense, making it the largest military establishment in Latin America second only to Brazil.

Since the early 1960s the Soviet Union has liberally supplied Cuba with stockpiles of military weapons. A substantial modernization program was launched in the aftermath of the Angolan War (1975–1976) and accelerated after the Horn of Africa War (1977–1978). After a brief pause, the Soviet-Cuban response to the Reagan Administration was to accelerate the rate of weapons deliveries, providing within two years all that had been planned for the entire 1981–1985 period.

In 1981 and 1982, more than 66,000 tons of weapons were shipped to Cuba annually. In 1983, the Soviets and their allies delivered over 50,000 metric tons, including 7 MiG-21s, 3 MiG-23s, 16 HiP helicopters, an unknown number of surface-to-air missiles, 100 T-62 tanks, and three PTH hydrofoils. According to the U.S. Defense Department, Soviet military assistance to Cuba has approximated $4 billion over the past five years.[29]

"ALL PEOPLE'S WAR"

In a policy that has baffled analysts, Castro has placed Cuba's defense posture on the concept of the "All People's War." Central to the concept is the creation of Territorial Militia Troops (MTT), ostensibly in response to what Castro terms "the aggressive policies" of the Reagan Administration and the danger of an "imminent" invasion by the United States. *"La guerra de todo el pueblo"* has incorporated nearly 1.5 million Cubans into the island's defense system, which has been divided into 1,300 defense zones. Modelled after Vietnamese defense concepts, it appears to be a comprehensive effort by Castro to mobilize and "martialize" Cuban society in order to leaven the contradictions and tensions that have been described above. It is aimed, moreover, at greater economic efficiency by in effect putting the economy on a wartime footing.[30]

In short, "All People's War" reflects the tried-and-true totalitarian method of applying a sweeping broom to all of society's outstanding problems. But if the method is standard, there are also some Castro wrinkles in its specific application. In the MTT, as the core of the "All People's War," Castro has created a new institution that is largely directed by the Party — and therefore less subject than the FAR to Soviet influence.

There is yet another possible implication of the founding of the MTT and "All People's War." As has been noted, Castro rationalized their creation with the alarm-bell of harsher American hostility toward Cuba and the danger of another U.S.-sponsored invasion of the island. It is at least moot that Castro truly believes in that heightened danger. What the MTT does concretely promise, however, is the possibility of freeing more of Cuba's regular forces for missions abroad.

FOUNDATIONS FOR MONUMENTS

During the past year the regime has intensified the ideological campaign within both the regular military and the MTT, stressing "internationalism" and the popular war doctrine as the cornerstones of the Revolution. While the MTT may be another mass organization formed in the "post-Mariel" period to tighten social control, it is also being used to revive revolutionary spirit and the "internationalist" mission within the population. Indeed, the total militarization of Cuban society suggests a progressive intermeshing of Cuba's domestic affairs and "internationalist" duties. As such, it may well signal a preparation of the populace for new adventures abroad.[31]

As has been noted, Castro's support for revolutionary movements and radical regimes is integral both to his self-image and his view of Cuba's role on the world stage. Thus, against the background of new Soviet demands on Cuba's economic policies, Castro has been intent on stressing his unswerving commitment to "internationalist" policies. He did so conspicuously after his speech to the Soviet Party Congress in March, when he stopped in Pyongyang, North Korea, on his way back to Cuba. After signing a friendship treaty with North Korea, whereby both countries pledged material support to national liberation movements, Castro thanked his hosts with a gift of 100,000 automatic rifles and millions of rounds of ammunition.[32]

The gesture may well have been another signal by Castro to the Soviet Union of his determination to continue on the path of "national liberations wars," notwithstanding economic woes and notwithstanding an apparent thawing of Soviet-American relations. It is noteworthy in the latter context that in October 1985 Soviet Foreign Minister Shevardnadze had visited Cuba, apparently to assure Castro that any discussions between the Soviets and the Americans would not compromise Cuban interests.[33]

In all, Castro's lobbying efforts in Moscow seem to have met with at least moderate success. With respect to Angola and Nicaragua, he apparently has extracted a stronger Soviet commitment and approval of Cuba's involvement. The Angolan issue was the subject of Soviet-Cuban talks in Moscow on January 27, 1986; agreement reportedly was reached on a process whereby Angola's defense needs would be coordinated in light of increased U.S. support to UNITA.[34]

At the same time, however, there have been reports that suggest both Castro's heightened ambitions in Africa and Moscow's efforts to keep them in check. According to the *London Observer,* the Soviets rebuffed a Castro initiative for an intensified Cuban role in Angola, and — more important — an expansion of conflict strategy into Namibia and South Africa. In an account attributed to an unnamed Cuban official, Havana approached Moscow to obtain "Soviet clearance and support to issue a formal declaration of war against South Africa to try to turn the struggle against the white regime into an international crusade, such as was fought against Hitler." Allegedly, the Cubans pressed the Soviets to support a full-scale war on the grounds it would "lift Cuban and Soviet prestige in the Third World and with anti-apartheid campaigners."[35]

While there may thus be both Soviet-imposed and domestic reins on Castro's broader ambitions in Africa, they do not apply in nearly the same measure to the Central American arena. Both the Soviet Union and Cuba have of late staggered their military assistance to the Nicaraguan regime, amid reports of an expanded involvement of Cuban military personnel in the regime's battle against the Contras.[36] There have been other signs of a more general strengthening of the Cuban presence in Nicaragua — even though the military expression of that presence may remain veiled for outside consumption, at least for the time being.

From Castro's vantagepoint, defense of the Sandinista regime clearly represents the pivot in his obsessive struggle against the United States. It is also the point-of-departure to the "one, two, three Vietnams" in Latin America pledged by Che Guevara. The "All People's War" in Cuba thus carries all the earmarks of a mobilization of the home base for prolonged external conflict. Especially with the achievements of the Revolution collapsing at home, there is all the more incentive for Castro to complete the personal monuments erected on revolutionary battlefields abroad.

NOTES

1. For Fidel Castro's closing address, see Havana Domestic Service, February 7, 1986.

2. For the lengthy foreign policy resolution passed by the Congress, see Radio Rebelde Network, February 7, 1986.

3. Radio Rebelde Network, February 8, 1986.

4. For Castro's address to the Soviet Party Congress, see Havana Tele-Rebelde Network, February 26, 1986.

5. Jorge Dominguez, "U.S., Soviet and Cuban Policies Toward Latin America," *East-West Tension in the Third World,* Marshall Shulman, ed. (New York: Norton & Company, 1986), p. 58.

6. Edward Gonzalez and David Ronfeldt, *Castro, Cuba and the World: Executive Summary* (Santa Monica: Rand, 1986), p. 5.

7. *Latin American Monitor,* July 1985, p. 188; Havana Television, February 7, 1986.

8. Sanchez Perez' syndicated interview appeared in *El Siglo* (Bogota), March 2, 1986.

9. "Policy Split in Cuba," *Latin American Times,* No. 71, March 11, 1986.

10. On the "youth movement," see *Caribbean Insight,* March 1986, pp. 5–6.

11. *New York City Tribune,* July 2, 1985; *The Washington Times,* December 4, 1985; *Latin American Weekly Report,* December 13, 1985, p. 9.

12. For Castro's remarks on Cuba's economic program, see Havana Domestic Service, February 4, 1986. Yegor Ligachev's praise of the new economic program appeared in *Tass,* February 5, 1986.

13. *Financial Times*, May 1, 1986; *Latin American Monitor*, April 1986; *Journal of Commerce*, April 16, 1986; *Wall Street Journal*, May 7, 1986; *New York City Tribune*, July 11, 1986.

14. *Washington Post*, April 12, 1986.

15. *Journal of Commerce*, April 16, 1986.

16. Ibid., June 12, 1985; *New York Times*, June 5, 1985; *Wall Street Journal*, June 12, 1985. For an extensive analysis of Cuba's oil economy, see Jorge F. Perez-Lopez, "Cuba as an Oil Trader," *Caribbean Review*, Spring 1986, p. 26ff.

17. *New York City Tribune*, July 11, 1986.

18. For Western bank reactions, see *Wall Street Journal*, May 7, 1986.

19. *New York City Tribune*, June 25, 1986.

20. *Radio Marti Quarterly Situation Report*, January 31, 1986, Section V, Social Development, pp. 6–7.

21. Ibid., October 22, 1985, Section I, Overview, p. 4.

22. "Policy Split in Cuba," *Latin American Times*, op. cit.

23. Ibid.

24. Sanchez, op. cit.

25. *Radio Marti Quarterly Situation Report*, January 31, 1986, Section 4, The Military, p. 16; *New York City Tribune*, June 25, 1986; "Political Prisoners in Cuba," Comite Pro Derechos Humanos en Cuba (Madrid: 1986).

26. For a discussion on the effects of Grenada on the Cuban military, see *Radio Marti Quarterly Situation Report*, April 20, 1985, Section 4, The Military.

27. Sanchez, op. cit.

28. *Radio Marti Quarterly Situation Report*, April 20, 1985, Section 4.

29. *Soviet Military Power*, Department of Defense, 1984; *Handbook on the Cuban Armed Forces*, Defense Intelligence Agency, May 1986.

30. Ibid., pp. 3–4.

31. For the ideological campaign in FAR and MTT, See *Radio Marti Quarterly Situation Report*, July 1, 1986, Section 4, The Military, p. 3ff.

32. See Pyongyang KCNA, March 12, 1986; and Pyongyang Domestic Service, March 11, 1986.

33. On Shevardnadze's trips, see Moscow *Tass*, October 29, 1985; Havana Television Service, October 30, 1985.

34. Havana Television, January 30, 1986; *Verde Olivo*, No. 5, February 6, 1986.

35. *The London Observer*, November 24, 1985.

36. For Soviet-Cuban involvement in Nicaragua, see *The Soviet-Cuban Connection in Central America and the Caribbean,* Department of State and Department of Defense, March 1985. For Soviet-Cuban construction of base and intelligence facilities in Nicaragua, see *New York City Tribune,* June 26, 1986. On the recent delivery of 15 Mi-17 helicopters, see *New York City Tribune,* June 27, 1986. For Lopez Cuba's replacement of Division General Arnaldo Ochoa as head of the Cuban military advisory mission in Nicaragua, see EFE, March 10, 1986, and *Barricada,* March 12, 1986. For Cuban involvement in an advisory capacity to the late March incursion of Nicaraguan troops in Honduras, see *Washington Times,* March 18–19, 1986. The use of Soviet An-30 reconnaissance planes in counterinsurgency campaigns, is described in *Time,* June 23, 1986.

10 The United States and Mexico

H. Eugene Douglas

The headlines today, more often than not, advertise disagreement between Washington and Mexico City over the security implications of the turmoil in Central America, or over the tone or substance of responses to Third World development issues. The crisis of the Mexican economy, following the deflation of the oil boom, has meant that events and attitudes in Mexico City have intruded more into Washington's global preoccupations than at any time since World War II.

Yet, there are risks to the new attention that is being given to developments south of the border. Indeed, a serious student of the history of U.S.-Mexican relations may well reach the conclusion that these two very different governments seem to get along best when Washington is preoccupied with a global, not just hemispheric, agenda.

To take just one graphic example: At the beginning of 1917 the United States was on the verge of going to war with Mexico. Public feeling was at a fever pitch when the Mexican Army joined Pancho Villa in killing and capturing U.S. Army troops under the command of General Pershing at Carrizal. Villa's raid on Columbus, New Mexico, and his massacre of 25 American mining engineers at Santa Ysabel in Sonora were still fresh in the public's mind. Old warriors like Teddy Roosevelt and Leonard Wood, Commander-in-Chief of the U.S. Army, were clamoring for a punitive expedition.

This chapter appeared as an article, entitled "The United States and Mexico: Conflict and Comity," in the Spring 1985 issue of Strategic Review.

President Wilson had federalized the National Guard a year earlier, but he did not wish to go to war with Mexico. He had campaigned and won the election of 1916 on a no-war platform. He was preoccupied with the war in Europe. At the same time in Mexican eyes, Wilson, the meddler of Vera Cruz, had become Wilson the paper-tiger. It was touch and go until British intelligence cleverly released the Zimmermann note, in which the German Foreign Minister promised a return to Mexico of all the lands lost in 1848 and 1853 if the Mexicans would support the Kaiser. President Carranza of Mexico, while flattered by the note, turned the offer down and engineered instead the constitution of Queretero, the basic document of the Mexican revolution. "Black Jack" Pershing took his 150,000 U.S. Army troops to Europe as the American Expeditionary Force, and the Yanks fought "over there" and not south of the border. Pancho Villa took his place in the pantheon of the Mexican revolution, while few in successive generations of Americans could even identify his name.

No American president since has seriously considered employing U.S. military force in U.S.-Mexican relations. A generation after World War I, when the real father of modern Mexico, Lazaro Cardenas, seized the oil fields at Tampico, President Franklin Roosevelt showed great restraint, not only in contrast to Wilson's early Mexican policy, but also in contrast to the British, who demanded immediate sanctions against Cardenas. President Roosevelt and his Secretary of State, Cordell Hull, insisted instead on "prompt and just compensation" under FDR's new Good Neighbor Policy. The newly established Export-Import Bank was instructed to make loans to U.S. exporters to Mexico, and trade negotiations began. President Roosevelt was preoccupied with the rise of Nazi Germany as much as with the pall of the Great Depression.

World War II, and the emergence of the United States as a global power, ushered in what the historians call "the era of good feeling" in U.S.-Mexican relations. The beginning of 40 years of sustained economic growth, averaging 6 per cent a year in Mexico, coincided with Washington's preoccupation with the Cold War. Comity, and Mexican growth, continued through the presidencies of John Kennedy, Lyndon Johnson and Richard Nixon during their preoccupations, first with the Soviet buildup in Cuba and then with Vietnam.

THE HEMISPHERIC SECURITY CONTEXT

The danger of too narrow or sharp a U.S. policy focus on Mexico is most obvious in security affairs. A vital U.S. role in this hemisphere must always be as its defender against dangerous major intrusions from without, meaning in current terms the Soviet-Cuban military link and the effects that link is exerting on developments in Central America and Mexico. Those who disparage the "East-West" dimension in hemispheric policy can hardly pose as true friends of Mexico. Just as the United States after World War II acted as guarantor of Western Europe's security against aggression from the East by the USSR, so do we find ourselves in a related role in this hemisphere. In Europe our strategic posture led to the Marshall Plan and NATO. Perhaps someday similar evolutions, appropriate to local conditions, will take place in the Americas. The fact that governments, like Mexico, are not requesting our protection, as did the governments of France and Italy during the later 1940s and early 1950s, does not rule out such evolutions. Indeed, if the day comes when governments south of the Rio Grande do clamor for our protection, it could well mean that the global position of the United States had already been catastrophically undermined.

This is not to say that U.S.-Mexican relations should be viewed solely or largely in an East-West context. Mexico's size, its resources and its geographic position make it inevitable that events south of the border are bound to intrude increasingly on Washington's consciousness, irrespective of developments in the rest of the world. In particular, the economic and financial crisis that followed Mexico's oil boom has raised altogether new questions about our relationship with that nation. But any reevaluation should start with a reaffirmation of the global perspective that must command the shaping of U.S. foreign policy.

A CONFLICTED RELATIONSHIP

"Asymmetry" and "dependency" are two words that recur in the academic literature on U.S.-Mexican relations. Mexicans are much more absorbed with their history than Americans are with theirs.

The merger of their Meso-American past with the invasion of Spanish culture has led to a continuing search for a unique Mexican role in the evolution of the globe. Mexican heroes never die, nor do they fade away. They comprise an anthropomorphic Supreme Court that delivers guidance and counsel on virtually every aspect of Mexican life. Our Founding Fathers have no such hold on United States citizens.

Mexico's constitution is less the "law of the land" than it is an expression of goals and ideals, some of which are very difficult to reconcile with one another. Through it all runs a thread of frustration, even of humiliation, especially at the hands of the Colossus of the North. Every Mexican is aware that a large part of his country was lost or "stolen" in the Nineteenth Century.

Mexicans cry out for understanding of their special history and of the ideals they cherish for their unique mestizo society. What they regard as indifference, compounded by a vast ignorance on the part of most Americans, serves as constant irritation, a continual frustration summed up in the word "dependency."

In light of the past, it was predictable that Mexico would be an early recruit to the Third World and seek to be a leader of that amorphous grouping of diverse nations. Third World imagery is congenial to the "custodians" (their word) of the Mexican revolution. The term "Third World" was coined by French intellectuals to whom the *"Thiers Monde"* was the projection of the French Revolution onto France's former colonies. The Mexican leadership holds the projection of the ideals of its own revolution, particularly in Latin America, as a continuing, if largely inactive goal. It is a goal, paradoxically, to be reached by pursuing a rigidly non-interventionist foreign policy.

Ignorance of Mexican history and insensitivity to Mexican ideals and political culture are all too frequent hallmarks of U.S. attitudes toward affairs in Mexico. In fact, it is an elementary misunderstanding of the Mexican body politic that fuels counterproductive pressures in the United States for government-to-government "solutions" of such headline capturing issues as Mexican immigration and alleged Mexican laxity in the war against narcotics and in the safeguarding of American tourists.

OLD ISSUES, NEW EMPHASIS

When one lists the issues on the diplomatic agenda of the two countries, it becomes clear that they are permanent features, not passing disputes. They have asserted themselves, in one form or another, for at least fifty years: immigration, water and fishing rights, energy policies, trade and investment policies and financial problems. Only the weight of emphasis changes from time to time.

Those issues, which will be reviewed below, illustrate a fact of the relationship that is of paramount importance: none of them is subject to a great deal of magesterial control from Washington or Mexico City. This is the result in large part of two contrasting philosophies of government, the one highly centralized, the other highly decentralized. The dominant political institution of Mexico, the PRI (literally the Institutionalized Revolutionary Party) is a unique and subtle combination of flexibility and authoritarianism which has given Mexico 50 years of peace and relative prosperity while rendering only the minimum concessions to decentralization of authority. The United States, in Mexican eyes, presents a bewildering conglomeration of political actors — state and local governments, regional authorities and commissions, and very powerful private business and banking interests — which seem to overshadow the federal government in Washington itself.

This "asymmetry" above all frustrates academic analysts on both sides of the border. Yet, the contrast in philosophy of government that exists between Washington and Mexico City is not likely to give way. The test of the U.S.-Mexican relationship is whether we in the United States can form a view of our relations with Mexico that serves our national interests and security, while reflecting at the same time an understanding of the realities and legitimate interests of Mexican society. It does not serve our fundamental interests to become involved in Mexican domestic politics — or to act as some kind of mentor for new political groupings. At the same time, wholly indigenous forces are at work within Mexico testing the strength, ethos, political vision and stability of the PRI — economic and political forces. Inevitably U.S. interests will influence those forces.

But let us examine the issues to see what sort of a policy they suggest.

IMMIGRATION

If our forefathers listened to the debate in the House of Representatives in June 1984 over the Simpson-Mazzoli Immigration Bill, they would have been heartened. The debate was in the style of America's early legislators; it defied partisan political analysis. Issues of principle clashed together and with parochial issues, reflecting the fact that immigration, as it used to be said of the tariff, is primarily a "local issue." The Bill's sponsors, reflecting legislative work covering more than a decade, struck a delicate balance between the claims of justice and the claims of security. Some legislators wanted more controls and less amnesty for currently illegal aliens in the United States; others wanted just the opposite. A few more Democrats voted against it than for it; slightly more Republicans voted for it than against it. But what emerged was a complicated consensus, worthy of the early debates in Philadelphia.

The Bill died, a victim of cynical election-year politics. But the compromise reached in the House (after having been accepted twice in the Senate by much wider margins) reflects some profound realities. The most important is that Washington, as a practical matter, can exercise only marginal control over the flow of people across the southern border of the United States. (A public opinion poll, commissioned by *Newsweek* in June 1984, found that 60 per cent of Americans believe that "controls won't work.")

Some critics of the Bill complained because it did not evolve from bilateral negotiations between Washington and Mexico City. This criticism profoundly misunderstands the attitudes in the two capitals. Neither capital has any interest in "politicizing" immigration at the level of national sovereignty. No recent Mexican government has suggested such a notion, nor has any administration in Washington. While some Mexican politicians may speak out on the treatment of undocumented Mexicans in the United States, no Mexican government has indicated a desire to negotiate such treatment as a sovereign matter. With their own population still growing at almost 2.5 per cent, Mexico's leaders know that the demand for Mexican labor in the U.S. market is a "safety valve" that they cannot risk destroying.

Nor is Washington likely to be pushed into making immigration a matter of "sovereign" negotiations with Mexico. The issue is not merely that there is a real demand for Mexican workers in the U.S. labor market, however difficult it may be to measure that demand. It is not merely that the demand is likely to grow as native-born entrants onto the labor market continue to decline as the result of the rapid fall in the U.S. birth-rate that began in the mid-1950s. More important, the rights and wrongs of the issue in terms of U.S. security and prosperity are not clear enough to warrant action from Washington that could threaten the stability of the Mexican Government.

Immigration is, indeed, a local issue in the United States. There will always be individual politicians and pressure groups in Washington who want to "politicize" the matter at the level of national sovereignty. The great virtue of the Simpson-Mazzoli Bill was that it would have made it more difficult for extremists of any stripe to reach that objective. As the new Congress prepares to consider a slimmed-down version of the Immigration Bill, it is useful to recall that, as a practical matter, neither Washington nor Mexico City are in a position to command dramatic and rapid changes in immigration, even if they desired to do so. Rather, they must find a resolution that is acceptable to their own domestic conditions and to the broader realities of international life.

WATER AND FISHING RIGHTS

It took nearly a century for the United States and Mexico to resolve even one dispute over water rights. At issue was some 600 acres of land called the Chamizal (or briar patch in English), which, after a flood on the Rio Grande in 1864 that changed the course of the river, ended up on the U.S. side between the cities of El Paso and Ciudad Juarez. The endless negotiations over this accident of nature resulted in an arbitration (by Canada in 1911), which the United States rejected, and the formation of the predecessor of the current International Boundary and Water Commission. The city of El Paso built a high school on the land, and its citizens remained intransigent until in 1963 President Kennedy, prodded by Thomas Mann,

his Texas-born Ambassador in Mexico City, proposed endorsing
the 1911 Arbitration Award by arranging for an equal exchange of
land. This agreement led to a wider compact between Presidents
Nixon and Diaz Ordaz demarcating the boundary lines in both the
Gulf of Mexico and the Pacific Ocean.

If boundary disputes have perhaps been laid to rest, a bewildering complex of questions involving water utilization, pollution and
fishing rights remain. While President Franklin Roosevelt, anx-
ious to obtain Mexico City's support for the establishment of the
United Nations, negotiated an agreement allocating to Mexico 1.5
million acre-feet a year of water from the Colorado River, nothing
was said about water quality. Rapid development of irrigated
agriculture in Arizona and southern California dramatically
increased the saline content of Mexico's allocation, and negotiations over that problem show every indication of challenging the
Chamizal as a test of endurance.

The saline content of water in the lower Rio Grande Basin has
also risen dramatically. But not all rivers cross the border from
north to south. There is the New River, which rises above the city
of Mexicali and empties into the Salton Sea in California, depositing
tons of pollution that threaten the Imperial Valley of California.
And there is the San Pedro River, rising among the copper mines
of Sonora, which carries copper wastes that threaten the water supply of Tuscon, Arizona.

Both El Paso and Ciudad Juarez compete for uncertain underground water supplies. Ciudad Juarez is a much larger city, but
El Paso is much richer, using perhaps three to four times as much
water per capita as its Mexican counterpart. How does one reach
agreement on water allocations in this situation, especially when
many residents of El Paso receive water from private wells, which
under Texas law are not subject to either measurement or regulation by public agencies?

If these issues are not complicated enough, one might consider
those relating to fishing rights. There has been a running "tuna
war" between the United States and Mexico, which is essentially
over the jurisdictional status of tuna while they are migrating through
Mexico's 200-mile Exclusive Economic Zone (EEZ). This problem
was addressed in the past by the Inter-American Tropical Tuna Com-

mission (IATTC), until Mexico withdrew, claiming that its legitimate rights were not being recognized. A migrating tuna, say the Mexicans, is a Mexican tuna while it swims in Mexico's EEZ. The United States contends that such a tuna is an international fish, subject to allocations among all fishermen. When the Mexican Navy seized some California tuna boats, the "war" was on. At present there is an uneasy armistice.

None of these water and fisheries disputes has been "politicized" to the point where it threatens U.S.-Mexican relations, but lobbyists on both sides are hard at work asserting their rights. Perhaps more important, none of these disputes is likely to facilitate greater cooperation between the two capitals. Again the reason is the contrast in philosophies of government. In Mexican eyes, these are all "sovereign" issues; on the U.S. side they are often seen as regional, state or local issues.

If the scientists are correct, fishing concerns on both sides of the border may face collapse as the source of supply disappears; this contingency might trigger action between the two governments. Some water disputes may become so serious as to prompt similar action. Meanwhile those on the U.S. side who daily confront these water and fishing problems look not so much to Washington as to state and local governments or regional commissions. The day has not dawned when Mexico City will accept subnational compacts. Nevertheless, Washington has little choice but to try to persuade the Mexicans that local agreements in these cases are more workable and more important than government-to-government meetings.

ENERGY POLICIES

Nothing originating in Mexico intruded on Washington's global preoccupations as dramatically as Mexico's oil boom. Between 1972, when Mexico's state-owned oil monopoly, PEMEX, announced its first large finds near Villahermosa in Tabasco state, and 1980, when Mexico's mean daily production reached one million barrels, it seemed that the balance in U.S.-Mexican relations had finally tilted in Mexico's favor and that Mexico, an emerging oil giant, was about to assert itself as an important factor in international trade and finance.

Today those perceptions are mere memory. Yet, as recently as 1981, at a conference on U.S.-Mexican relations hosted by the U.S. Academy of Political Science, the Deputy Director General for Planning at Mexico's Ministry of Finance confidently asserted:

The economic and energy crises in the United States, as well as the development of the Mexican economy, will bring about a situation in which the United States needs Mexico more than Mexico needs the United States. This will be true not only in the area of energy but also in foreign trade and foreign investment. . . .

A U.S. participant in the conference, comparing the outlook for the economy in the two countries, had this to say:

As the United States moves even further into a recession at the beginning of the 1980s, it is difficult to keep an eye on the far horizon. . . . From the perspective of the Mexican economy, the picture is by no means as dismal. . . . The Mexican Government has set growth targets for the gross national product that vary between 8 and 9 per cent a year; if sustained for a generation, that would lead to a quadrupling of the present GNP by the year 2000. . . .

Indeed, the horizon was clouded, but not for the reasons stated. The Mexican oil boom heightened expectations in Washington only less than in Mexico City. President Carter saw in the new oil discoveries a welcome alternative to Western dependence on Middle East supplies. His administration attempted to negotiate a vast agreement to import Mexican natural gas. And the President appointed in the State Department a Special Coordinator for Mexican Affairs, former Representative Robert Kruger of Texas.

The latter's unhappy tenure illustrates the degree to which those heightened expectations were unrealistic. Among his travails, Mr. Kruger had the task of trying to persuade the Mexican Government to take some responsibility for the oil spill at PEMEX's Ixtoc I well, which was approaching the coasts of Texas and Louisiana. The ensuing dispute, coming in the midst of negotiations over natural gas, drew a predictable reply from Mexico City. The Mexican Foreign Ministry proclaimed that there was no "basis in international law to recognize the existence of a legal responsibility. . . ." President Lopez-Portillo recalled that the United States took no responsibility for the damage done to Mexico by the dramatic increase in salinity in the waters diverted to Mexico from the Colorado River. The oil spill balanced the poisoning of the waters of the Colorado. (The post of special Coordinator for Mexican Affairs was abolished by the Reagan Administration.)

The negotiations over natural gas came to nearly naught because Mexico City was no more willing to let market forces determine any part of gas prices than it was willing to let those forces determine Mexican oil prices. Oil and gas are part of the "national patrimony" — meaning that prices are to be set by the government and not the market. This was, and remains, prevailing doctrine throughout most of the Third World, and it doomed many energy negotiations during the oil boom.

This attitude has been part and parcel of many developing countries' demand for a "new international economic order," of which President Lopez-Portillo was a fervent advocate. Before the United Nations General Assembly in 1979, Lopez-Portillo set forth his own "Global Energy Plan," which was designed "to ensure fair, integrated, progressive and orderly transition from one state to another in the history of humanity" — i.e., until solar, nuclear and geothermal power become generally available. His plan guaranteed each nation's sovereignty over its natural resources; proposed easier access to, and transfer of, energy technology; offered assistance to developing and fuel-importing countries in meeting their long-term and emergency needs; and promised reduced speculation in the Rotterdam spot market.

President Carter called the speech "the most profound and beautiful I have ever read." But the OPEC members, from Libya to Saudi Arabia, would have nothing to do with a Mexican initiative that did not address their particular concerns in the Middle East. The plan was stillborn.

Meanwhile, Washington's heightened expectations of formal agreements with Mexico on energy policy proved unrealistic. But the dashed expectations in Washington bore no comparison to the mood in Mexico where, after years of patently unstable growth, the boom gave way to the most severe economic crisis in modern Mexican history.

THE DEBT CRISIS

One of the most important American officials in U.S.-Mexican relations in recent years has been Paul Volcker, Chairman of the Federal Reserve Board. In 1982 Volcker fashioned with newly elected Mexican President de la Madrid the complicated financial package which saved Mexico from economic disaster. This signal act of cooperation between the two governments is unprecedented: it was designed to prevent the worst, and it succeeded. And therein, perhaps, lies a lesson.

The enduring objective of U.S. policy toward Mexico remains what it has been for at least fifty years: the maintenance of political stability. The proposition stated at the outset — that this objective is served best when Washington is absorbed with its own global agenda — remains valid, even after the chaotic years of the Mexican oil boom. Yet, when elemental political stability in Mexico is seriously threatened, Washington must act, as it did in October 1982.

It is not the purpose of this article to explore the roots of the intensifying international financial crisis or even of its impact on Mexico. Nevertheless, several points should be posited.

The first point to be made about the crisis is that it was not the two OPEC-engineered oil price shocks per se that threatened to bring down the system; rather it was the recycling, or "intermediation," of the huge OPEC financial surpluses. The tacit agreement of all OECD countries was to leave recycling to the commercial banking system. For a time this worked, but the result was an intolerable inflation, which brought on a global recession that quickly exposed the vulnerability of the system.

"Financial intermediation" by the commercial banks made them for the first time in modern history the major suppliers of balance-of-payments support for a group of rapidly developing countries, of which Mexico was a prime example. Before the 1970s these countries received capital from abroad largely through direct foreign investment, selling their bonds, or from various official lending agencies ("foreign aid"). Commercial bank loans are much less demanding than these other sources of finance. With bankers pressing money on them, it is not surprising that many countries accepted such loans.

The political and economic consequences of these huge banking transactions differed from country to country, but in general (and in Mexico) middle- and upper-class living standards were maintained at artificially high levels; wage increases far outstripped productivity; development was skewed toward the public sector as bankers preferred "sovereign" loans to the more risky private-sector variety; and unrealistic exchange rates fostered capital flight and widespread corruption. The latter was particularly important in countries as diverse as Mexico and Nigeria. Borrowing governments in the 1970s succumbed to the temptation to obtain money at what amounted to negative real interest rates, and they used the loans to buy relatively cheaply abroad and sell relatively expensively at home. People with wealth in countries like Mexico and Nigeria were practically invited to ship it to safe havens abroad.

These points need to be stressed, because at times of crisis there is a great temptation to pin blame, and that is a very dangerous temptation today. It is far better to accept the fact that the policies in the 1970s of almost all concerned were to blame. The bankers, while believing that they were carrying out a patriotic duty, made large profits from risky loans. The borrowers, while protesting that "development" was their only objective, plunged into "investments" which at best could be made to look "productive" only so long as everyone was banking on inflation.

So much fuel for mutual recrimination abounds today that it will take the highest form of statesmanship to prevent the worst in a great many countries. That is why the Volcker-de la Madrid agreement was so important. Even so, it only bought time. A little over two years later, Mexico, thanks to the austerity policies imposed by President de la Madrid, is cast as a positive actor in the international financial drama. Yet, we have only emerged from the first act of the drama; it will take more imaginative financial diplomacy before one can conclude confidently that the crisis in Mexico has been left behind.

Today probably 80 per cent of Mexico's public enterprises (large employers of Mexico's 19 million labor force, half of which is probably unemployed or underemployed) are operating in debt. Perhaps one out of three, or more, of Mexico's private industrial enterprises are in effect bankrupt, not earning enough to keep their creditors at bay. While in 1975, 12.5 Mexican pesos purchased one dollar, the figure today hovers at 200 pesos — a devaluation without any precedent in U.S.-Mexican relations.

I have no solution to offer to the present financial crisis, but it is doubtful that we can escape our predicament on a "case-by-case" basis. One senses that only as Washington and the other OECD capitals turn their full attention to the security of the financial system itself will there be real progress toward an improved world economy. For U.S. relations with Mexico, this might be the best outcome — again because relations seem to be best when Washington is immersed in a broader agenda. Yet, one fears that bilateral banking diplomacy, even under the international umbrella of the IMF, will prove inadequate.

The outcome of the present debt crisis has portentous implications for U.S.-Mexican relations. Whatever the outcome, however, we can predict with certainty that, in the absence of really productive, direct foreign investment, Mexico's dreams will remain unrealized.

TRADE AND INVESTMENT

At the 1981 conference on U.S.-Mexican relations referred to earlier, one group of participants made a particularly apt observation:

> Mexico City is a haven for planners; Washington, D.C., is a haven for lawyers. Washington trade officials think in terms of *rules* of the game — free trade but fair trade. Mexican trade officials think in terms of *targets* — sector-by-sector, and even company-by-company. . . .

Nowhere do the contrasting philosophies of government in Washington and Mexico City clash more consistently or vocally than in trade and investment matters. Mexico's commercial policy and the Government's attitude toward foreign investment are always justified in terms of the current development plan. The chosen instruments of Mexican trade and investment policies are subsidies, tax incentives, local content regulations and export "requirements" — the whole paraphernalia of protectionism. Those instruments squarely conflict with President Reagan's concepts of fair trade, and with the conclusions reached by the GATT after more than thirty years of tedious negotiations. It is not difficult to understand why Mexico refuses to join GATT and why Washington's persistence in trying to persuade Mexico to do so has never borne fruit.

If Washington can do little about the reigning "development" philosophy in Mexico City, Mexico City can do even less about its dependence on the U.S. market, notwithstanding constant efforts to lighten that dependence. The collapse of the oil boom and the international debt crisis have removed all illusions on this score. It is not just that upward of 70 per cent of all Mexican exports flow north to the United States; more important, only the United States capital market offers a reliable source for the massive development capital Mexico so desperately needs.

While the oil boom and the debt crisis only confirmed Mexican dependence on the United States, they have not in equal measure confirmed interrelatedness between the two neighboring economies. U.S. exports to Mexico plunged by more than 40 per cent between 1981 and 1983. Much has been made of American jobs presumably lost as a result of this decline. To be sure, along the border U.S. commercial interests were hurt badly: communities like Laredo, Texas, and El Paso have suffered levels of unemployment equal to the highest in the nation, thanks largely to the devaluation of the peso. Yet, Austin, Texas, barely 200 miles distant, boasts of one of the lowest unemployment levels in the country.

A peculiarity of the current economic recovery in the United States is that unemployment has fallen from about 10 per cent to 7 per cent even as U.S. exports have been hard hit by an overly strong dollar and a drastic fall in purchasing power in once booming markets like Mexico's. It can be argued that the statistics obscure some qualitative factors — that jobs in export industries are usually "better," in terms of pay and skills, than those in service industries. Nevertheless, the loss of Mexican markets, while impacting on individual companies, has had very little effect overall on the U.S. manufacturing industries.

The short answer to the current, very serious dilemma is "investor confidence." Viewed from north of the border, a vital task of the Mexican Government is to restore confidence in the Mexican private sector, which has been devastated by the crisis of recent years. It is clear that President de la Madrid wishes to bring about this restored confidence. It can also be taken for granted that Washington has a vested interest in doing all it can to assist the Mexican President. And if U.S. banks will have to absorb more blows to their earnings as a result of the billions in Mexico's debt that they so ill-advisedly assumed, it is better that this be done quickly rather than prolonging the agony of all concerned.

Progress is being made in these directions. But again the fact remains that in U.S.-Mexican relations in trade and investment, as in other matters, Washington and Mexico City cannot really do more than prevent the worst. Resuming healthy economic growth and expansion depends on myriad interactions between private U.S. businesses and banks and the private sector in Mexico.

Diplomacy's Role in Restored Confidence

Must we conclude, as the above survey of the issues may suggest, that the styles of government in the two countries are so different that the best the United States and Mexico can expect in their relations is to agree to disagree?

The answer is probably a qualified affirmative. As was stressed earlier, the prospects for working out policy norms in formal inter-governmental agreements are dim. Yet, this conclusion does not necessarily validate the worst-case scenarios in U.S.-Mexican relations projected by many analysts. Washington must never cease trying to persuade Mexico City to accept both the fact and the virtues of the decentralized economic system of the United States, just as it must not fail to view U.S.-Mexican relations in the context of U.S. global policies.

Mexico is an integral part of North America, and our present diplomacy recognizes that fact. Like the United States and Canada,

Mexico is a large country, rich in resources. Commanding both an Atlantic and Pacific coast, it should, like the United States and Canada, look both eastward and westward in developing its own wealth. Indeed, there may be more appropriate development models for Mexico in East Asia than in Western Europe.

While it may be premature to speculate about the formalization of a North American common market, nevertheless a great deal can be undertaken toward improved U.S.-Mexican economic cooperation. If Washington can do little directly with respect to creating jobs in Mexico, it can do more to encourage private capital to assist in that objective. Direct foreign investment for productive purposes is Mexico's priority need: it is available as nearby as in Texas and California, and as far away as Hong Kong.

In the future that capital will not follow the dominant flow of the recent past — that is, from the commercial banks. It is doubtful that, in this century at least, the commercial banks will again become the dominant suppliers, net of debt repayments, of balance-of-payments finance to countries like Mexico. Thanks to its oil, and given correct policies, Mexico can look forward to becoming less dependent on foreign capital, but not for a great many years. It can, of course, sell its bonds if it can afford the high price of a very competitive market. Yet, the obvious source of productive capital is direct foreign investment.

The notion of foreign investment in Mexico may sound like an appeal to the past rather than to the future. Yet, the notion does not center on large inflow of capital for the development of Mexico's natural resources: that flow stopped many years ago and probably will never again become of primary importance. Nor does one imagine a revival of foreign capital currents into industries producing primarily for the Mexican market. That was the feature of foreign investment in the 1950s and 1960s: it fed a highly protected, highly artificial industrial structure that could not withstand the collapse of the oil boom.

Rather, the capital must be attracted to future-oriented productive purposes, and that means commercializing technology for export and for the domestic market. Technology is the key to Mexico's future. Mexico should be an integral part of a unified North American technology market, producing not just labor-intensive subassemblies, but completed "made-in-Mexico" products, just as producers throughout East Asia have done.

U.S. diplomacy should stress the fact that economic growth today depends more on capitalizing on technology than on the ownership of resources. Japan and Korea are the models, not the OPEC members. The question, "who owns the resources?" — which has so dominated U.S.-Mexican relations — should give way to "who is capitalizing on technology?" The Mexicans have already given their answer to the first question: "capturing" their oil from foreign investors was the great physical achievement of their revolution. With respect to the second question, the answers are not likely to be forthcoming from the two governments. Perhaps if there were a shared philosophy at the level of government, the two capitals could set the rules for the development of a truly interdependent technological market. But no such shared philosophy exists, and it is not discernible in the foreseeable future. Still, Washington can at least say the right things, even if it can do little to right the situation.

There is already a multitude of formal and informal contacts between the U.S. and Mexico that do not involve "sovereign" delegations. Washington should do more homework and listen more closely to those involved day-to-day in the geographical embrace between the United States and Mexico. As just one example, the State of Indiana has a "smokestack" industry problem; therefore, the state government is working with local businesses to organize counter-trade with Mexico involving Indiana machinery for Mexican products of a wide variety. Counter-trade may not be the preferred way to conduct modern commerce, but as a short-term measure made necessary by the international debt crisis, we will have to live with it. What we should do is use it to encourage relationships from which new investment and trade can grow.

Of course, it is to Texas, New Mexico, Arizona and California that one would look most for new cross-border initiatives. Washington's role should be that of supporting actor, not lead actor. The governors of these states meet regularly with their Mexican counterparts. Even though none of the latter possess the authority of the U.S. governors, Washington should make clear that it regards these meetings as very important.

And the U.S. Government can and should do more to promote Mexican trade and investment outside Mexico. The channels of trade between Mexico and Canada often run through the United States, especially the shipments of Mexican produce to Canada. We can help smooth those channels by removing red-tape obstacles on our side of the border. And we should encourage joint ventures in third countries between U.S. and Mexican firms, especially in technology.

The way to promote a more unified North American market is to act now as though it were in a process of evolution. This is a matter both of style and of substance. It is important that Washington help set the style or tone in U.S.-Mexican relations. The place to begin is by raising public consciousness in the United States that a job created in Mexico is, in the final analysis, as important to our security and wellbeing as a job created in the United States, and to focus attention on capitalizing technology, rather than on the ownership of resources.

11 Mexican Immigration: A Fortress America?

SOL SANDERS

In the Fall 1982 issue of *Strategic Review,* H. Eugene Douglas, then U.S. Coordinator for Refugee Affairs in the U.S. Department of State, performed the pioneer — and courageous — task of examining the growing problem of worldwide refugee and immigration flows in a sober, "strategic" context. He began with a prediction:

> . . .It is difficult to see how in the year 2000 the sovereign right of nations to control their own borders will be viewed as a right that can be enforced unilaterally over time. The control of borders, like the control of economies, will become more and more a matter of consultation (if not confrontation) and negotiation between nations.[1]

Ambassador Douglas cast his thesis on a global scale, but he clearly was thinking primarily of the growing predicament of the United States — a nation of immigrants which etched the right of asylum into its very ethos (as symbolized by the tall statue in New York harbor), but which now finds itself under increasing assault by refugee waves over porous borders and sparsely guarded shores. And Douglas referred specifically to Mexico as the "acid test" for U.S. policy:

> Pressures on our borders from the Caribbean and Central America — particularly Mexico — make it certain that in the foreseeable future, as never before in the past, the United States is going to have to maintain a foreign policy, including preemptive

This chapter appeared as an article, entitled "Mexican Immigration: Specter of a Fortress America?" in the Winter 1986 issue of Strategic Review.

and prophylactic measures, which has as one of its objectives the protection of our frontiers against excessive illegal immigration. The tensions within our society resulting from illegal immigration could grow to dangerous proportions.[2]

This kind of projection has been disparaged as a "scare scenario," designed primarily to win support for the present U.S. Administration's Central American policies, particularly in the politically powerful sectors of the American Southwest. It is argued that there is a tendency to exaggerate both the magnitude of the problem of illegal Mexican immigration and its potential socioeconomic impact on the United States.

But is the problem exaggerated in its current status, let alone its likely future dimensions? The answer can only be found in the problem's wellspring: namely, developments in Mexico itself. And there the discernible trends suggest that the fears expressed by Ambassador Douglas and others are, if anything, understatements of the tinder of crisis along the "soft" southern border of the United States.

The Mexican Population Explosion

Among the various factors that account for human migration in the modern setting, rapid population growth obviously is a major generator of the phenomenon. Not only does such growth provide direct prods for demographic movements that ultimately strain against a nation's borders, but it also feeds the fires of economic distress and socio-political conflict which are apt to turn refugee waves into floods.

Just as the population explosion is at the root of so many domestic Mexican problems today, so it is an underlying determinant of the new relationship emergent between the United States and Mexico. In 1910, at the beginning of the period to which Mexicans reverently refer as their Revolution, Mexico had only 15 million people (compared to 92 million for the United States). Between the end of World War II and 1970, the Mexican population, largely as a result of a decline in infant mortality, had doubled to 53 million. Today it stands at 80 million.

There is a prevalent view among observers of the Mexican scene that the former population growth rates — which were as high as 3.3 per cent a year only a decade ago — have declined as urban patterns cut into traditional rural customs and fertility drops. This conclusion, however, is subject to considerable debate. Mexican statistics are highly suspect, and the experience in other parts of the world has been that urbanization, at least initially, has the opposite effect on fertility — that families moving in from rural areas tend to grow even more rapidly because, no matter how squalid urban slum conditions may appear to Westerners, it is rare that they are not an improvement in terms of nutrition and hygiene over the rural areas from which the migrants come. In any case, there is a general consensus that Mexico's population will grow at well over 2 per cent annually into the next century.

Concomitants of Population Growth

The old traffic metaphor is apt: will the brakes applied to a speeding automobile, however effective, bring it to a halt before it crashes into the wall? By the year 2000, Mexico will have at least 100 million people — perhaps as many as 126 million. One Mexican authority estimates that if this higher projection holds, Mexico will move by the mid-Twenty-first Century to a total population of 500–600 million.[3]

Today more than half of Mexico's population is under 15 years of age. The population explosion and the inadequacies of economic development combine to make poverty universal in the country. Mexican per capita income — a not very adequate gauge of the quality of life but a measure of relative wealth — was only $1,640 in 1979. That means that the total national economic product divided by the number of inhabitants was about a tenth of the same figure for Americans, or a half of that for Venezuelans. And given the disparity of income within the country, the situation is even worse than the per capita figures indicate. Some 20 per cent of the population with higher incomes accounted for more than 57 per cent of total national household income in the 1970s. In 1980, 11.7 per cent of all Mexicans lived without water in their homes; 48 per cent had no sewage disposal; and about a third of the country's families lived in single rooms.

Furthermore, the distribution of the Mexican population complicates any attempt to improve their livelihood and standards of living. Only 15 per cent of Mexicans live on the coastal plains where there is abundance of water, readily available energy and a large part of the arable land. More than 60 per cent is crowded on the high central plateau around Mexico City, where an infrastructure is at best difficult to provide.

Despite the squalid conditions for the poor in Mexico's major cities, the urbanization continues with mass migration into these cities. By 1980, 66 per cent of all Mexicans were living in urban areas. Mexico City, whose metropolitan area now contains some 20 per cent of the total population, has been growing at the rate of 30 per cent annually during the last ten years. It expanded from 8.9 million in 1970 to 16.4 million in 1980 and, barring some radical changes in present trends, there will be a megalopolis of 40 million people living in the Valley of Mexico by the turn of the century.

The effect of all this is clear to the naked eye of the most casual observer, even to a tourist who manages to steer clear of the wretched, makeshift slums that gird much of Mexico City. More and more people are living on the streets, even in the more fashionable areas. "Marias," the Indian or meztizo women who come down from the mountains to sell handicrafts or lottery tickets on the streets with three or four small children in tow, are becoming an increasingly common sight even in better neighborhoods. The quality of the air, a grave problem aggravated by the absence of oxygen at the 8,000-foot altitude, has reached abominable conditions with almost two million cars — more than half of all those in Mexico — concentrated in the area.

Virtually no new rental apartments have been built in the last decade due to the lack of incentives for private investors. Rents have skyrocketed. Mexico City's Planning Director, Javier Caraveo Aguero, stated in 1984 that there is no solution for the housing shortage: "Let us say that the 800,000 housing units now needed could be built in 50 years. By that time the population would have grown, and housing needs would have again increased, so there would still remain a shortage. . . . Each one of us in Mexico City has less than two square meters of green space — and, according to some international organizations, there should be a minimum of 10 square meters for each inhabitant."

Following the earthquake in September 1985, the Government announced that it would expropriate 7,000 privately owned buildings in downtown Mexico City for a total of 625 acres in order to build 180,000 housing units for the estimated 200,000 people rendered homeless by the catastrophe. It is clear that even if this radical project were accomplished (owners promise to seek court injunctions to delay if not prevent the expropriation) it would only exacerbate the immense housing problem in the tradition of previous, bungling Government attempts at intervention.

The water supply is in jeopardy, and because Mexico City lies in a valley on the plateau, waste has to be pumped up over the mountains for disposal. The only major source of water that can be tapped in the future is at Tecolutla, almost 300 miles away. Meanwhile, the city continues to pump water from its subsoil — water that was once abundant when the pre-Columbian city of the Aztecs was built on islands in a lake on the plateau. The pumping has caused the gradual sinking of major structures throughout the city. When the subject of water rationing comes up — as it does perennially during periods of shortage — the idea is immediately abandoned because there is no infrastructure that would permit any equitable division of the existing supply.

DEARTH OF REMEDIES

None of the remedies which have been suggested, plotted and partially implemented have even begun to meet this population challenge. Birth control programs have foundered on the same shoals that mark other nonindustrial societies: traditional attitudes which see children as economic units adding to the productivity of the family; disproportionate illiteracy and suspicion by precisely those whom the program must target; politics and corruption and incompetence among the bureaucracy recruited for the program; and the still inherent inadequacies of current contraceptive devices in this kind of environment.

A Mexican Government official charged with the propagation of birth control literature and devices claims that the traditional opposition of the Catholic Church is not a major factor in the problem. He said that he welcomed the anti-contraception statements of Pope John Paul II, arguing that the Church's anti-contraception program helps the government program by simply drawing attention to the problem. Given all the other, relatively greater problems of the population control program, this claim does not seem farfetched.

THE UNEMPLOYMENT SPIRAL

Unemployment is increasing in Mexico as enormous numbers of new workers swell the labor market. The labor force has expanded since 1970 at an even faster rate on an average annual basis than has the general population — 6.2 per cent versus 3.8 per cent. Official government estimates set unemployment at 7 per cent. This is sheer invention: based on income statistics in the census of 1970, there appeared to be 4.9 to 5.8 million (37 to 45 per cent of the labor force) unemployed or underemployed — that is, people whose contribution to the gross domestic product is nil, or who work less than 40 hours a week, or who earn less than the minimum wage. Both the Echeverria and the Lopez Portillo Administrations attempted job creation through enormous deficit financing schemes, which brought about the runaway inflation and the enormous foreign borrowing.

One way of measuring the failure of that program to create new jobs is to set the number of 731,000 new jobs estimated to have been created by the Mexican economy in 1981 against the deportation of 866,000 Mexican illegals from the United States, reported by the U.S. Immigration and Naturalization Service that same year. The statistics of the United States Immigration Service do not attempt to cull out those illegals who have been deported more than once — a very large number, according to those familiar with the problem. Yet, the rough comparison does suggest the extent to which the Mexican government program has failed even during a boom year — and the significance of illegal migration to the United States as a safety valve for the Mexican population problem.

FACTORS IN EMIGRATION

Any discussion of the problem of Mexican emigration to the United States must start with the proposition subscribed to by most expert observers in Mexico and in the United States: namely, that large-scale Mexican emigration to the United States will continue. That proposition is based on five factors:

• The enormity of the Mexican population "surplus" and the "porous" nature of the long land border with the United States virtually dictate that large numbers of Mexican nationals will continue to enter the United States in future years.

• Mexican analysts, as well as many students of Mexico's problems on this side of the border, argue that the exploding Mexican population must have the U.S. "safety valve" if any kind of stability is to be maintained below the border.

• The American tradition of hosting new arrivals will continue with respect to Mexicans and other Latin Americans, notwithstanding other American traditions of prejudice and discrimination against them, particularly in the Southwest.

• The effect new immigrants can provide for the U.S. economy — "stoop labor" for Southwestern agriculture and untrained but cheap labor for the service industries — will be an important supporting factor.

• Although it is more ambiguous toward the problem than many Hispanic spokesmen in Washington admit, the Mexican-American community has strong familial ties to Mexico and will, to an unknown extent, support a continuing emigration.

HISTORICAL BACKGROUND OF THE PROBLEM

Emigration from what is now Mexico into what is now the Southwest of the United States is as old as the Spanish conquest in the Sixteenth Century. Yet, contrary to popular folklore, the claim of Mexican-American "nationalists" to a privileged role in the Southwest — because they preceded other Americans there — is flimsy at best.

Partisans of a more liberal policy toward Mexican immigration often invoke the argument that "it belonged to them" in order to justify "an open border" or the right of Mexicans to immigrate and populate the American Southwest without restriction. More specifically, the argument is that, at the time of the American annexation, there were probably not more than 100,000 people in the whole area between Louisiana and San Francisco, and a large part of them were Indians who drew little distinction between the two colonizing centers coming at them from the north and south. Therefore, it is contended, the region is one that "belongs" equally to the ethnic groups that now inhabit it.

The point is, however, precisely that there was little in the region, prior to its annexation by the United States, that can be pointed to as an ethnic or cultural claim. In 1821, when the first "Anglos" (English-speaking settlers) from the United States began to colonize the territory, Texas had less than 4,000 Spanish-speaking inhabitants; by the time of the Texas Revolution in 1836, "Anglos" already outnumbered the Spanish-speaking inhabitants five to one. There were only 61,000 inhabitants of New Mexico and southern Colorado, the most successful of the Spanish-Mexican colonies in the region, when the Treaty of Guadalupe Hidalgo was signed in 1848, ending the U.S. war against Mexico, and already substantial numers of "Anglos" lived among them. Arizona had only 2,000 non-Indian inhabitants even after the Gadsden Purchase extended the border southward to include Tucson. And there were perhaps 7,500 Spanish-speaking settlers in California at the time of the American takeover. Indeed, few Mexican-Americans in the entire Southwest can make claims to the area on the basis of their ancestry: like their fellow Americans in the region, they are the descendants of immigrants who settled there after it was joined to the United States.

The history of Mexican migration to the Southwest is confused by other factors. Until the 1930s large stretches of the border were simply lines on paper in Washington, and no adequate records were kept. From 1886 to 1893 no statistics were maintained on border crossings, and even later in the century most figures are estimates based on the small "head tax" charged immigrants who passed through official checkpoints. No visas were required from U.S. consulates. Nor was there great population movement on the Mexican side of the border, since northern Mexico was sparsely populated.

Cheap labor for U.S. expansion of agriculture in the Southwest and for the railroads was recruited in China and the Philippines. The construction of railroads from the United States into Mexico during the 1900–1910 period began to make migration northward easier, and estimates are that some 24,000 Mexicans took (legal) advantage of this new mode of travel. Because the railways were employers as well as the avenue of approach to the United States, concentrations of Mexican-Americans manifested themselves as early as the 1920s, and they continued to grow in such relatively remote places as Chicago (which now has the largest Mexican-American population of any city in the United States except Los Angeles). This also helps to explain why "barrios" have grown up in areas of America's large cities near the railroad facilities or the stockyards, and why the caste differences arose which are so pronounced in the Mexican-American community. As one analysis puts it:

Drawn to these segregated enclaves, later arrivals either from Mexico or rural areas in the United States faced problems which were not identical with those of the more experienced earlier residents, despite the identity in culture and traditional institutions. . . . Among other national groups the relative suddenness of their urbanization suggests that an overwhelming proportion started out occupying approximately equal status and were confronted by common problems of adjustment, with differentiation developing later.[4]

MIGRATION TRENDS IN THIS CENTURY

But it was the violent period in Mexico, beginning in 1910, that spurred the movement which generated today's large Mexican-American minority in the Southwest. Perhaps as much as 3 per cent of Mexico's population moved north annually in some of the troubled years, reaching a peak in the 1920s — even though by then the actual fighting in Mexico had stopped and pressures mounted in the United States to put a brake on the inflow. Official U.S. statistics, probably still only vague approximations, indicate that at the very least a million permanently resident Mexicans must have entered by 1930 as the economic and social effects of the Mexican civil war continued to disrupt life below the border.

An intensified effort, beginning in 1924, to control the border resulted in a growing number of illegal entries. This trend was abetted by labor contractors seeking recruits for the expanding large-scale agriculture of California and Texas. "Coyotes" — local runners who helped emigrants across borders and showed them how to escape visa fees, the literacy test and a head tax — were the precursors of today's army of smugglers of people, drugs and arms, as well as less valuable contraband, across the border. But as the effects of the U.S. depression began to impact after 1928, along with the consequent mass movement to California of poor whites from the drought-destroyed farms of the South and West, Mexican emigration dropped off sharply.[5]

Official figures for the 1930s record only 27,000 Mexicans entering the country on permanent visas. As the depression deepened and the unemployed Mexicans in urban areas of the Southwest became a more visible drain on local government budgets, a program for forced repatriation developed between the federal Border Patrol and local authorities — and even Mexican consular authorities. Between 1931 and 1934, the city of Los Angeles sent 15 trains, with an average 1,000 Mexicans aboard, southward over the border. Other cities as remote from the border as Detroit and St. Paul, Minnesota, also pressured Mexicans to return to Mexico in programs of repatriation of indigents. Again, there are no accurate statistics, but guesses are that as many as 300,000 persons returned to Mexico in this manner during this period — even though some of them came back to the United States either as immigrants or by their ability to establish American nationality and obtain repatriation.

World War II brought a new development: the *bracero* (fieldhand) program by which the U.S. Government arranged the importation of Mexican agricultural workers to replace large numbers of Americans drafted for the military. An executive agreement between Mexico and the United States, ratified by the Congress in August 1942 and later extended in 1951, was not to end for 22 years. The peak of the exchange was reached in 1959, when more than 135,000 men were admitted to work in the United States and then returned to Mexico. The volume declined markedly toward the end of the period but was replaced, at least in part, by the "wetbacks" (*mojados,* a term of derision in Mexico) — illegal workers who crossed often for the same kind of work but without legal authorization. In 1953, an official U.S. Government report estimated that for every agricultural laborer admitted legally, four aliens were being taken into custody by the Border Patrol.

Another twist came in 1964 when the Department of Labor administratively imposed a new criterion for legal entry of temporary workers, requiring certification that jobs for which they were being recruited could not be filled by domestic labor. The end of the *bracero* program and this new regulation altered the conditions of Mexican entry and has led to a plateau for legal entrants of under 50,000 a year. But, of course, the illegal migration has continued apace, and although all numbers are suspect, it must be assumed that it has reached into the millions. The number of forced repatriations reached the million mark in 1984. The probability is that for every illegal returned, some four or five successfully establish at least temporary residence in the United States.

THE CONTEMPORARY SCENE

Thus, Mexican emigration to the United States has a varied past: It has fluctuated violently, generally in accordance with developments south of the border. Because of the geographic proximity of their homeland, Mexicans — far more than Europeans or Asians who have come to the United States — have tended to think of themselves as temporary migrants, and the back-and-forth movement traditionally has been very large, increasingly so with the ease and low cost of transportation. And Mexican immigrants — because of their language, the constant flow of new arrivals into relatively concentrated geographical areas, and the history of widespread discrimination against them in the Southwest — have tended to remain less assimilated into the general U.S. population, and more a national subgroup than most other immigrant groups.

But even this complicated background hardly prepares one for the rat's nest of claims and counterclaims for the actual situation today. One U.S. Government estimate is that 900,000 Mexican nationals illegally living in the United States were counted in the 1980 census, but this is considered only a minimum figure for the number of Mexican illegals in the country.[6] Mexican government estimates set the figure at between 800,000 and 1.9 million "undocumented" Mexicans working in the United States over the course of a given year, contending that most of these sooner or later return to Mexico. Another estimate is that by 1975 the U.S. already hosted 3.5 million Mexicans, both legal and illegal, permanent as well as temporary, in the work force.

Notwithstanding these disparate figures, there is agreement among most students of the Mexican migration problem that several new patterns have come onto the scene in the past decade:

• There has been a sharp increase in the illegal immigration into the United States, reflected in the greater number of illegals being apprehended and returned to Mexico by the Immigration and Naturalization Service.

• There has been a shift toward more permanent residence and longer periods of residence in the United States by the newer arrivals, apparently reflecting both the increasing economic pressures in Mexico and the new opportunities for integration in the United States.

• Immigrants are arriving in greater numbers from non-traditional centers of emigration — the southwest and southeast of Mexico instead of northern and central sections from which they had come in the great migrations of the 1920s and 1930s.

• The Mexican immigration to the United States is becoming more diffused throughout the country rather than remaining in the traditional *barrios* in the Southwest built up over the last 60 years.

• Although relatively small in statistical terms, the United States is now receiving a heavy migration of upper-middle-class and upper-class Mexicans, uncharacteristic of Mexican emigration.

Again, quantifying these observations is difficult, and expert observers vary widely in their estimates. But it is obvious that, if the economic situation continues to deteriorate in Mexico, the human outflow will rise substantially. Following the 1982 devaluations of the Mexican peso, the border surveillance organizations on the U.S. side were reporting a 50 per cent increase in the flow of illegal crossings. Figures for deportations also seem to reflect this, although these increased numbers of returnees might be attributed to greater vigilance on the part of the U.S. officials. Many observers saw even the proposals contained in the Simpson-Masoli immigration bill, which was defeated in the U.S. Congress in 1984, as a stimulus to those in Mexico who were thinking of crossing the border to try to reach the United States before more stringent U.S. legislation went into force.

The fact that larger numbers of emigrants are now coming from the states of Oaxaca, Chiapas and Tabasco in southern Mexico presents a host of new problems. The populations of these states are culturally different from the older sources of Mexican migration to the United States: they tend to be poorer, less integrated into the modern Mexican economy and more "Indian" — both culturally and racially — than the people in the north and the central plateau. Some Mexicanists would argue, too, that because they come from areas of the country which were pre-Columbian Mayan-speaking rather than Nahuatl-speaking (the language of the Aztecs and many of their conquered peoples), they constitute a quite different ethnic group with different problems of integration in any U.S. environment.

Although the statistical information is scarce and subject to debate, indications that the Mexican emigrants are staying longer and more permanently than in the past are implicit in the growing evidence that they are moving into occupational areas other than simple agricultural labor, which was once virtually their only source of employment. With respect to the dispersion of the Mexican immigration beyond the Southwest, again the statistical evidence is poor. But constant news reports — for example, of expulsions and difficulties experienced by Mexican labor in the timber industry of Oregon, Washington and other parts of the Northwest — as well as the increasing visibility of Mexicans in eastern U.S. cities attest to such a trend.

Perhaps no trend is as difficult to document as the arrival in the United States of a new caste of emigrants: namely, members of the

Mexican elite. Their numbers may be small, but there is constant gossip in professional circles in Mexico City of members who have bought homes in the United States or who have sent their children. A representative of one of the international Jewish welfare organizations reports that non-Jewish Mexican friends — mostly upper-middle-class — constantly approach him with inquiries about the mood and the intentions of the small but relatively influential Jewish community in Mexico. "The Jews have a nose for catastrophe, and I want to know what they are doing," was the way one typical inquirer put the questions to him.[7] During the pre-1981 boom, individual purchases of homes in the United States by wealthier Mexicans through American banking facilities in the Southwest reached into the billions of dollars at market values. And Houston, for example, is the scene of thousands of young and middle-aged Mexican professionals who have entered businesses there in what would appear to be a permanent exile.

SOMBER SCENARIOS

What is clear from this brief resume is that Mexican immigration to the United States is a function both of the "push" of Mexican conditions and the "pull" of conditions in the United States. In the past, however, the level of emigration has been dictated largely by the "push" of conditions in Mexico. The real threat to U.S. stability lies not so much in a continuing Mexican immigration which would supply the United States with a replenishing reservoir of new workers and enrich its cultural diversity. Rather, looking back to the Mexican rebellion of 1910–1924 — and to the enormous immigration flow it triggered in the face of much greater obstacles than exist today — what would happen in a new period of instability in Mexico? Would Washington wake up one morning, after the first shots had been fired in a new upheaval in Mexico, to find literally millions of refugees swarming across the poorly defended U.S. border?

The extent to which the idea of flight has become commonplace among Mexicans is demonstrated by two recent novels by Manuel Sanchez Ponton: *El Golpe: Operation Incruenta* and a sequel appropriately entitled *Estampida*.[8] The novels present a scenario in which a rightwing coup fails to rescue Mexico from its present crisis. This time the huddled "pacificos" who simply tried to keep out of the way of the fighting and the banditry of an earlier period are poised to flee across the northern border to the United States. Not only is the Mexican population five times bigger than it was in 1910, but the restraints on movements which existed in that largely rural Mexico no longer obtain.

That is the nightmare that Americans have to consider. Nor is it clear what the American response would be in that kind of emergency — a catastrophe for which little preparation has been made in Washington, Austin or Sacramento.

Moreover, the contingency is not a function strictly of developments indigenous to Mexico. Today Mexico is still a buffer — if a sometimes troublesome one — between the United States and upheavals in Central America. Yet, the fragile fabric of Mexico's economic and political society is very much prey to developments in the larger Central American environment. What would happen if regional conflagration were to spill into Mexico itself — especially a conflagration fueled and exploited by the outside forces that are active today in Nicaragua, El Salvador and elsewhere in the region? We may recall Fidel Castro's innovative and cynical use of refugees as a weapons system against the United States in the exodus from Mariel in 1980. What would happen in the event of an immensely magnified Mexican version of such a strategem?

What such scenarios paint is a more direct, and darker, picture of a potential "Fortress America" than has usually been adduced in the strategic literature. Exaggerated or not, the scenarios give salience to U.S. efforts to contain the destabilizing developments — and forces — on our strategic doorstep. Although the task calls for delicate statesmanship and sensitivity to the proud sovereignties of our hemispheric neighbors — particularly so in the case of Mexico — nevertheless the time is long past for the comfortable notion of a "benign neglect" by the United States — the notion that the problems south of our border will somehow right themselves, if only we will not interfere. The problems are not likely to resolve themselves, and we are very much within the path of their potential explosion.

NOTES

1. H. Eugene Douglas, "The Problem of Refugees in a Strategic Perspective," *Strategic Review,* Fall 1982, p. 12.

2. Ibid., p. 17.

3. Franciso Alba, *The Population of Mexico: Trends, Issues and Policies* (New Brunswick, NJ: Transactions, Inc., 1982), p. 131.

4. Leo Grebler et al, *The Mexican-American People: The Nation's Second-Largest Minority* (New York: Macmillan Publishing Co., 1970), p. 85.

5. In the mass "Okie" migration to California were also large numbers of Mexican-Americans from Texas, the parents and grandparents of many Mexican-Americans in California today. They form a distinct sub-caste in the highly heterogeneous Mexican-American population of the Southwest.

6. Jeffrey S. Passel and Robert Warren, "Estimates of Illegal Aliens from Mexico counted in the 1980 Census," a paper presented at the Annual Meeting of the Population Association of America in Pittsburgh, PA, April 14–16, 1983.

7. Both the Jewish and Lebanese communities were threatened by the highest Mexican authorities during the mass flight of capital in 1981–1982 in an effort to discourage their remittance of assets overseas. An official of the Mexican Government, talking to U.S. Jewish organization officials, used the fact that Lebanese as well as Jews were pressured by the Mexican authorities to "prove" that there was no anti-Semitism involved.

8. Both novels were published by EDAMEX (Mexico City) in 1983.

PART IV

U.S. Policy Issues

12 U.S. Options — and Illusions — in Central America

David C. Jordan

The fires of revolutionary conflict are spreading in Central America, threatening to engulf widening parts of this vital area at the strategic doorstep of the United States. Conventional weapons are flooding into the region from worldwide communist suppliers. At the same time, the United States seems to be vainly casting about for a political and economic policy which can help stamp out the fires while bolstering on a more durable basis those regional forces that can resist revolutionary Marxist advances and Soviet-Cuban inroads.

The advent of the Reagan Administration in 1981 marked a sharp shift in official U.S. perspectives of the accelerating current of developments in the Caribbean-Central American region and of the requisite U.S. policies to deal with these developments: one might call it the shift from a "regionalist" to a "globalist" perspective. In contrast with the Carter Administration, which at least until its final months tended to view developments in the Southern Hemisphere in essentially a regional context and outside the super-power competition, there seems to be a consensus in the higher strata of the Reagan Administration that the key to U.S. regional policies is to be found in the Soviet threat and in what the Soviets call the "global correlation of forces." Latin America in general, and the Caribbean-Central American region in particular are now seen as arenas of an ever bolder Soviet strategy directed at the "strategic rear" of the United States.

This chapter appeared as an article in the Spring 1982 issue of Strategic Review.

In this "globalist" perspective, direct and indirect Soviet expansion, with emphasis on the use of surrogates, aims at two paramount and entwined strategic objectives: 1) the erosion of the resource base of America's economic and military power, and 2) the build-up of the resource base for the Soviet security system. From Moscow's vantagepoint, the two objectives need not interact in a "zero-sum" sense: that is, an erosion of the U.S. position does not necessarily have to translate into a direct and immediate gain for the Soviet Union. Thus, anti-U.S. states can be tied in loose ways to the Soviet Union and its proxies — principally Cuba — or even tolerated in a "nonaligned" stance while nevertheless catering to Soviet security goals.

It will be the thrust of the analysis that follows that, while this recognition in Washington of the forces and stakes involved in the ascending conflict in the Southern Hemisphere is a positive (if belated) development, nevertheless the Reagan Administration's unfolding policies toward the region continue to be flawed both by misperceptions and by a drift toward "pragmatism" — which tends to become a euphemism for the absence of a policy.

The United States must come up with a coherent strategy designed not only to undercut the geopolitical designs of its adversaries, but also to build up those political and economic forces in the Caribbean-Central American region able and willing to sustain constitutional and free enterprise systems. A coherent U.S. policy must deal certainly with communist expansion, but even more it must recognize and discard those policy concepts and initiatives which make Latin America increasingly vulnerable to Marxist revolution.

The imperative of such a policy requires: 1) a forthright discussion of the various U.S. options for blocking Soviet-backed revolution, and 2) the replacement of strategic pragmatism with a sound U.S. historical perspective and doctrine. In the absence of such historical perspective and coherent doctrine, U.S. policy will continue to be at the mercy of revolutionary tides as well as powerful special interests. There is still time to hammer together the essential elements of an embracive and effective strategy, but the accumulating warning signals from the Southern Hemisphere mark that task as an excruciatingly urgent one.

THE SOVIET OFFENSIVE

The Reagan Administration has accurately focused upon the Soviet Union as the principal progenitor of conflict and conflagration in the world at large, including the Caribbean-Central American basin. Yet, implicit in the Administration's views has been an emphasis on the overt tentacles of expanding Soviet military and political power and influence, including those extended through Moscow's clients and surrogates. A coherent U.S. hemispheric policy, however, demands a more integrated understanding of a phenomenon that has been fundamentally alien to the American sensibility and experience: namely, the basic phenomenon of imperialism. For what the Soviet Union is plying today is imperialism in its atavistic manifestations of the expansion of the imperial state, but with a powerful modern instrument: the export and exploitation of revolution.

Soviet imperialism carries both overt and covert dimensions. In its overt form, the Soviets have militarized Marxism-Leninism. The original Marxist-Leninist concept regarding the "inevitability" of historical development has been replaced with military Marxism, the concept of the Marxist state fashioned by military conquest or coup d'etat from above rather than social revolution from below. Clausewitz has been reversed by the Soviets: politics becomes the continuation of war by other means. Having brought state socialism to a repressive zenith at home, and having expanded it through the "Brezhnev Doctrine" to the subjugation of neighboring parts of the empire, overt Soviet imperialism has become the ultra-imperialism of our era.

In its covert form Soviet imperialism disguises aggressive expansion as "national liberation" and as directed at democratic and popular causes rather than dictatorial or totalitarian outcomes. Covert Soviet imperialism toward targeted countries has several remarkable features. Conflict is vertical — that is, a Soviet-backed insurgency is depicted as internal or civil war, and not as the cutting edge of a horizontal, transnational process. The pattern of the ultimate takeover is flexible, depending on the vulnerability, feasibility and desirability of the prize. The vulnerability of the target nation is both opportunistically recognized and carefully prepared, and the mode of exploitation depends on the desirability of the prize and the feasibility of its taking.

The preparation of vulnerability is the most interesting aspect of covert Soviet imperialism: in each case, the target country is systematically undermined politically and ideologically, infiltrated in its culture and institutions, and eventually disrupted. Because the Soviets work adaptively in the wings of a targeted society, they are able to make use of forces and groups that are ostensibly opposed to them. This is particularly applicable when the forces in question lean toward Marxist values or Marxist "mind-sets," notwithstanding their ostensible allegiances to ideological mainsprings or embodiments other than the Soviet model. At the present juncture in the Caribbean-Central American region, the Socialist International especially fits this mold. More will be said on this topic below.

More generally, covert Soviet imperialism battens on opportunity — and opportunity is paved by circumstances not only in the target area, but in the broader international environment, with heavy emphasis on prevalent policy attitudes in the United States and other significant nations. This tactic was heralded in the Russo-Cuban intervention in Angola. In that operation in the mid-1970s, not only was the United States inhibited by internal politics from moving against the intervention, but other, regional forces capable of resisting had been politically discredited in the United States to the point where even indirect U.S. intervention was barred. The Soviets and their surrogates obviously are trying to erect the same kinds of barriers and inhibitions to possible U.S. intervention in El Salvador, Guatemala and other targets of their conflict strategy in Central America.

Counterpointing covert Soviet imperialism are its overt manifestations — notably the growing reach of Soviet conventional military power, which long ago has breached the erstwhile U.S. strategic "containment." By matching, and in many areas surpassing, U.S. naval power, Soviet military forces combine with the covert means to effect and sustain political conquests — and are doing so in an expanding geographical arc that is approaching ever closer the core bases of U.S. power.

The orchestration of the overt and covert prongs of its offensive yields to the Soviet Union another tactical advantage: it conditions U.S. policy and public opinion — as well as those of the target countries and other relevant nations — to focus on the overt manifestations of Soviet power at the expense of the more shadowy salients of attack. And it is in this context that the Reagan Administration has been doing a disservice to its own, presumed objectives in the accelerating struggle for the Caribbean-Central American region. By placing the emphasis on the "blatant" aspects of the growing Soviet involvement in the region, sight has been lost of the intricate field of covert battle within the threatened societies themselves. Moreover, the imbalance in emphasis makes it easier for opinion circles in the United States, as well as in other Western countries, to cling tenaciously to the myth that what is happening in threatened societies simply represents a continuation of a "legitimate" revolutionary process that is strictly indigenous to the societies themselves.

History makes it clear that Soviet conflict strategy is rarely, if ever, "blatant" — that is, until opportunity enables them to cast aside both caution and pretense.

THE GEOPOLITICAL OUTLINES

As was noted at the outset, the Soviet imperial strategy is aimed at the indirect defeat of the United States through 1) seizing, or barring U.S. and Western access to, strategic resources — particularly oil and industrial minerals — and 2) gaining control over, or the ability to interdict, the world's searoutes. The Caribbean-Central American and South Atlantic-Latin American regions fit integrally into this design.

There has been a dearth of geopolitical thinking in the United States in recent years. Although Americans are increasingly sensing the overall impact of patterned changes in power relationships in various geographical regions of the world, few are familiar with the precepts of the classical geopolitical writers, let alone with the scattered writing of their contemporary disciples. Indeed, it can be argued that the lack of a geopolitical framework of policy perception has, as much as any other factor, been responsible for the inconsistent, often incoherent U.S. foreign policy initiatives of the past three decades.

It is an elementary fact of geopolitics that the sealanes of the Caribbean are indispensable to the U.S. military and economic position. Truly a single geopolitical region, the Caribbean contains the islands and the littoral states. Certain patterns of control over these islands and states permit either the opening or the closing of the Atlantic-Pacific and north-south maritime routes. The north-south searoute includes the major South Atlantic sealane connecting the Persian Gulf with the Caribbean Sea and Gulf Coast ports via the Cape of Good Hope. The Caribbean Sea is both a major transshipment point for Middle East oil and a principal refining center. Refineries and transshipment installations are located in St. Croix, Aruba, Curacao, Trinidad and Tobago, Venezuela and the Bahamas. Nearly one-half of the total oil destined for the U.S. East and Gulf Coasts is refined in the Caribbean basin.

The direct military importance of this region looms large, for example, in the context of the defense of Western Europe. Not only would a large contingent of the U.S. troops earmarked for NATO reinforcement embark from Gulf ports, but also great quantities of materials necessary to sustain NATO forces depart on vessels from those harbors. In short, for the United States the Caribbean sealanes are essential to commerce in peacetime and to the projection of U.S. military power to deter or to prevail in war.

These vital sealanes can be jeopardized in a wide variety of ways. The mini-island states, if they should tumble under the control of hostile forces, could be transformed into convenient platforms for the harassment of naval or commercial traffic. Already the tiny island nation of Grenada, with Cuban support, is helping to spread revolution in the Lesser Antilles, with St. Vincent a focal point of anti-U.S. activity. The littoral states of the Caribbean basin are all targeted in varying degrees by Soviet-Cuban conflict strategy. All of them suffer from a variety of serious internal problems which are ripe for exploitation.

Nicaragua has become the pivot for this conflict strategy on the Central American mainland. The *Washington Post* reports that the military build-up in Nicaragua has created a standing army of 45,000 to 50,000 troops — some three times the size of the former forces under Anastasio Somoza.[1] According to this report, Nicaraguan pilots are being trained in Bulgaria to fly MiG jets, and Cuban military advisers number in the thousands. (*Editor's Note:* Updated

U.S. estimates in September 1986 put Nicaragua's military forces at 75,000 active duty personnel and 45,000 reserves and militia.) Thousands of foreign revolutionaries are being trained in Nicaragua. Bases have been constructed at the four corners of Nicaragua: at Punta Nata in the northwest, which looks across the Gulf of Fonseca into El Salvador; Rancho San Martin in the southwest, which may sustain Soviet-built MiGs; Puerta Cabezas in the northeast, providing access to Honduras; and Colonia-Agricola in the southeast facing Costa Rica. These bases portend a Soviet-Cuban potential for generating wars in Honduras, Guatemala, Costa Rica and Colombia — not to mention the on-going conflict in El Salvador.

Indeed, there are signs that Nicaragua might largely take up Cuba's cudgels as sponsor and warehouse of insurgency in Central America. Meanwhile, however, Cuba's fueling of insurgency has become increasingly sophisticated. Every insurgent movement is encouraged to develop in accordance with its own environment and its own aims. No revolutionary process is seen as an exact model for another.

Certainly, there is ample tinder for conflict to be exploited in the region, some of it in places that are not prominent in the news. One, for example, is the Venezuela-Guyana dispute over Esequibo, a contested territory between the eastern border of Venezuela and the western border of Guyana. Not only has Castro backed Guyana against Venezuela in this dispute, but several training camps for indoctrination, guerrillas and communications have been established at Tumatumari, Kimba and Konawaruk respectively in Guyana.

Similarly, newly independent Belize has become an object of regional concern. The belief is strong in Guatemala that Belize provides a base for infiltrating terrorists into that country and serves as a transshipment point for terrorist weapons and supplies.

These and other security issues trace an ominous pattern. Should a Soviet surrogate become firmly established on mainland Latin America — as now seems probable in Nicaragua as well as elsewhere — the U.S. strategic position in this hemisphere would be fundamentally at risk. A pan-Caribbean communist movement linking the scores of depressed microstates and economically devastated but ideologically impressionable littoral states would create for the United States the gravest problem it has ever faced in the region.

SOME OF THE OPTIONS FOR THE UNITED STATES

The current dialogue — within the U.S. policy community and at large — over appropriate U.S. policies toward the rapidly deteriorating situation in the Caribbean-Central American region has identified several policy options. They are not necessarily discrete or mutually exclusive; as will be seen, some apply to tactics that might be invoked at different stages of a given revolutionary process. Nevertheless, in shorthand form these options are the following:

1. *Preemptive Revolution.* This option applies particularly to a situation featuring a given country under heavy attack by revolutionary and insurgent forces that are clearly supported by Moscow and Havana. The general estimate is that the given government cannot hold out for long against the combined assault of these forces, all of which are marked by radical Marxist ideologies, although not necessarily (or in the same degree) friendly to the objectives of their suppliers in the Soviet Union and Cuba. Some observers suggest that this description fits the situation in El Salvador today.

Under the circumstances, the United States may have the choice (or may believe it has the choice) of supporting one insurgent faction in the hope that, once having assumed control of the country, it will pursue policies that are both moderate and pro-American (or at least not anti-American). In Latin America, this is generally referred to as the "Mugabe solution" — after the leader of the Zimbabwe insurgents in southern Africa who, after having established his power in his "liberated" country, has been displaying ostensibly moderate policies (at least thus far).

As a general proposition, the tactic may seem enticing in the abstract. Yet, even assuming that the Mugabe episode has been a "success" for the West (an assumption that is contestable), does the analogy apply to Central America? More important, is the United States really in a position — in terms of image, resources and available influence in the field — to enter the game of "competitive revolution"? And even if it were feasible, could the Reagan Administration play at this game — without coming under debilitating fire from both left and right at home?

2. *Counter-Penetration.* This option is not dissimilar to the "preemptive revolution" option above, but it involves different timing and somewhat different instrumentalities. The basic idea is to accept the victory of a given revolutionary movement in a given country as a *fait accompli,* but to try to influence the regime, through both internal and external means, in directions more favorable to U.S. interests. Essentially this is the option that is being discussed as an alternative to confrontation with the Sandinista regime in Nicaragua today.

The trouble with this option is that the means available to the United States tend to be sorely limited. This applies particularly in a situation like that obtaining in Nicaragua, where not only the Sandinista regime has consolidated its hold over the country, but where also the Cubans (and less directly the Soviets) have consolidated their hold over the regime and the movement. In that case, the only conceivable levers available to the United States, beyond whatever scattered covert assets may exist inside the country, are external forces that are ideologically compatible with the regime and the society. But by very virtue of that compatibility, those external forces tend to be of doubtful value and probably counterproductive to U.S. interests. This will be brought out in the discussion of the Socialist International below.

3. *Categorical Alliance with Authoritarian Forces.* This is the option that the United States ostensibly has been following in the case of El Salvador and which has come under increasing domestic and international attack. In its more explicit and more widely applicable connotations, the option holds that the United States should 1) recognize that the polarization of forces in the Central American-Caribbean region leaves some form of authoritarian rule of the center or the right as the only realistic alternative to the entrenchment of communist or quasi-communist forces, and 2) therefore make both clear and durable its support of such regimes, notwithstanding domestic brickbats and international censures.

The travails which the United States continues to encounter in its support of the Duarte Government in El Salvador may be specific to the circumstances in that unfortunate country, but they are also reflective of the fragility of this option in its more general application in the region. For example, to the extent that it will be pursued in Guatemala, the option may be placed to an even more excruciating test there.

The trouble is that evolving circumstances indicate clearly that the option can hardly be sustained, in and of itself, "notwithstanding domestic brickbats and international censures." Rather, particularly under the duress of domestic pressures, the U.S. Administration finds itself constantly wavering in its support of the given regime and/or trying to place the best image on this support by imposing internal reforms, elections, etc., which usually have the effect of weakening the regime without providing for a more "democratic" alternative.

American policymakers may look back nostalgically upon the times when U.S. policy enjoyed a relatively "free ride" in the exercise of its political choices in the Southern Hemisphere. Yet, the drumbeats of the American media (which in turn reflect to one extent or another powerful special interests), along with the "internationalization" of the Central American-Caribbean problems, have sharply curtailed this former luxury. A clear lesson that is emerging from the embattled U.S. policy in El Salvador is that U.S. assistance to regimes in the region must be encased in a larger rationale that is both more positive and compelling than simply the encouragement and support of "anti-revolutionary" regimes.

4. *A Negotiated Modus Vivendi with the Revolutionary Regimes and Forces.* This is, in effect, the option with which the United States flirted in its tentative acceptance in 1982 of Mexico's offer to act as an intermediary between Washington on the one hand and Havana and Managua on the other. (*Editor's Note:* The unilateral Mexican initiative described here by the author has since been abandoned. His discussion of the initiative below is retained because it still bears relevantly on both the "negotiated modus vivendi" option and Mexico's general stance.)

The outlines of the regional "settlement" adumbrated by Mexico called essentially for 1) the cessation of arms supplies by Cuba and Nicaragua to the Salvadoran rebels, 2) the conclusion of a non-aggression pact between the United States and Nicaragua, 3) U.S.-Cuban negotiations (by implication to lead possibly to the resumption of formal diplomatic ties), and 4) the reinstitution of U.S. economic assistance to Nicaragua.

Among the larger Latin American nations, Mexico has been conspicuous in its equivocal view of the Soviet-Cuban offensive. Thus, former President Lopez Portillo, in his fifth annual State of the Nation address, deplored "the new climate of the Cold War," praised Cuba, Nicaragua and the leftist insurgents in El Salvador, and in a separate action joined France in recognizing the Revolutionary Front led by Guillermo Manuel Ungo as a "representative political force" in El Salvador.[2] Nine Latin American nations immediately condemned the Mexican-French recognition of the Revolutionary Front, charging that a declaration which tended to favor one of the subversive extremes that operate in El Salvador in an "armed struggle for the conquest of the government" was unacceptable intervention. The statement was signed by the foreign ministers of Argentina, Bolivia, Colombia, Chile, Guatemala, Honduras, the Dominican Republic, Paraguay and Venezuela. The number of signatories has since reached twelve.

Beyond Mexico's historic sympathy for revolutionary causes of all sorts, it is easy to speculate that Mexico's leaders are increasingly feeling the vulnerability of their own country to Soviet and Cuban propaganda and subversion. Benevolence toward Castro and the Sandinistas helps the regime buy time and ward off leftist militants both inside and outside the ruling Institutional Revolutionary Party (PRI). It is probably in this context that President Lopez Portillo's words in his fifth annual State of the Nation address should be understood:

> By further tightening the links of friendship and cooperation that bind us with the revolutions of Cuba and Nicaragua, we have underscored Mexico's attachment to the political principle of a free people's free determination. For sympathy and affinity with the essence of their struggle — social justice — [Mexico] has helped them and will continue doing so.[3]

These considerations throw a large shadow on Mexico's willingness — or, in the final analysis, its ability — to play a strictly even-handed role as an intermediary between the United States and its revolutionary opponents in the Central American-Caribbean region. Yet, even if the intermediary efforts might be successful, what could be the extent of that "success"?

The realities of the situation speak compellingly for the prospect that such a negotiated "settlement" would prove at best a transitory lull in the storm, and at worst a cover for a *de facto* retreat by the United States from the region. First of all, there would be no way in which a cessation of the arms flow to El Salvador, and increasingly elsewhere in the region, could be effectively verified, let alone enforced. Indeed, it can be conjectured that the "export of revolution" by Havana and Nicaragua (as well as, of course, Moscow) would be emboldened by a new "legitimacy," by lessened fears of U.S. reprisals, and by a progressive erosion and demoralization of those regional regimes that might still be determined to resist the revolutionary offensive.

In short, not only will the cancer spread more quickly (if perhaps less visibly), but the United States would face inexorably a much sharpened dilemma, with the alternatives ever more painfully reminiscent of Vietnam: it could react to the inevitable "breaches" of the agreements with direct military intervention as the only really viable response, or it could turn its back and accept the same kind of outcome that was imposed in Southeast Asia in 1975.

The Penalties of Pragmatism

It was stressed in the foregoing discussion of the options for the United States that they are not necessarily mutually exclusive. In fact, each of them has been adopted — or flirted with — in one measure or another by the Carter and Reagan Administrations. The total picture adds up to a "strategy of pragmatism."

That "strategy" not only is one by default, but it tends to be elevated into a virtue. The theme is echoing ever more in Washington that in as "diverse" a region as Central America and the Caribbean there can be no fruitful overarching strategy: each case must be approached on its own merits, and each specific policy determined on the basis of its own cost-benefit analysis. Moreover, it is argued, the necessity for pragmatism is reinforced by the tides of American domestic opinion which place sharp limits on any broader policy design — assuming that one were available.

Perhaps there is sincerity behind those avowals, particularly as they relate to the constraints set by American domestic opinion. Yet, as far as domestic factors in the United States are concerned, there is one that places the underlying assumptions of "pragmatism" into a different light. That factor has to do with a traditionally powerful element in the equation of U.S. regional policies: namely, special U.S. business and commercial interests.

That subject can only be approached in a tentative way. Nevertheless, it seems clear that a disquieting attitude has evolved in wide circles of the American business and banking communities on the question of revolutionary Marxist change in areas abroad, on the nature of the revolutionary statist regimes that have sprouted, and on the ability of U.S. and Western commercial interests (particularly those represented in multinational corporations and banking combines) to "do business" with those regimes.

This perspective was revealed in a startling way by David Rockefeller, the retired chairman of Chase Manhattan Bank. During a 1982 tour through Africa, Rockefeller, whose bank has helped finance purchases of airliners and oil equipment for the Marxist regime in Angola, made some far-ranging comments about the phenomenon of Marxist-revolutionary movements and regimes. He downgraded the ideological fervor and pro-Soviet orientation of such regimes by asserting: "the more I've seen of countries which are allegedly Marxist in Africa, the more I have the feeling it is more labels and trappings than reality."[4] And then, noting that Chase Manhattan was the first American bank in Moscow and Peking, he declared:

> I don't think an international bank such as ours ought to try to set itself up as a judge of what kind of government a country wishes to have. We have found we can deal with just about any kind of government, provided they are orderly and responsible.[5]

It is not difficult to transplant this attitude from Africa to Latin America and the Caribbean where, if anything, U.S. commercial and financial interests have a longer history, where they believe that they are operating on more familiar ground, and where there may be more (superficial) grist for the assumption that the "Latin way" of revolution is inherently indigenous to the given and specific social environment and not likely to accede to any enduring fealty to Moscow. The fact that the same assumption was widely applied to Castro's revolution in Cuba more than twenty years ago is seldom drawn into account.

No hard evidence obviously can be drawn as to 1) whether the view articulated by Rockefeller is representative of a broader "mind-set" on the part of U.S. business interests with large stakes in the Central American-Caribbean region, and 2) if so, to what extent this "mind-set" is, in turn, a force behind the apparent predilections toward "pragmatism" in U.S. policy. The least that can be said, however, is that the role of U.S. commercial interests in the evolving politics of the region, and in the policies emanating from Washington, is open to probing question.

Another source of encouragement of U.S. "pragmatism" comes from Europe: namely, from the Socialist International, which has endeavored to arrogate to itself the role of "mediator" between the United States and regional revolutionary movements. This role was prominent during the Carter Administration, when hopes were pinned in Washington on the ability of the Socialist International and its operatives to influence, and perhaps transform, the fledgling Sandinista regime in Nicaragua.

In June 1981, Felipe Gonzalez, head of the Socialist Party (PSOE) in Spain, proclaimed in Managua that the Socialist International supported the Sandinista revolution and will be its "protective umbrella." Gonzalez' position could hardly be otherwise, as the Socialist International had taken the lead in the battle against Somoza.

The Socialist International has taken a strong pro-revolutionary position in El Salvador as well. Since the failure of the major revolutionary military offensive in that country just before President Reagan's inauguration, the Socialist International has been ostensibly bending its efforts toward a negotiated internal settlement. It should be noted that the titular leader of the communist-dominated Democratic Revolutionary Front in El Salvador is Guillermo Ungo, chief of the Socialist International's Salvadoran affiliate.

The charge is rife in parts of the Latin American press that the Socialist International, along with the Mexican-led Permanent Conference on Political Parties of Latin America (COPPPAL), have become coopted by the Marxist offensive in Central America. Thus, for example, the National Liberation Party of Costa Rica belongs to both these organizations: its delegates helped form the Solidarity Committee with the Sandinista Revolution in December 1980 in Madrid. It bears noting that France's President, Francois Mitterand, is also a member of the International Committee to Defend the Sandinista Revolution.

According to prominent press reports, the Friedrich Ebert Foundation, which is tied to the West German Social Democratic Party (SPD), plays an important role in behalf of the Socialist International in Latin America. In 1982 a letter was published from the representative of the Foundation in Mexico to the Secretary-General of the Socialist International, Bernt Carlsson; it indicated the people close to the Socialist International were friends and advisers of the candidates for the presidency of Mexico. There is general agreement in Mexico that this initiative forced the early designation of the next PRI candidate for President.

More generally, the regime in Mexico has sustained a strong cooperative role with the Socialist International in Central America. This connection has been maintained indirectly through COPPPAL. Tomes Borge, the Nicaraguan Sandinista leader of the Popular Prolonged War Faction, is a member of the Executive Council of COPPPAL.

The dominant ideological strains in the Socialist International clearly are Marxist, notwithstanding a minority representation of more moderate social-democratic viewpoints from some Western parties. With respect to the basic thrust of the International's activities in Central America, the verdict of a knowledgeable analyst is worth citing at length:

Socialist International officials assert that they are attempting to prevent Castroism or Soviet influence in El Salvador. In 1979, they made the same assertions with regard to Nicaragua. It is noteworthy, however, that in the entire stream of SI denunciations of Chile, Argentina, Guatemala, Paraguay, Uruguay and

Honduras there has *never* been an SI condemnation of Castroism, *never* a call for pluralism in Cuba. And in the general resolution adopted in November 1980 by the SI Congress in Madrid, Cuba is not mentioned. The effort by Fanny Simon of the Social Democrats USA to include criticism of Cuban policy in the Latin American-Caribbean region during the pre-Congress Bureau meeting was rejected on the instigation of the British Labor Party and Jamaican People's National Party representatives.

. . .The consistently expressed SI support for national liberation movements has been as uncompromising as the CPSU support for these movements, even though the motivations and purposes of the two organizations may differ. The word "parallelism" may well describe the SI's and the CPSU's support of these movements. In Nicaragua, El Salvador and Chile, "convergence" may even be the better term.[6]

In the light of such evidence, the characterization of the Socialist International as an "ally" of the United States in the effort to resolve the problems of the area carries an ironic twist. Moreover, it tends to reinforce the conclusion that, to the extent that U.S. "pragmatism" is, in whole or in part, hostage to such forces, it represents the path of inexorable capitulation to the revolutionary forces and their manipulators in Moscow and Havana.

The Untapped Potential of Nationalism

The United States needs an overarching rationale that can lend both credence and coherence to its initiatives on the Central American battleground, with emphasis on the crucial psychological dimensions of that arena. It is perhaps ironic that the immediacy of that battle might finally awaken the United States to the potential of a powerful but latent ally in the global struggle: the force of nationalism. This is a complex subject, but it can be spelled out concisely in the Central American context.

A U.S. strategy to defeat the Soviet imperial policy in Central America can harness nationalism in two salients: in thrusts against the core and intrinsic linkages of the Soviet imperial system itself, and in bolstering the "natural" regional defenses against the intrusion of a new extra-hemispheric colonialism into the hemisphere. It is this rationale which places Poland and El Salvador on the same battlefield, but which needs to be spelled out explicitly.

The momentous significance of the events in Poland is that they have not only spiked the economic myth that is communism's *raison d'etre,* but also painted the vulnerabilities of the Soviet empire in unmistakable colors. Soviet imperialism requires a confederation of client states in a hierarchy similar to that which bonded the feudal *ancien regime.* The Soviet Union's international feudal order is brittle at its center, in its links and within those peripheries where clients are employed as mercenaries.

The vast Soviet military enterprise has pauperized a people whose repression at home is justified with the ideological banners of "revolutionary" wars abroad. The promise of "peaceful socialism" is progressively revealed as a sham because the feudal order could not subsist without the demonstrated "enemy," whose existence rationalizes massive expenditures for a military machine, which in turn ensures the continued abject economic status of captive peoples. Both at the center and in the peripheries of the Soviet empire the most powerful forces are precisely those struggling to effect fundamental economic, political, administrative and even constitutional changes.

It is a great irony of our age as well that the Soviets have recognized only too keenly their own, rending imperial contradictions and have turned for help to an unusual source — to the "enemy" himself. Soviet military power owes much to economic assistance from the West. The Soviet forces that invaded Afghanistan came in trucks built at the Kama River plant, a facility constructed with U.S. technology and financing. The Export-Import Bank financed the Soviet purchase of diesel engines for those trucks to the tune of $153,950,000.[7] Bertram D. Wolfe has speculated on the tendency of American businessmen to assist Marxist regimes because they "hoped to ingratiate themselves and then make huge profits by tapping the supposedly 'inexhaustible' Russian market, a story that repeated itself during the 'detente' illusions of the seventies."[8]

The United States and its allies clearly are in a position to sharpen the Soviet imperial dilemma by blocking the funnels of credit. Perhaps existing loans may not be called, but the extension of new credit certainly should be curtailed. More generally, U.S. geopolitical doctrine must be directed at the internal and external stresses in the Soviet imperial design; those weaknesses must be exploited as systematically and with the same sense of strategic coherence that has animated the offensive of the global opponent.

Meanwhile, on the immediate battlefield, the most powerful indigenous force in Latin America is still nationalism. It exists in the region in its classic manifestation as a *cultural* phenomenon that postulates the hierarchy of values for defining the state, for judging the conduct of the state's foreign and domestic policy, for authorizing state autonomy, and for protecting the cultural values themselves. In Latin America, nationalism is also a shared, hemispheric phenomenon that derives from common historical roots and a struggle against colonial yokes imposed from abroad. The Soviet Union has endeavored to exploit this force — while concentrating on dividing the target societies from within — but the masks of "national liberation" and of the use of local surrogates are transparent. And the Soviet Union cannot hide the fact that it is an extra-hemispheric power.

By contrast, the deepest and most honest impulse in the ethos of the United States is that which embraces and respects national self-determination and national autonomy. Nonetheless, it must be recognized that, in the eyes of Latin American observers, the countenance of that ethos tends often to be distorted by multinational economic interests that are perceived as dominant in the U.S. foreign policy process — interests that are equated in their sinister implications with those of other transnational intruders into the region.

The policy of the United States in the Southern Hemisphere must hew to a clear rationale that categorically favors those Latin American nationalisms which aspire to state autonomy, internal growth and the sustenance of traditional cultural wellsprings. Such nationalisms are intrinsically opposed to the various manifestations of the international revolutionary movement. The United States can hope for strengthened relations with the Latin American states if it stresses the sanctity of national sovereignty, of the right to economic development, and of the protection of cultural heritage.

Such an unmistakable policy rationale has the potential not only for attracting substantial Latin American support, but also for defining the real lines of the unfolding battle — as well as for fostering a positive pan-American nationalism steeped in common hemispheric interests and cultural legacies. In the meantime, the United States must spurn the temptations of "internationalist solutions" that may or may not ease its immediate policy dilemmas, but that certainly, in the not-much-longer run, will play into the hands of extra-hemispheric opponents and their regional surrogates.

POSTSCRIPT

Since the above was written, the United States has moved to confront the Central American crisis within the framework of support for democracy and military assistance to those countries and forces resisting communist revolution and expansion. The encasing of U.S. policy as support for democracy has conveyed only an implicit encouragement of local nationalisms. The possibilities of formulating and promoting the larger nationalist themes of unity, economic development, cultural identity and enlightened self-interest have been muted.

Probably the latter task remains elusive because of special U.S. interests in the region, particularly that of managing the debt crisis, which engender priorities that seem to be incompatible with an embracive nationalist theme as the *leitmotif* of U.S. policies in the region. But until such a theme is explicitly developed and adopted, the danger that Latin nationalisms will be moved increasingly toward the revolutionary Marxist-Leninist camp will grow and our real position in the region will decline.

NOTES

1. *Washington Post,* November 22, 1981.
2. Christopher Dickey, "Lopez Portillo Underlines Growing Rift with U.S.," *Washington Post,* September 2, 1981.
3. Ibid.

4. *Washington Post,* March 3, 1982.

5. Ibid.

6. Arnold M. Silver, "The New Face of the Socialist International" (Washington, D.C.: The Heritage Foundation, October 1981).

7. *Wall Street Journal,* February 8, 1980.

8. Bertram D. Wolfe, *A Life in Two Centuries* (New York: Stein and Day, 1981), p. 166.

13 The Reagan Doctrine in Outline

William R. Bode

The term "Reagan Doctrine" began to be applied in the Administration's first term to several aspects of its foreign policy which had in common the theme of "prevailing" in political and military competition with the Soviet Union. Thus, a news analysis in the *New York Times* in the fall of 1982 stated that, "as Administration officials explain the theory of prevailing, it means pushing Russian influence back inside the borders of the Soviet Union with the combined pressure of a military buildup along with diplomatic, economic and propaganda measures."[1]

Other early references to a "Reagan Doctrine" included a version proffered by Nicaragua's Vice Foreign Minister Hugo Tinoco in November 1983, shortly after the U.S. military rescue operation in Grenada. Tinoco described the new doctrine as "gunboat diplomacy," asserting that "whenever conditions are ripe in another country, it [the United States] will be ready to send its expeditionary forces to establish peace, order and democracy."[2] A *Washington Post* editorial on May 7, 1983, titled "A 'Reagan Doctrine,'" had come closer to the mark when it noted an offhand comment by the President that the treatment of guerrillas should be based on "what kind of a government they are opposing." Regarding the Sandinistas in Nicaragua, the President was quoted as asking: "Other than being in control of the capital, you might say, and having a handle on all the levers — what makes them any more a legitimate government than the people of Nicaragua who are asking for a chance to vote for the kind of government they want?"

This chapter appeared as an article, entitled "The Reagan Doctrine," in the Winter 1986 issue of Strategic Review.

THE DOCTRINE TAKES SHAPE

The Administration began to develop this theme in earnest early in the second term. The President alluded to broad support of "freedom fighters" in his State of the Union address on February 6, 1985. A week earlier, Secretary of State George Shultz had told the Senate Foreign Relations Committee that "experience shows we cannot deter or undo Soviet geopolitical encroachments except by helping, in one way or another, those resisting directly on the ground."[3] President Reagan began his radio address on February 16, 1985, with the statement that "freedom fighters in Afghanistan, Ethiopia, Cambodia and Angola...are fighting to undo the infamous Brezhnev Doctrine, which says that once a nation falls into the darkness of communist tyranny, it can never again see the light of freedom."[4]

Several days later, Secretary Shultz, who has emerged as the chief protagonist of the evolving Reagan Doctrine in the Administration, provided its clearest exposition in a speech to the Commonwealth Club of San Francisco. Citing a 200-year-old history of American support for "those around the world struggling for freedom and independence," he affirmed a "moral responsibility" for Americans to accept leadership of the Free World, including the support of "people who have made their own decision to stand and fight rather than see their cultures and freedoms 'quietly erased'." U.S. support should be given "not only out of our historical sympathy for democracy and freedom but also, in many cases, in the interests of national security," because "promoting insurgencies against non-communist governments in important strategic areas has become a low-cost way for the Soviets to extend the reach of their power and to weaken their adversaries." "Wars of national liberation" have become "the pretext for subverting any noncommunist country in the name of so-called 'socialist internationalism'," while the Brezhnev Doctrine holds that "once you're in the so-called 'socialist camp,' you're not allowed to leave."[5]

From these and other statements, the Reagan Doctrine emerges as more than an expression of moral and diplomatic support for freedom fighters resisting Soviet military power and repression exercised directly or through Soviet surrogates. Rather, the major elements of the Doctrine appear to be the following: a clear endorsement of the victory of democratic values worldwide; support (in varying forms) of forces of freedom fighters striving to shake off Marxist rule; a determination to lift the mask of subversive aggression in order to identify the nation behind violent attacks and to hold it to account for aggression; as well as an assertion of American rights under international law to use force unilaterally in self-defense.

It needs to be noted that the right to unilateral action in self-defense is also becoming a conspicuous element in the Reagan Administration's evolving counterterrorist policy. This raises the question of the relationship between the Reagan Doctrine and the counterterrorist arena. Clearly there are congruences between the two, expecially inasmuch as some Soviet client states, notably Libya, are heavily involved in the conduct, harboring, training and other support of international terrorist operations. To that extent, the battle against terrorism may well add impetus to the Reagan Doctrine.

Still, counterterrorism calls for specific and selective tactics, with emphasis on unilateral U.S. actions, that are somewhat distinct from the broader objectives and strategy adumbrated by the Reagan Doctrine. The discussion that follows centers on that broader strategy.

Soviet Strategy in the Developing World

The Reagan Doctrine thus challenges not only the Brezhnev Doctrine on the irreversibility of "socialist gains," but also a major element of Soviet grand strategy: namely Soviet expansion into the developing world. Soviet investments in this salient date back to the founding of the Soviet Union, and its objectives have been fairly constant over time: to separate the Western capitalist nations from their sources of critical raw materials; to pro-pagate communism as the "wave of the future" in colonial or ex-colonial regions deemed ripe for such ideological inroads; to deny the West military outposts in those regions (especially those that threatened an "encirclement" of the Soviet home base); and ultimately to create the strongpoints with which to sustain an offensive aimed at outflanking, and eventually encircling, the centers of capitalist power in Europe and North America.

In the decades before World War II, when the Soviet leadership was preoccupied with consolidating its power and remolding Russia's society in the Bolshevik model, the strategy was pursued primarily at the political, ideological and subversive levels. After the war, the dramatic rise in Soviet military capabilities, and the accelerating breakup of colonial empires, opened vast new opportunities. The strategy was taken up explicitly by Nikita S. Khrushchev in the late 1950s — especially after the Stalinist offensive had ground to a halt in Central Europe in the face of West European consolidation and American military power — and achieved early successes in such places as Egypt and Cuba. Khrushchev's successors methodically extended the strategy's reach more deeply into Africa, the Middle East, and South and Southeast Asia — notwithstanding some setbacks and obstacles that emerged particularly in the wake of the Sino-Soviet split.

By the 1970s, during the United States' embroilment in Vietnam and subsequent global retrenchment, the Soviet Union established solid political footholds in several strategically important regions of the developing world. Those Soviet clients — Angola, Ethiopia, Mozambique, South Yemen, Libya, Afghanistan, Vietnam and Nicaragua, in addition to Cuba — now provide not only sanctuaries for subversive operations against neighboring states — as well as the infrastructure for a global terrorist network — but also military bases for routine and contingency use by Soviet military forces. In combination with improvements in military technology, those forward bases enable Soviet deployment of naval and air forces capable of waging strategically significant military operations against "the deep rear of the enemy," the United States. From the perspective of the United States, it is above all the fact of this extending infrastructure for Soviet power projection that hangs over developments in a country such as Nicaragua.

This expansive Soviet strategy in the Third World has leaned heavily on the use of proxies or surrogate forces. The Soviet Union has operated, as Harry Summers said of North Vietnam, behind "the smokescreen of revolutionary war to mask their own aggression."[6] "National liberation fronts" have been used to impose Marxist regimes while screening Soviet involvement from the society under attack and from the world-at-large. This deception, used as successfully in Nicaragua as in South Vietnam — and now being practiced in El Salvador — pays substantial dividends at both the tactical and strategic levels: it enhances the force of surrogate, "popular" revolution leading to the ultimate Marxist takeover, while minimizing the risk of direct confrontation with the United States.

VULNERABILITIES OF THE SOVIET STRATEGY

As has already been noted, the Soviet offensive in the Third World reaped its most prominent successes in the 1970s, a period when any attempt by the United States at an effective, let alone concerted, countereffort was stifled by the war in Vietnam and its subsequent consequences for the political climate within the United States. A political landmark of that period was the passage in the U.S. Senate of the Clark Amendment, which prohibited the expenditure of even covert funds to assist the forces battling the communist-dominated MPLA and Cuban brigades in Angola. The lack of U.S. response not only eased the Soviet-supported takeovers in such places as Angola, Mozambique and later Nicaragua, but it also had the effect of conferring on the regimes installed in those countries an instant legitimacy, permitting them to draw on broad sources of international support.

In the wake of the Soviet successes, however, has come evidence of vulnerabilities. The basic vulnerability lies in the incompatibility of Marxism with fundamental popular expectations and aspirations. In virtually all the countries in question, including those in which a tradition of personal freedom had not been firmly rooted, popular forces are resisting the imposed regime. It is a phenomenon that prompted Secretary of State Shultz to note: "the yearning for freedom is the most powerful political force all across the planet."[7]

Marxist ideology is behind a second and related Soviet vulnerability, in that it renders the Soviet leadership, and its local conflict managers, prone to serious miscalculations of popular attitudes in the target countries. Thus, the Soviet leaders as well as their invading forces apparently were genuinely surprised by the determined resistance mounted by the population of Afghanistan to the Soviet invasion. It was a case of ideological misperception leading to a major military miscalculation. Although the Soviets are prepared to wage a protracted war in Afghanistan, and are in no risk of losing this struggle militarily in the foreseeable future, clearly Moscow can ill afford additional engagements on the model, let alone scale, of the Afghanistan conflict.

A third vulnerability is economic. The Soviets are endeavoring to defray the costs of their expanding empire by imposing on their clients a major share of the latter's own military outlays. Angola, for example, is paying for Cuban troops from oil revenues.

Impoverished Soviet clients cannot, however, shoulder this burden indefinitely. They are forced, in effect, to "eat their seed corn" — diverting into the military resources and investments critically needed for basic economic infrastructure and, thereby, for the consolidation of political power. Trade and investment drawn from Western sources can help to stave off disaster, but the steady economic drainage eventually must cut debilitatingly into the provision of even basic civic services, while combat is continued against insurgent forces which further disrupt those services. As that predicament deepens, the Soviet Union faces the choice of assuming increasingly heavy economic burdens or countenancing the economic and military collapse of its clients. This dilemma already may account for the markedly increased urgency with which Soviet client regimes — e.g., in Angola and Nicaragua — have recently mounted military campaigns against "counterrevolutionary" forces.

These ideological, political and economic liabilities of the Soviet empire translate into conspicuous military vulnerability. What is remarkable about the anti-regime forces that have sprung up not only in the remote extensions of the Soviet empire in Africa and Central America, but also at the very border of the Soviet Union in Afghanistan, is their spontaneity and their ability to function with only a modicum of outside assistance, notwithstanding the standard, shrill Soviet claims about "imperialist machinations."

This spontaneous combustion not only threatens every new Soviet expansionist venture, but it also holds the potential of spilling back into the core of the Soviet empire. In today's communications environment, the spark of resistance can traverse great distances, e.g., from Angola to Cuba. And it leaps more directly: the phenomenon of spreading infection confronts the Soviets particularly in Afghanistan, where Afghan resistance commanders report increasing contacts with — and presumably channels of assistance from — kindred Moslem populations on the other side of the Soviet-Afghan border.[8]

Spontaneity, however, typically entails penalties of weakness in the organization, training, discipline and armaments of democratic resistance forces. These are also elements, especially training and weapons, that can be supplied from outside the conflict arena. And they can be furnished quickly — before a given Marxist regime can consolidate its grip on the political and economic levers of power.

TAKING THE OFFENSIVE

A survey of emergent battlefields in the Third World — with both their overarching dangers to the United States in the context of Soviet strategy as well as Soviet vulnerabilities — yields compelling logic for a concerted American counteroffensive centered on the powerful assets offered by democratic resistance movements.

Such a counteroffensive must be sensitive to two important principles of war: mass and economy of force. At the level of insurgency warfare, guerrillas apply the principle of mass, or concentration of effort, by engaging government forces directly only in places of decisive advantage. They execute the principle of economy of force in skirmishes, ambushes and raids that, although not in themselves decisive, bog down and exhaust the enemy's forces. On the larger strategic plane adumbrated by the Reagan Doctrine, those principles mean that a counteroffensive cannot be effective if it is simultaneously directed against Soviet and proxy forces everywhere in the developing world; rather, it must concentrate on defeating those salients that either are most vulnerable or most threatening to U.S. interests, while acting in other regions to tie down Soviet resources.

Taking the offensive is consonant with economic as well as military criteria. In effect, an offensive strategy of assisting anticommunist guerrilla forces takes advantage of the widely assumed (if not universally applicable) ratio of 10:1 in manpower required by conventional forces to cope with an insurgency. Moreover, government troops are more costly to train, equip and maintain than are guerrilla forces, and the regime-under-attack bears the additional burden of maintaining and guarding the nation's economic infrastructure, part of which is exploited by the guerrillas.

A guerrilla force typically is armed predominantly with easily portable weapons; it resorts to armor or heavy artillery only as these are captured from the regime's forces, abandoning them when they become liabilities. Hence its logistical demands are much lighter than those of the defending forces. The guerrilla force also tends not to put heavy, unanticipated demands on its logistics lines. By gradually amassing supplies, then launching coordinated attacks against such valuable installations as airfields or supply depots, it can suddenly and substantially deplete a government's store of critical supplies. In the current strategic context, the need to replenish those supplies urgently will impose serious strains on Soviet airlift capabilities, especially in areas remote from the Soviet power base and if the demand arises simultaneously from more than one client state.

The strategic, military and economic advantages flowing to the United States from the support of resistance movements in Soviet client states alone do not validate the Reagan Doctrine. It rests as well on moral principles of the universality of human rights and freedom of human choice — values that are integral to the American ethos. And it offers a counterstrategy on the Soviets' chosen battleground — a strategy that can defend and prevail short of a general war.

OBJECTIVES OF THE REAGAN DOCTRINE

The fundamental objective in any military conflict is victory, achieved by destroying the enemy's ability and will to wage war. In past decades, the military forces of the United States often have been asked to place themselves in harm's way for objectives short of victory, such as "raising the costs of aggression" or "demonstrating American resolve." However, as Harry Summers has observed; "The political objective cannot be merely a platitude, but must be stated in concrete terms."[9]

Many of the lessons of the war in Vietnam apply to our conflict with the Soviet Union in the developing world. Again it is instructive to read Harry Summers:

> North Vietnam concentrated on one objective — the conquest of South Vietnam. By comparison the United States was caught up in the conflicting and sometimes contradictory objectives of resisting aggression and counterinsurgency.... The United States unwittingly confused the tactical offensive for the strategic offensive and conducted the war on the strategic defensive in pursuit of a negative aim — counterinsurgency — with results that should have been foreseen. Despite our enormous technological advantage the North Vietnamese were able to apply *Mass, Economy of Force and Maneuver* to greater strategic effect than we were, particularly in their use of the guerrilla screen as an economy of force effort that caused us to dissipate our efforts.[10]

At the United Nations, President Reagan stated that one American objective is the "elimination of the foreign military presence and restraint on the flow of outside arms" to troubled nations where the wars are "the consequence of an ideology imposed from without, dividing nations and creating regimes that are, almost from the day they take power, at war with their own people." If possible, this objective is to be accomplished through a "regional peace process" that begins with negotiations among the warring parties, but "until such time as these negotiations result in definitive progress, America's support for struggling democratic resistance forces must not and shall not cease."[11]

The stated objective is tactical: to isolate the battlefield. The strategic objective, implied in this quotation and stated in other Administration pronouncements, is victory for the democratic resistance forces. An equally important political objective is to demonstrate to communist and noncommunist nations alike that communism is not, as the Soviets propagate, the "wave of the future," and that communist rule, once installed, is reversible.

PRIORITIES OF THE REAGAN DOCTRINE

While the basic objectives of the Reagan Doctrine may be reasonably clear, its priorities are still implicit at best. The Administration's praise of resistance movements in Afghanistan, Cambodia, Ethiopia, Angola and Nicaragua gives little indication of the relative scale and urgency of assistance merited by those movements.

Nevertheless, the principles outlined above suggest some priorities. Thus, it would be reasonable to assign top priority to those areas in which vital U.S. security interests are at stake. Nicaragua clearly qualifies for this criterion because of the threat to U.S. sea lines of communication posed by Soviet bases in that nation, as well as the specter of subversion and insurgencies directed against other Central American nations and Mexico.

A second priority could apply to the most vulnerable Soviet clients — not only in accordance with the principle of economy of force, but also in consideration of the psychological implications of a clear defeat for the Soviet Union in the Third World. Within this category, Angola may head the list, especially given the reverberations that a reversal there would carry not only for Soviet influence in Africa, but for the prestige of Fidel Castro and Cuba's role as a global surrogate for the Soviet Union.

A third category of priorities relates to conflict arenas that entail vulnerabilities to the Soviet Union proper. For reasons that have already been outlined, Afghanistan represents such a conflict arena.

THE ROLE OF DIPLOMACY

Secretary Shultz's statement that "the United States will always seek political solutions to problems" is as much a historical observation of American reluctance to use force as it is a statement of policy.[12] If force is to remain our last resort, it follows that an important objective of diplomacy must be the preservation of this option. The agreement that ended the Cuban Missile Crisis of 1962, which involved a pledge by the United States not to invade Cuba, clearly breached this principle, not only by foreclosing a U.S. military option, but relieving the Castro regime of the ultimate restraint upon its export of revolution and subversion in the hemisphere and elsewhere. The consequences confront the United States in Central America today.

Clearly we cannot permit an opponent to lock us into diplomatic embrace while he exploits his military advantage. The critical determination of when a political solution is no longer possible, and the application of force is essential to achieve our objective, requires hard judgment of the prospects for negotiations — a judgment that must lean, in turn, on hard assessment of the intentions of the opponent and of the impact of the negotiations on the military situation.

Soviet and American strategies lack what Clausewitz called "polarity": U.S. strategy tends to be predominantly political and defensive, while Soviet strategy is predominantly military and offensive. Negotiations between the United States and the Soviet Union or its surrogates reflect this lack of polarity. We generally seek a return to the status quo ante; our adversaries seek consolidation of "socialist gains." We insist that political change occur peacefully through a democratic process; they pursue change through the use of force euphemized as "revolution" and reject democratic processes except as a temporary screen for the consolidation of power.

THE REWARDS OF LEGITIMACY

A standard negotiation objective of a Soviet client — one that is achieved in part through the very fact of negotiations — is to gain international acceptance of the regime's legitimacy, and thus to gain the time to defeat armed internal opposition. Typically, a Soviet client will insist on negotiating with the United States in order to wrest legitimacy and to tie our hands, while refusing to negotiate with its internal opponents in order to deny them the same legitimacy. The need for legitimacy explains why the Sandinista Government in Nicaragua adamantly has been rejecting negotiations with its Contra opponents, at the same time that the rebel forces in El Salvador fervently have been suing for negotiations with the Salvadoran Government.

Legitimacy thus offers obvious advantages for a client regime: it enables it to solidify its power base, discourages U.S. and other intervention, and opens doors to Western economic assistance. The "concessions" offered in return for such legitimacy typically do not seriously impinge on the regime's hold on internal control, and/or they can be ignored or retracted later. This is to be expected, because at stake for the Soviet client regime is its very survival.

The stakes in negotiations for the resistance force tend to be equally high. Although Marxist guerrillas can be pulled back from a conflict as a concession, then reinserted later, democratic resistance forces are not as flexible. They tend to be less disciplined, trained and organized. Once disbanded, they cannot easily be reconstituted — all the more so to the extent that the Marxist regime is able meanwhile to consolidate its hold over the society.

Moreover, the longer negotiations are protracted, the higher rises the political cost to nations supporting resistance forces operating against that regime. Particularly in democratic societies, the costs and risks of providing such support become more difficult to justify when a "peaceful resolution" seems within reach: this applies all the more sharply to neighboring states that offer safe havens and operating bases for the resistance forces. For all these reasons, concessions offered by a Soviet client regime may prove ephemeral, whereas those rendered by or on behalf of resistance forces can effectively spell the latter's elimination.

The objectives vested in negotiations by a Soviet client regime under internal attack are manifest in the current diplomatic and propaganda campaign conducted by the Sandinista regime in Nicaragua. The obvious aim of this campaign is to isolate the Contras through diplomacy in order to defeat them militarily. Political isolation is pursued through a diplomatic campaign, reinforced by propaganda, to cut off assistance to the Contras from democratic Central American nations and the United States. Thus, isolation of the battlefield, an objective which the Sandinistas cannot attain militarily, is being pursued through diplomatic efforts to deprive the Contras of logistic support and safe havens in neighboring states prior to their decisive defeat in battle.

The conditions for negotiations may vary from one conflict to another. Nevertheless, the Reagan Doctrine, in integrating diplomacy with the military, economic, political and psychological prongs of the overall strategy, must take into account the unequal stakes that inhere in negotiations with Soviet client states, and the prospect that a "peaceful resolution" not only can mean the entrenchment of another Soviet military outpost, but lead to far greater future conflict and dangers.

PUBLIC AND CONGRESSIONAL SUPPORT

At a time when public and Congressional support for U.S. security assistance to other nations is uncertain at best, the Reagan Doctrine has raised a new issue: support of democratic resistance forces struggling against Soviet oppression. Yet, public opinion regarding assistance to governments may prove an unreliable guide to sentiments concerning "freedom fighters." Traditional American attachment to individual liberties, combined with an American inclination to favor the underdog, may generate public support of the Reagan Doctrine. Whatever the current attitudes may be, firm leadership by the Administration in the public debate on this issue is likely to shape American public opinion for years to come.

Among the problems that the Administration must anticipate is a major Soviet propaganda campaign. Like the Strategic Defense Initiative, the Reagan Doctrine confronts the Soviet Union with a serious competition on a field where it previously had enjoyed a virtual monopoly. Already, the Nicaraguan resistance is being muddied with charges of large-scale drug smuggling and rampant human rights abuses, and UNITA in Angola is denounced for ties to South Africa. Other resistance groups are described as incapable of winning, or of governing if they were to win. Only the Afghan Mujahidin seem invulnerable to criticism: television images of Soviet helicopters and armored forces attacking poorly equipped tribesmen and of the desolate landscape produced by the Soviet scorched-earth campaign against defenseless villagers cannot be erased by clever slogans.

Yet if U.S. public and Congressional opinion can be mobilized only in support of freedom fighters directly resisting Soviet armies, the Reagan Doctrine faces substantial obstacles. Afghanistan, after all, represents the exception to the customary Soviet use of surrogate force in the developing world.

A basic problem in gaining popular support relates to the ambiguities sponsored by covert forms of assistance. Senator Malcolm

Wallop, for one, has criticized a "broad disposition in the U.S. Government to embrace covert action not only as a 'safe' option — something between diplomacy and sending in the Marines — but in effect as a substitute for policy itself, while thus avoiding or deferring a clear policy choice."[13] The elaboration of the Reagan Doctrine, as a commitment in principle to support freedom fighters in five nations, already has addressed the problem of clarity in an overall policy sense. There will be intense debate on the appropriate elements and recipients of that support, but there no longer can be any question about the Administration's basic intent and objectives.

Still, a public consensus has yet to cover the urgent components of the strategy that has been outlined. In the U.S. political system, such a consensus can only be shaped by informed and responsible debate. For this reason, while some cases may require that U.S. assistance to the given resistance movement be largely covert, wherever possible a component of overt support should be provided, without compromise to sensitive covert programs, as a focus for public and Congressional dialogue. Beyond inhibiting public debate, covert assistance tends to blur the issue of the full range of options that may have to be faced. Again citing Senator Wallop: "Covert action makes sense only as a calculated addition to diplomatic and economic efforts — and only if it is backed by the will to use overt military force if need be."[14]

More intense public debate of American security interests in such regions as Central America, Southern Africa and Southwest Asia is essential if we are to provide assistance on the scale and for the duration that will be needed.

REMAINING REQUIREMENTS

There are other notable gaps, beyond consensus-building, between the declaratory Reagan Doctrine and its implementation. These gaps relate to U.S. weaknesses in such realms as paramilitary operations, psychological warfare and intelligence networks, which were largely dismantled in the 1970s. Much construction and reconstruction are needed in those capability areas.

The construction process must be sensitive to principles of strategy other than those cited above. Security, for example, suggests that legislation, executive orders and procedures be put in place to safeguard the integrity of covert programs. Unity of command dictates that someone below the President be given the responsibility for ensuring cooperation and coordination among the various agencies of the Executive Branch involved in the implementation of the Doctrine. Problems in applying these principles are common to all aspects of national strategy for a democracy.

The basic principles of objective and offensive must be applied conscientiously if the Reagan Doctrine is to have any prospect of success. Secretary of State Shultz has stated that "we must seek a sustainable strategy geared to *American* goals and interests, in the light of Soviet behavior but not just in reaction to it."[15] The Reagan Doctrine represents a major step toward such strategy, compatible with the logic of global realities, with American resources and with fundamental American values.

POSTSCRIPT

In the months since the above was written, the "Socialist Fraternity" — that is, the Soviet dominated axis that ranges around the globe from Cuba through Syria to Vietnam — has made important strides along the path charted by the Brezhnev/Gorbachev Doctrine. Major commitments to international terrorist and subversive warfare against the United States were made openly at the 27th Congress of the CPSU, the Third Party Congress of the Cuban Communist Party, a conference in Nicaragua that was a followup to the Cuban Congress, and an international conference of terrorist and socialist organizations in Libya. These conferences were not simply occasions for belaboring a "declaratory policy" but genuine working sessions. They reaffirmed and elaborated Soviet grand strategy for attacking the United States through the Third World.

Soviet leaders understand that "creating new objective realities," not debating, will determine the outcome of the global struggle. Rhetoric only counts to the extent that it incites or guides actions. Even modest armed forces on the ground are worth more than fine phrases, and Soviet leaders have been working assiduously to insert or strengthen armed forces, whether proxy or their own, wherever an opening presents itself. They work equally diligently to prevent and disrupt the building of democratic forces as barriers to their objectives.

In the face of communist consolidation in Central America, flourishing terrorism and subversion in Europe, and Soviet expansion into the Pacific region, the Reagan Administration's greatest achievement in foreign affairs has been to foster and bolster democratic government. If the world were at peace, that would constitute a lasting contribution. In the current state of undeclared war, however, it may prove to be ephemeral. Notwithstanding their longer-range promise of a peaceful world order compatible with the ideals and interests of the United States, in the critical short run democracies — especially young and struggling ones — are demonstrably vulnerable to communist subversion and armed assault. Without the determined protection provided by the United States, they cannot survive. That protection cannot be solely in the form of security assistance which ensures a war of attrition that they are certain to lose. The best protection they could have — in fact, their only hope, as well as ours — is the overthrow of the communist governments that threaten them.

The Reagan Doctrine is at least a conceptual step in that direction. It is an open question whether the Reagan Administration, in the brief time still available to it and in the face of the global tides, can overcome bureaucratic, Congressional and other obstacles and move from declaration to execution.

NOTES

1. *New York Times*, September 23, 1982.
2. As quoted by Associated Press, November 17, 1983.
3. Secretary of State George Shultz, "The Future of American Foreign Policy: New Realities and New Ways of Thinking," statement before the Senate Foreign Relations Committee, January 31, 1985, *State Department Current Policy*, No. 650.

4. Weekly Compilation of Presidential Documents, Vol. 21, No. 8, February 25, 1985, p. 186.

5. George Shultz, "America and the Struggle for Freedom," address before the Commonwealth Club of San Francisco, February 22, 1985, *State Department Current Policy,* No. 659.

6. Harry G. Summers, Jr., *On Strategy: A Critical Analysis of the Vietnam War* (Novato, CA: Presidio Press, 1982), p. 96.

7. *State Department Current Policy,* No. 650.

8. Abdul Rashid, "An Afghan Resistance Commander Looks at the War and Its Strategic Implications," *Strategic Review,* Winter 1985, pp. 30–39.

9. Summers, op. cit., p. 185.

10. Ibid.

11. President Reagan, "A Foundation for Enduring Peace," address before the U.N. General Assembly, October 24, 1985, *State Department Current Policy,* No. 756.

12. George Shultz, "New Realities and New Ways of Thinking," *Foreign Affairs,* Spring 1985, p. 719.

13. Malcolm Wallop, "U.S. Covert Action: Policy Tool or Policy Hedge?," *Strategic Review,* Summer 1984, p. 10.

14. Ibid.

15. Schultz, "New Realities and New Ways of Thinking," op. cit., p. 717.

14 Covert Action: A Substitute for Clear U.S. Policy

MALCOLM WALLOP

Today in Afghanistan, Angola and Nicaragua, to mention only the most prominent arenas, thousands of ordinary people are volunteers in irregular wars against the Soviet Army or Soviet-supported regimes. Whereas in the 1960s and 1970s anti-Western causes attracted recruits throughout the Third World, the 1980s have emerged as the decade of guerrillas who fight against communist regimes and who, if victorious, would give their countries a pro-Western orientation. The movements in these and other countries represent the responses of peoples subjugated by the Soviet Bloc's major conquests of the 1970s. They are threatening to undo the Soviet Union's most important accomplishments since World War II: the acquisition of strategic promontories in relation to the Persian Gulf and the Indian Subcontinent, the Cape of Good Hope and the Panama Canal. Hence the outcomes of these popular wars of national liberation are of substantial interest to the United States.

Unfortunately discussions of this interest, in both the Executive and Legislative Branches of the U.S. Government, have been unenlightening. Sad to say, these discussions have betrayed no really concerted intention, never mind plans, by the U.S. Government to break the Soviet Union's newly gained and locally contested holds on these strategic crossroads of the world. Worse yet, opinion among the public and in the Congress has been badly distracted from the true substance of these conflicts.

This chapter appeared as an article, entitled "U.S. Covert Action: Policy Tool or Policy Hedge?" in the Summer 1984 issue of Strategic Review.

A major reason for this distraction is that the debate has fastened on basically only one among the many instruments of policy available to the United States: covert action. This focus, in turn, is the consequence of a broad disposition in the U.S. Government to embrace covert action not only as a "safe" option — something between diplomacy and sending in the Marines — but in effect as a substitute for policy itself, while thus avoiding or deferring a clear policy choice.

Experience provides some sharp lessons in this respect. Covert action, when it has been successful, has not been an option chosen *in lieu of* diplomatic or military efforts. Rather, covert action makes sense only as a *calculated addition* to diplomatic and economic efforts — and only if it is *backed by the will to use overt military force if need be.* What is argued below is that in two of the three major armed struggles in the world today — Angola and Afghanistan — the United States' employment of covert action has cloaked the unwillingness or inability by American decisionmakers to formulate a self-consistent policy: that is, the thoughtful thread connecting between what we as a nation want and what we do. And this process is being repeated with respect to the immediate arena of Nicaragua today.

THE CASE OF ANGOLA

In 1974, the United States' response to the Soviet-Cuban intervention into the Angolan civil war in behalf of the communist-dominated MPLA of Agostinho Neto was to ask the Central Intelligence Agency to supply some arms and advisers to the other two factions in the conflict, primarily Holden Roberto's FNLA and, to a lesser extent, Jonas Savimbi's UNITA. This aid was on a scale vastly inferior to that invested by the Soviet Union and its surrogates. The conflict was decided, at least for a decade, by some 20,000 Cuban troops in Angola, as well as by the passage of the Clark Amendment in the U.S. Senate that prohibited the expenditure of covert funds for actions in Angola.

The Clark Amendment did not prohibit the expenditure of *overt* funds for the non-communist Angolans. Yet, neither the Ford Administration nor its successors have tried to argue before

Congress that, because the victory of Jonas Savimbi over the Soviet coalition is both in the United States' interest and morally preferable to its alternative, a certain amount of funds, and perhaps a treaty, ought to back the United States' resolve to take *whatever* political, economic or military measures might be necessary for Savimbi to succeed. Congress never rejected such an argument because it was never made. Instead, the Congress was, and continues to be, faced simply with the question: shall the United States support covert action in Angola?

By the time the Clark Amendment came to a vote, the United States, through the CIA, had already been active in Angola for some months. The forces supported by us, badly outmatched, were in retreat. At that point, President Ford wanted authority to undertake more in Angola, but he was unwilling to state his case openly. This reticence implied that the Administration was unsure about both the effectiveness and the moral legitimacy of the requested authority for additional measures. Senator Clark charged that the covert action had failed and that continuing it might lead to deeper involvement in a moral and material quagmire. The Administration did not respond with a logical and comprehensive brief of U.S. interests at stake in Angola and what would be required to safeguard those interests. Hence Angola was abandoned. It should be noted, however, that inasmuch as Jonas Savimbi has done very well on his own since then, the issue is not merely historical.

RESPONSE TO AFGHANISTAN

A very different situation elsewhere illuminates the same problem. Soon after the Soviet Army drove into Afghanistan in December 1979, Senator Birch Bayh, then Chairman of the Senate Select Committee on Intelligence, revealed publicly that the United States was supplying covert assistance to the Mujahideen, the freedom fighters resisting the Soviet occupation. There was no outcry then from the American public against this U.S. assistance, nor has there been since. Quite the contrary: four years later, 67 Senators are cosponsoring a resolution which declares that the U.S. Government should give effective material assistance to the Afghan freedom fighters — and that it is wrong to give them enough to fight and die, but not enough to prevail. It is worth noting that this resolution was not inspired by "hawks" within the Executive Branch, but rather by a Vietnam veteran working through the office of liberal Democratic Senator Paul Tsongas.

The only opposition to the resolution has come essentially from the CIA and the Department of State. These agencies do not dispute the Mujahideen's claims that, although they are winning most of the battles, the Soviets are winning the war by exacting a three-to-one ratio of casualties from the resistance and by depopulating the countryside (thus "draining the pond in which the resistance swims"). Nevertheless the agencies argue that any substantial increase in material assistance to the Afghan resistance, e.g., the provision of effective anti-aircraft weapons, would be harmful because the Soviets, frustrated, would turn on Pakistan. Besides, the argument runs, a heavier flow of arms into Afghanistan would make it more difficult for the Pakistanis to sustain their denial to the Soviets that they are taking sides in the Afghan war. The United States would then be forced to protect Pakistan against Soviet reprisals. Hence the Afghan freedom fighters should not be provided with the extent of covert assistance that could incite an overt Soviet move, which we could only counter with a massive, overt commitment.

This argument is abjectly flawed. When the Soviets invaded Afghanistan, they stopped at the Khyber Pass — not so much out of modesty or fear of the Pakistani Army, but because they believed that an impingement upon Pakistan would risk war with the United States. Moreover, the Soviets are under no illusion whatever about the fact that such aid as reaches the Afghan resistance comes via the two million Afghans now on the Pakistani side of the border. No doubt the Pakistani Government derives some comfort from its argument that it is wholly uninvolved in military assistance to the Afghans. But it knows very well that its security lies in the tacit understanding that it is protected by the United States.

Yet, if the United States is not willing to commit itself to the ultimate protection of Pakistan against a Soviet invasion, why consider *any* assistance at all to the Afghans? If the goal of such assistance is not the eventual end to the Soviet occupation — if instead it is assumed that the Soviet strategy of attrition will

ultimately succeed — then why not spare the Afghan people a protracted blood-letting? In that case, Afghanistan's smoother transformation into a Soviet Socialist Republic would at least leave millions of Afghans alive to fight again another day.

But could it be that the real purpose behind the nourishing of
the Afghan resistance does not turn so much on the good of the
Afghans themselves? Could there be a "larger Western interest"
in keeping some 150,000 Soviet troops "bogged down" for a decade
or so? No, not only would such cynicism be contrary to the very
values that we project to the world, but it would mask arrant naivete.
The West would gain little by providing one-tenth of the Soviet
ground forces with live-fire training exercises every year.

All this aside, one looks in vain for a substantive basis to the
arguments concerning Afghanistan that have so far emanated from
the Executive Branch. Occasionally, a high official will admit to
this paucity of fundamental policy, but he will then try to turn the
question (and the onus) around: would Congress be ready to accept
the possible (overt) consequences of a stepped-up (covert) assistance
to the Afghan freedom fighters? The implication therefore is that,
on the assumption that the nation as a whole is not prepared to
face up to the risks of purposeful policy, the Government is relieved
of the task of formulating it. Whether that assumption is valid or
not in the specific case (and the U.S. public response to the U.S.
move in Grenada certainly does not bear it out), the leadership of
a democracy hardly is exercising its mandate by an *anticipatory*
deference to the mood of a public that it is supposed to lead. Meanwhile, what is the purpose of covert action — beyond perhaps
"harassing" or "inconveniencing" the outposts of expanding Soviet
power?

It should be stressed that very rarely is the argument for limiting
covert action to quiet failures and inconsequential successes made
as clearly and honestly as it has been represented above. Sadly,
the very way U.S. foreign policy is formulated militates against such
clarity. A variety of officials within the White House, the Department of State and the Department of Defense, not to mention their
respective allies in the Congress, carry into the policymaking
process their own preferences and phobias, perhaps not so much
concerning overall policy as about individual measures to be taken.

The overall course of the United States' actions, then, is the *resultant* (in the geometric sense) of innumerable pushes and pulls over specific policy measures and actions. This way of doing business, of course, is the antithesis of policy. Precisely for this reason, covert action tends to be used as a convenient substitute for policy — or, rather, as a vehicle forced to carry the full, surrogate burden of commitments that the U.S. Government has been unable or unwilling to formulate. It lends itself to the postponement of hard questions about policy. Hence, not by design but by the logic of the situation, covert action can become the medium for institutionalizing indecisiveness and accepting defeat.

NICARAGUA: THE STAKES OF CONFLICT

Let us now turn to our immediate case: the civil war between Nicaragua's Sandinista government and its democratic opponents, the so-called Contras. Should the United States help the Contras, for what purpose and to what extent?

The area between the Rio Grande and the Panama Canal clearly is the one global region the control of which by the Soviet Union would prove most menacing to the United States. The astuteness of the Kissinger Commission's Report and the documents captured in the invasion of Grenada were not really needed to reveal the fact that the Soviets are making a concerted effort to push their power and influence into the region. The victory of the Sandinistas, long-time disciplined members of the Nicaraguan Communist Party and international communist organizations, was managed directly from Havana. The Soviets and their Cuban allies took this victory as a sign that nearby countries were ripe for similar campaigns.

The Sandinistas are now receiving Soviet arms at the rate of 15,000 tons per year — the same rate at which Cuba was being supplied in the 1970s. Nicaragua today is host to specialists from throughout the Soviet Union's international coalition. East Germans are setting up systems for internal security and population control. The PLO is training Nicaraguans, Salvadorans, Hondurans, Guatemalans and Costa Ricans in the specialities perfected in Israeli marketplaces, airports and Olympic quarters. Vietnamese soldiers bring the lessons and the spoils of their victory over the United

States to instruct Central American recruits in long-range patrolling. The Cubans train the conventional armed forces and supervise every ministry. Libyans and Bulgarians carry out special logistics and construction. The Soviets direct the enterprise and reap the geopolitical benefits.

The division of labor in Nicaragua is the same that has been instituted everywhere the Soviets have taken hold — from tiny Grenada to Ethiopia and Angola. In Central America, however, the potential geopolitical harvest is great, indeed. If the Soviet sphere of influence were to advance to Mexico's southern border, Mexican elites would be less likely to expose themselves to danger by opposing this great new anti-Gringo force, and more likely to ally themselves with it. At least this seems to be the Soviet Union's expectation.

There is no need here to describe how a hostile southern border would hamstring the United States in its ability to exercise its global commitments. Because Cuba is now a well-defended base for Soviet submarines and aircraft, in any future war our logistic support of overseas commitments already is certain to be incomparably more difficult than it was in the worst days of World War II. If, in addition, the United States were to face a hostile southern border, the resupply of overseas allies would become prohibitively difficult. Moreover, in those circumstances, our overseas commitments would simply drop down in our list of priorities.

Nor need we dwell here on the scenario of a twilight struggle against Latin terrorists in an American Southwest swollen by refugees, and on the social consequences of such a struggle. Let us simply note the conclusion of the Kissinger Commission to the effect that relatively little stands in the way of the Soviet drive to isolate the United States in its own hemisphere — and that Nicaragua is the continental spearhead of that drive.

THE EVOLUTION OF COVERT ACTION AGAINST NICARAGUA

Given the clarity and seriousness of the Central American problem, it is remarkable not only that the United States lacks an agreed-upon policy for dealing with it, but also that policymakers are not debating alternative policies and their consequences. Instead they are debating covert action. Let us see how this preoccupation developed.

The Carter Administration openly welcomed the Sandinistas' seizure of power in Managua in 1979 and channeled to the new regime more aid in a year than the United States had given to the previous government in a decade. Clearly the Carter Administration officials believed either that the Marxist Sandinistas were men of good will who would not lend themselves to the role of Soviet surrogates, or that they could be bribed or charmed away from any inclination toward such a role, or that the unarmed non-Marxists in the governing junta might somehow restrain their armed comrades. Within several months, however, the Carter Administration had to admit that its hopes were not well founded. It had to recognize that the Sandinistas were instituting classic communist measures to control the population, such as people's courts, rationing and a pervasive secret police, and that Nicaraguan society was being rapidly militarized with the help of the Soviet Bloc. The suppression of the few Trotskyites in the country suggested to those even slightly acquainted with the workings of the communist world that the Sandinista regime was going to be an orthodox disciple of Moscow to a fault.

The Carter Administration did not instantly abandon all its illusions in the face of facts. For FY 1980, for example, it obtained from the Congress an additional $75 million in aid, ostensibly for the private sector in Nicaragua. Yet, at the same time, in December 1979 President Carter reported to the Congress that he had begun a covert action program against Nicaragua.

It is important to note why President Carter acted as he did. His decision was *not* aimed at combating the Sandinistas' attempts to destabilize neighboring countries, because at that time those efforts had not yet begun. The Carter Administration, in its early response to the Sandinista regime, demonstrated its willingness to countenance the establishment of a government in Managua professing a strong Marxist orientation. Yet, by the summer and fall of 1979 even the Carter Administration recognized that the United States could not abide the prospect of Nicaragua ruled on the Soviet model and allied with the Soviet Union — precisely because such

a regime would inevitably make war upon its neighbors. Therefore, it decided to take steps to alter the Nicaraguan Government's
totalitarianism and/or its alliance with the Soviet Union.

Although the Carter Administration did not settle on a particular
strategy for effecting these changes — and while it continued to
do its best to stay on friendly terms with the Sandinistas, hoping
for the best — it began political efforts aimed at propping up the
opposition in Nicaragua and creating the infrastructure for
paramilitary action. At its inception, then, covert action was a
mechanism that enabled a new policy option to arise as the Administration's illusions disintegrated.

By 1980 the Sandinistas were bearing out President Carter's worst
fears by enabling their longtime allies, the Salvadoran communists,
to mount a serious military challenge to their government. Moreover
the Sandinistas' repression drove thousands of Nicaraguans to seek
help. Hence by 1980 both dissident Nicaraguans and Nicaragua's
neighbors were asking for U.S. assistance against the Sandinistas.
Stories soon began to appear in the press about Americans and
Argentinians aiding the counterrevolutionaries — the "Contras."

CHOICES FOR THE REAGAN ADMINISTRATION

The Reagan Administration inherited its predecessor's problems
and its program of help to the Contras, both of which had grown.
By late 1981 the new Administration's judgment with respect both
to the problem and to the solution was summed up by Thomas
Enders, Assistant Secretary of State for Inter-American Affairs: Do
unto Nicaragua what Nicaragua is trying to do to El Salvador. The
Reagan Administration's aims were the same as those of the Carter
Administration: to foster pluralism in Nicaragua both for its own
sake and as the surest safeguard against the Sandinistas' proclivity
for fomenting regional conflict. By this time, however, there was
no more room for hope that the Sandinistas might be bribed away
from their objectives or that they would allow themselves to be influenced by their more moderate supporters.

The Sandinistas had dispelled whatever doubts might have remained about their intentions. Their army (25,000 regulars, 50,000
militia) was on its way to becoming larger than those of the rest

of Central America combined. The command, control and logistical structure for the war in El Salvador was operating openly in Managua. The democratic allies who had given the Sandinistas the veneer of pluralism during the revolution had been cast off. Every vestige of independent social activity, from the church to private business, had been restricted and harassed. Thousands of Miskito Indians, their villages burned, had been massacred for refusing to move into concentration camps, and the remainder took to the swamps to fight back. Meanwhile, the Contras had swollen to a few thousand men in Honduras and Costa Rica. In late 1981 the Contras began to give serious battle to the Sandinista militia.

Logically, by that time any remaining foundation for the Carter Administration's original policy toward the Sandinistas had crumbled. Nonetheless, powerful groups in the Executive and Legislative Branches began to oppose strenuously and publicly any support of the Contras. By and large they did not challenge the assessment of the nature of the regime in Managua and of its dangerous implications. Nevertheless, they charged, and have continued to charge, that U.S. support of the Contras is fundamentally wrong because it forecloses the option of negotiations. The Administration has countered by claiming that support of covert action is essential if there is to be any hope of negotiations.

COVERT ACTION AND "NEGOTIATIONS"

Paradoxically, the U.S. policy argument has thus centered on whether the "forceful option" would or would not help achieve the goals of the original "friendly option." Not surprisingly, the argument has been unenlightening. Perhaps the most confusing part of the debate has been the stress on "negotiations" with the Sandinistas. Nearly everyone seems to favor them, but few specify the objectives that negotiations might achieve and the incentives involved. Let us see why.

The Sandinistas view themselves as the local chapter of a worldwide communist coalition led by the Soviet Union, which helped them into power, sustains them and holds out to them the wherewithal for the achievement of their regional ambitions. No one seriously suggests that there exists a set of words that, if presented to the Sandinistas, would convince them to put at risk their membership in the Soviet coalition or their control over their people. No advocate of negotiations suggests that the Sandinista leaders would take any set of earthly goods in exchange for assured control of the Nicaraguan people and visible progress in their regional offensive.

What, then, could negotiations be about? Above all, the Sandinistas desire a pledge that the United States will not invade, nor assist Nicaraguans who challenge their control of the country. "We ask only that you respect our sovereignty," they say. In return, they are willing to consider doing anything — so long as it would not compromise their control of the country and their alliance with the Soviets. Specifically, they have broadly hinted that they would exchange the cessation of their support of the war in El Salvador for the United States' cessation of its support of the Contras.

If such an agreement could be worked out, inspectors might well certify that Salvadoran commanders moved out of their villas and command posts in Managua on the way to Cuba, that the arms traffic ceased, and that a number of Salvadoran insurgents trooped back to their Nicaraguan sanctuary. But each of these moves could easily be reversed after a tactical pause because the basic infrastructure of command and professional cadres for the insurgency in El Salvador would still be there, ready for reassembly and reactivation. On the other hand, the Contras are not likely to survive the withdrawal of U.S. aid as a fighting force. Most of the Contras are not professional fighters, but rather ordinary people who will seek out ordinary lives elsewhere once they become convinced of the futility — let alone the betrayal — of the cause of freedom for their country. In short, they will follow the example of the Cuban survivors of the Bay of Pigs before them and disperse into exile.

Negotiations might also guarantee that elections are held in Nicaragua. Elections are also held in East Germany, which helped draw up Nicaragua's laws on elections and on political parties — laws which provide essentially that candidates from non-Sandinista parties must be acceptable to the Sandinistas and may not criticize them.

In sum, those who propose negotiations with the Sandinistas must be willing to provide brutal incentives for the latter to jeopardize the power that they have seized at the cost of many lives in a bitter conflict and to abandon an ideology that forbids the relinquishment of that power. Just as important, advocates of negotiations must provide for the continuation-in-being of those brutal incentives after the agreement is concluded. In innumerable discussions among American policymakers, support for the Contras has been promoted as the violent incentive necessary to bring the Sandinistas to the negotiating table. Yet, such discussions rarely take into account that those concessions that the United States really wants are the ones that the Sandinistas cannot afford to yield, while the central concessions the Sandinistas desire would remove our ability to press them for any concessions at all.

COVERT ACTION AND "CONTAINMENT"

It has been suggested that how the Sandinistas rule 2.5 million Nicaraguans is not the affair of the United States—so long as they halt their efforts to destabilize their neighbors. Common sense and experience suggest, however, that a passive containment of a well-entrenched, Soviet-allied Sandinista regime would be futile. In this respect the Kissinger Commission's Report is worth citing at length:

> . . .There would be little incentive for the Sandinistas to act responsibly, even over a period of time, and much inducement to escalate their efforts to subvert Nicaragua's neighbors. To contain the export of revolution would require a level of vigilance and sustained effort that would be difficult for Nicaragua's neighbors and even for the United States. A fully militarized and equipped Nicaragua, with excellent intelligence and command and control organizations, would weigh heavily on the neighboring countries of the region. . . . We would then face the prospect, over time, of the collapse of the other countries of Central America, bringing with it the specter of Marxist domination of the entire region and thus the danger of a larger war.

According to the Commission, only "the involvement of U.S. forces as surrogate policemen" on a repeated basis would prevent the projected domino-pattern. A corollary conclusion must be that mere covert operations cannot aspire to the task.

The Kissinger Commission did not consider the suggestion by Secretary of State Alexander Haig in 1981 that the United States deal with the problem of Central America by "going to the source." That can mean facing the Sandinistas with the choice of ceasing the export of revolution or being invaded by the United States. It can also mean facing Cuba with the same choice. Moreover, since the ultimate "source" of the problem is the Soviet Union, the silence with respect to Secretary Haig's suggestion is understandable.

THE EMERGING SCENARIO

The political discussion in the United States has obscured the fact that the military struggle between the Contras and the Sandinistas will be won by one side or the other. In two-sided wars, nothing so harms the interests of third parties as indecisiveness. If the Sandinistas are to win, the United States will have committed a profound mistake in aiding the Contras at all. A victory over the "traitors backed by the colossus to the North" will have the effect of entrenching and emboldening the Sandinista regime, just as Fidel Castro's victory in the Bay of Pigs led to the consolidation of his regime and the emergence of Cuba into the powerful Soviet outpost that it is today. If it is the objective of the United States to prevent the establishment of "another Cuba" on the hemispheric mainland, then there is ample historical precedent for how *not* to pursue that goal.

The officialdom in Washington seems no better prepared for a victory by the Contras. In briefings of the Congress, Executive Branch officials have evinced trepidation at the prospect of either the imminent victory *or* defeat of the Contras, as if once formed they could stay in place forever or disappear without consequences. Failure to deal forthrightly with the basic goals of the covert operation has engendered innumerable quarrels within and among the Legislative and Executive Branches, most recently over the mining of Nicaragua's harbors.

The emerging scenario of the covert operation itself calls for decisiveness. By early 1984 the Contras commanded almost 20,000 men under three commands: the Miskito Indians in the north, the forces of Eden Pastora in the southwest, and the National

Democratic force of Adolfo Calero in the northwest. Apparently the expansion of these forces is limited only by the availability of weapons. The Contras have no difficulty gathering recruits or intelligence: a battalion of Sandinista militiamen even defected to the Contras with their weapons. The Contras' number, out of a Nicaraguan population of 2.5 million, is all the more impressive when compared to the number of communist guerrillas in El Salvador: 8,000 in a population of 5 million.

The Contras now roam more or less freely in the least populated parts of Nicaragua, where they encounter only the Sandinista militia. But they do not now command the logistics to reach, or the heavy weapons to attack, the regular Nicaraguan Army in the Managua area. The regime, for its part, has avoided risking the regulars' morale and allegiance by throwing them into the fight. The Sandinistas' strategy generally seems to be to expose themselves as little as possible while convincing the Nicaraguan people that the Contras' international supporters will abandon them. Hence, both sides consider the news about debates in the U.S. Congress more important indicators of the struggle than body-counts. The key political prize in this, as in other insurgencies, is hope. Whichever side can convince first its own fighters, and then the people-at-large, that it will win in the longer run gains a potentially decisive advantage.

THE LESSONS

And here we come to the overarching lesson explicit in the three case studies of U.S. covert action that we have considered. In a democracy there is no substitute for fully articulated, vigorously defended policy. Good intentions, eloquent declarations, diplomatic skills, covert action, military force—these are *elements* of policy. Yet, they must be understood and practiced together as integrated parts of a success-oriented plan. Such a plan is essential to obtaining agreement from the Congress and the public for any expenditures, sacrifices or risks.

The first step in such a plan is to decide and to define what we want to achieve. In all three of the cases, the victory of the anti-Soviet forces is so preferable to its alternative, both in terms of our interests and from a moral standpoint, that U.S. officials should have no difficulty in espousing it publicly. In a democracy, no action, however covert, ought to be undertaken unless, if need be, it can be confidently defended in public. A successful public defense requires a clear exposition of the ends to be achieved, of the means to be employed and of why those means are likely to be effective. Proponents and opponents of the U.S. involvement in these areas, never mind those who take a neutral stance, ask the same question: Are the measures being urged by the U.S. Administration reasonably likely to bring about the desired results? That question deserves an answer.

Although some aspects of the U.S. involvement in these regions must remain unacknowledged out of respect for the needs of third parties and in order not to identify targets for the enemies, nevertheless the reasoning that guides our involvement must be much more overt and explicit than it has been heretofore. In the case of Central America for example, would it be useful for us to attempt to contain the Sandinista regime or to try to change its nature? Which of the contenders for power in Nicaragua is the legitimate representative of the Nicaraguan people? Is it really possible to prevent the Sandinistas, and the coalition of Soviet auxiliaries of which they are part, from expanding over Central America without defeating them militarily? Can and should the battle be carried by the Contras or, if necessary, by American troops? Does it make sense to will a set of ends without committing means reasonably calculated to achieve them?

As we have applied pressures and our opponents have countered them, and as our efforts have become better known, it has become imperative to explain to ourselves what we have done and what we are ultimately willing to do in order to achieve our objectives. Thus far, the Administration — but not the President — has tended to frame its public position in terms of adherence to restrictions in the scope of covert action. But *any* activity in these areas, small or large, overt or covert, can only be justified by the reasonable expectation of ultimate success. To attempt to justify activities in any other terms invites both substantive failure and popular rejection.

15 The Reagan Doctrine: It Awaits Implementation

ANGELO CODEVILLA

Over the past several years, the fact that most of the guerrilla wars in the world today are being waged against Soviet or Soviet proxy forces has provided a strong theme in the pronouncements of the Reagan Administration. In the Presidential campaign of 1984, the Administration's leading spokesmen invoked this fact as further proof that America's previously battered image had been refurbished by their competent stewardship, that the "correlation of forces" on the globe was shifting against the Soviet Union, and that American-style democracy was once again ascendant as the wave of the future. Throughout 1985 the Administration spoke increasingly about "anti-communist resistance movements," and "aid to freedom fighters" rose into a major political issue in Washington.

President Reagan, for his part, went so far as to call Nicaragua's Contras "brothers." In his 1986 State of the Union message he announced what has come to be known as the Reagan Doctrine: that any people fighting to free itself from communist rule could count on the Administration's effective aid. Using the (original) words of the resolution on Afghanistan that the Congress had passed in September 1984, the President asserted that the aid would be not just enough to help the freedom fighters fight and die, but enough to help them win.

Shortly thereafter, Jonas Savimbi, the charismatic leader of Angola's anticommunist forces, received a her's reception in

This chapter appeared as an article, entitled "The Reagan Doctrine — (As Yet) A Declaratory Policy," in the Summer 1986 issue of Strategic Review.

Washington. President Reagan introduced the three civilian leaders of Nicaragua's Contras by declaring that he was one of them. In May 1986 he received three leaders of the Afghan Resistance in the Oval Office. In June the President won hard-fought support from the House of Representatives to expend $100 million for the Contras. Earlier in the year, the *New York Times* reported that the Reagan Administration had agreed to send Stinger shoulder-fired anti-aircraft missiles to Angolan and Afghan (if not yet Nicaraguan) anticommunist forces.

LIBERATION AND THE POLICYMAKING "BARONIES"

The very word "doctrine" over these Presidential statements has conveyed the image of a determined Administration policy aimed at the objective of driving the Soviets and their surrogates out of Afghanistan, Angola and Nicaragua. Yet, the test of policy in a democracy lies less in the declaratory statements of the head-of-state (irrespective of his sincerity) and more in the substantial decisions and actions taken by the government. Particularly in the current U.S. Administration, with its strong emphasis on the "cabinet approach," foreign policy is the "resultant," in the geometric sense, of the policy preferences of the major "baronies" involved in the policymaking process: the State Department, the Defense Department, the Central Intelligence Agency, and their respective allies in the National Security Council and the U.S. Congress.

Of course, it is risky — and perhaps less than fair to individual policymakers who may diverge from the given "corporate" line — to generalize the policy preferences within the "baronies" and their interplay over the issue of U.S. assistance to anticommunist forces. Still, close observation of the interagency process in the Reagan Administration with respect to the issue has yielded consistent evidence of basic positions and themes.

There is first of all the Department of State. Given the central place of diplomacy in that agency's mandate and functions, there has evolved among its members — especially in the professional ranks of the Foreign Service — a disposition that assigns to negotiations the primary role in foreign policy. Short of being the instruments of "last resort," military power and armed force are seen as at best inputs into the negotiating process — as "strengthening the bargaining hand." But the principal purpose of negotiations is to defuse conflict and tensions — from the vantagepoint of U.S. national interests, to ameliorate and constrain through negotiated agreement the threats posed to those U.S. interests.

It is in the very nature of negotiated agreements, moreover, that they are addressed to the status quo — to its stabilization rather than its revision. Applied to the situations in Afghanistan, Angola and Nicaragua, it leads to what may be called a "minimalist" view in the State Department, which holds that the "insurrections" in those places may be harnessed to the search for regional arrangements which, while continuing the given Marxist-Leninist regime in power, might render it less threatening to its neighbors and to U.S. interests. There is also a "maximalist" view in the Department which suggests that the combined phenomenon of anti-communist movements may lead to a new global U.S.-Soviet *modus vivendi* based upon respect for the status quo. In neither the "minimalist" nor "maximalist" view, however, is there really room for victory by the anticommunist forces. In fact, it is fair to say that some would deem such victory "destabilizing" in the larger U.S.-Soviet context.

In contrast with such themes in the State Department, the civilians in charge of the U.S. Defense Department's policy generally favor the liberation of the three countries from communist control. They have pressed for formulation of national policy along those lines, but do not have a charter for dispensing aid. Moreover, they can count on resistance from the military services to giving liberation movements the weapons and other resources from their own hard-won shares of the military budget.

The Director of the Central Intelligence Agency, William Casey, is firmly aligned with the officials in the Defense Department, and personally seems to favor the victory of liberation movements. His Agency has the charter for dispensing the aid. But from among the CIA's senior personnel have come strong echoes of the State Department's view of the role of liberation movements in U.S.-Soviet relations. In their dealings with Congress and the NSC, CIA officials have often outdone even their colleagues in the State Department in reticence to provide aid to such movements quantitatively and qualitatively sufficient for victory, declaring that the Agency would rather be rid of the burden of supplying such aid at all. Nevertheless, the CIA has strenuously opposed proposals that the Defense Department be given primary responsibility for providing such assistance.

All of this is to say that, in the absence of more forceful Presidential leadership, the "resultant" of such contradictory forces within the Administration is a de facto policy neither of liberation nor of abandonment, but of what might be characterized as providing enough to anticommunist liberation movements to "keep the pot boiling," or to "raise the cost" to the Soviet Union and its surrogates of consolidating their holds over areas where such movements operate. Of course, few in the foreign policy establishment would be prepared explicitly to argue the case for such a "policy," given its cynical implications for those fighting the liberation cause, as well as the prospect of thereby conceding to the Soviet Union ultimate victories more meaningful — and more discrediting to the United States — than they would have been in the absence of any U.S. involvement. Yet, the various participants in the policy process seem reasonably content with governmental decisions that make such an outcome inevitable, because they represent "reasonable" compromises of intragovernmental differences.

Such compromises avoid the most vexing burden of policymaking: namely, casting the hard choices concerning the ends sought and the means likely to achieve them, and accepting the responsibility for success or failure. Instead, the Administration's foreign policymakers generally have dealt with their differences by adopting in foreign affairs in general, and with respect to the issue of anticommunist liberation movements in particular, the habits of domestic policymaking, which consist of giving a little to each side in a given controversy. This sort of policymaking permits the hard choices to be postponed — and ultimately to be foreclosed by the march of time and events. In foreign affairs, however, it has the effect of conceding to the opponent all the advantages of rationality that we deny to ourselves. But let us see how the phenomenon has applied in practice.

NICARAGUA: GENESIS OF THE PROBLEM

All too soon after the Carter Administration had in effect helped the Sandinistas' victory in Nicaragua by isolating the Somoza regime from all possible sources of support, it was forced to confront the implications of a now-recognized fact that it had so recently dismissed: namely, that the Sandinista leaders were dedicated communists tightly allied with the Soviet Union. Clearly the Carter Administration decided that no U.S. government could agree to the establishment in Central America of a regime able to coerce its people into serving as the spearhead of a Soviet intrusion onto the hemispheric mainland and into the vulnerable "strategic backyard" of the United States itself.

Acting on that recognition, the Carter Administration in December 1978 notified Congress that it would engage in covert activities to forestall the "emerging totalitarian nature" of the Sandinista regime by giving assistance to democratic forces in Nicaragua. In 1979 most of the emergent democratic opposition to the Sandinistas was nonviolent. But already then the Sandinistas had begun labeling any and all who stood in the way of their consolidation of power and alignment with the Soviet Bloc as *"contra-revolucionarios,"* or simply *"contras."* Over the following months, the opposition which the United States was helping gradually but inexorably became a paramilitary resistance.

By the time the Reagan Administration began to review its own program of assistance to the Contras, some thousand Nicaraguans per month, not to mention entire tribes of Miskito Indians, were asking for weapons with which to reclaim the freedoms they thought they had recently won. The Administration was generally favorable to meeting the demand, and its formulation of objectives did not differ from that of the Carter Administration: namely to change the Nicaraguan government. At the time, a spokesman for the Administration described its objective as follows: "do unto the Sandinistas what they are trying to do to El Salvador." Listeners were free to draw the conclusion: "change the government."

EARLY DERAILING OF THE REAGAN NICARAGUA POLICY

Yet, a variety of people within the Administration, along with Democratic members of Congress who felt freer to oppose a

Republican administration then their own, began to charge that it was illegitimate for the United States to seek to affect the nature of a foreign government by supporting armed actions against it. Although the opposition was to the *ends* of the Administration's policy, it was couched in objections to the paramilitary *means* to be employed. Thus, no sooner had the Reagan Administration announced that its intentions did not differ from its predecessor's than it felt pressure, both from within and without the Administration, to qualify or somehow blur those intentions.

The principal tactic of the opponents of actions against the Sandinista regime consisted of convincing the Administration that it could obtain appropriated assistance for the Contras only at the cost of pledging that this aid would not be used in an effort to change the Nicaraguan government. Throughout 1982 members of Congress led the Administration's witnesses into statements that the United States did not seek to involve itself in Nicaragua's internal affairs, but only intended to stop Nicaragua's intervention into El Salvador's internal affairs. Support for the Contras was a means of sending this message, and also of interdicting the flow of arms from Nicaragua to El Salvador.

In 1982, the annual appropriations for the Department of Defense were delayed until December's "lame duck" session of the Congress. At that time, Congressman (later Senator) Tom Harkin (D-Iowa) proposed an amendment prohibiting any and all expenditures for anyone seeking to overthrow Nicaragua's government. This was defeated easily, as was Senator Edward Kennedy's dentical motion in the Senate. Thereupon the President was persuaded, reportedly by recommendations from the State Department and the CIA, to support an amendment offered by Congressman Robert Boland (D-Mass.) which barred the United States from expending any funds in order to overthrow the government of Nicaragua. The argument advanced to the President was that, inasmuch as the Administration's official line mentioned not "overthrowing," but "changing" and "democratizing" — which could theoretically be effected without overthrow — the Boland Amendment would strengthen rather than weaken the Administration's position by putting it beyond reproach. Predictably, however "the law," as the Boland Amendment was quickly dubbed by opponents of aid to the

Contras, was elevated into a test for the Administration that it prove by deeds that it was *not* working to overthrow the Sandinista regime.

That burden of "proof" exacted a series of statements from the Reagan Administration in 1983–1984 to the effect that assistance to the Contras indeed was *not* intended at the overthrow of the Sandinistas — meaning in practical terms that the Contras would not win their struggle. The principal evidence for this was invoked in the Administration's refusal to supply the Contras with the heavy weapons, anti-aircraft and logistics essential to victory. Again and again the Administration contended that its policy was to seek a negotiated settlement, and that aid to the Contras was the primary prod toward such a settlement. Beyond that, in testimony before the Congress spokesmen for the Administration found themselves responding to questions — logically consequent to the Administration's stance — regarding the circumstances under which it would curtail aid to the Contras. It is noteworthy that the Sandinista radio in Managua repeatedly broadcast words by CIA Director William Casey to the effect of such a curtailment, making the point to friend and foe alike that the Contras were mere tools of the United States fighting for a hopeless cause.

That cause never seemed less hopeful than during the summer of 1984, when the Reagan Administration, having attached a request for arms for the Contras to an urgent supplemental appropriations bill in the Senate (in order to force the issue into a conference with the Democratic-controlled House of Representatives), thereupon agreed to have its request stripped from the bill. In October 1984, State Department officials were putting pressure on Honduras and Costa Rica to sign a treaty drafted by the representatives of Mexico, Colombia, Venezuela, and Panama, which would have cut off support for the Contras in exchange for a "commitment" by the Sandinistas to discuss reducing the role of its foreign supporters and better treatment of the opposition. Only when the Honduran Ambassador in Washington protested to the NSC staff and to members of Congress, who then protested to the President, did the State Department back off. The incident eventually led to the replacement of Langhorne A. Motley, the then Assistant Secretary of State for Inter-American Affairs who became identified with the maneuver, with Elliot Abrams.

THE 1985 ASSISTANCE DECISION

The October 1984 State Department initiative and its aftermath also led President Reagan to depict in clearer terms the struggle in Nicaragua as one between the Sandinistas and their legitimate internal opposition, and to insist that the United States would never deal with the Sandinistas behind the back of that opposition. More generally, the White House sometime in 1985 came face-to-face with the recognition that time was working for the Sandinistas and the Soviets and against U.S. interests in Central America — that while the United States had halted its help to the Contras, the Soviets were shipping ever mounting stockpiles of sophisticated weapons to Nicaragua to be used against the Contras. Once again the Administration had to confront squarely the dire implications of a consolidated, unchallenged Sandinista government and of the ensconcement of Soviet power in Nicaragua. The recognition prompted an increase in Administration pressure on the Congress, particularly on Democratic members seeking to avoid being placed on the wrong side of the line drawn by the President — namely that those refusing support to the Contras would bear ultimate responsibility for the establishment and expansion of communist totalitarianism close to America's southern border. Hence the Congress' agreement in the summer of 1986 to supply $100 million worth of food and weapons to the Contras.

Yet, in and of itself, this clearly did not — and could not — represent a decision either by Congress, or by the Administration, to seek the Sandinistas' ouster, nor even to declare to the world, to the Nicaraguan populace, or to the American people that the Sandinista regime is illegitimate. This was not a decision to give the Contras anything resembling the military odds that the Sandinistas had enjoyed in their rising against the Somoza regime. Had the United States made such a decision, it would be providing the surface-to-air missiles, the anti-aircraft weapons, the artillery, the transportation and the training necessary for fighting a modern army lavishly supplied by the Soviet Bloc.

One hundred million dollars worth of military aid over eighteen months — even assuming that it represents a significant fraction of what the Contras need to mount a serious military challenge —

can be easily offset by increases in the tide of materiel (and men) from the Soviet Bloc to Nicaragua. A commitment to victory — or even the possibility of victory — would entail either a decision to supply the Contras with whatever they need to counter the Soviet Bloc flow, or a decision to limit that flow by a naval-air blockade or by even the threat thereof. In the absence of such decisions, the commitment of $100 million may be enough to "keep the pot boiling" in Nicaragua — at least for the time being.

THE NEGOTIATIONS TRACK INTO THE WILDERNESS

According to at least one explanation of U.S. policy, there may be even less to the $100 million than meets the eye. In a speech to the World Affairs Council of Northern California on June 16, 1986, the President's Special Ambassador to Central America, Phillip Habib, argued for the assistance funds, and for the Contras themselves, as indispensable means to a negotiated arrangement in Central America. As did the Carter Administration, the Kissinger Commission and President Reagan, Habib explained that the United States — not to mention Nicaragua's immediate neighbors — cannot abide a Nicaraguan government both totalitarian and allied with Moscow. The Contras are worthy of support because they are legitimate Nicaraguan democrats and because, unless the Nicaraguan government turns to democracy, its neighbors can place no faith in its promises of coexistence.

The United States, Habib continued, fully supports the efforts of Mexico, Colombia, Venezuela, and Panama (the so-called Contadora countries) to fashion an agreement between Nicaragua and its neighbors that would end support for violence on all sides and rid the area of foreign, including U.S., military interference. The United States would abide by such an agreement while not being party to it. But, Habib emphasized, there is no getting away from the fact that the democratically elected presidents of Honduras and Costa Rica insist that any treaty involve not just agreements between nations, but also the democratization of Nicaraguan politics, without which neither of their countries could rest secure. They insist that any provision for Nicaraguan democratization come into force simultaneously with those requiring the neighboring countries to stop harboring the Contras, and they insist that any treaty provide for verifiable evidence that Nicaragua is living up to all of its provisions. Thus, the thrust of Habib's presentation of U.S. policy was that the price of a U.S. dismantling of the Contras is a Contadora treaty that is "comprehensive, simultaneous and verifiable."

Habib made no mention of who would *enforce* such a treaty. It has become standard in State Department formulations that the concept of verification crowds out the less comfortable one of enforcement of compliance. State Department officials tend to argue that if all provisions of a treaty, including arrangements for verification, go into force simultaneously, the treaty is self-enforcing: the U.S. side will not perform its obligations unless the other side performs its obligations. It is difficult to believe that those who wield this argument fail to foresee what would happen once the United States announced its intention to sponsor the dismantling of the Contras in exchange for Sandinista promises of democratization — promises whose fulfillment (or lack thereof) the United States might verify but would be in no effective position to enforce.

The Contras for the most part are not professional fighters whose campaign can be turned on and off, but ordinary people who have taken up arms in the hope of freer lives for themselves and a better life for their country. It is remarkable that they have fought for five years with so little tangible hope. An agreement that provided for their disbandment and the cut-off of American support would spell their end. Thus, by the time realization of the communist side's betrayal of the treaty's provision were to filter through the U.S. national security bureaucracy, the Contra option would no longer be available. The United States would have to choose in effect between doing nothing and going to war.

Of course, due to the objections from democratic Honduras and Costa Rica, a treaty is not around the corner. It hovers near enough, however, to help keep the U.S. foreign policy bureaucracy from focusing on reality and to justify giving the Contras enough to fight and die, day after day, as the Sandinistas and their Soviet Bloc allies tighten their hold on Nicaragua and prepare for the next step.

A CLEARER ISSUE IN ANGOLA

In late 1985, even as President Reagan and Secretary of State George Shultz were echoing the widespread sentiment that Jonas Savimbi's Union for the Total Independence of Angola (UNITA) deserves the Free World's support in its fight against a Soviet-supported Cuban army of occupation — and as the Democratic-controlled House of Representatives was about to consider a proposal by Congressman Claude Pepper (D-Fla.) to provide some aid to Savimbi — Secretary Shultz wrote a secret letter to Congressman Robert Michel (R-Ill.), the leader of the House Republicans, asking him to quietly oppose aid to Savimbi. Congressman Michel, outraged, published the letter. This led a patently embarrassed Secretary of State to a series of meetings on Capitol Hill lasting into March of 1986, in which he sought both to remedy the impression of hypocrisy created by his letter to Michel, and to channel the Congressional pressure for aid to Savimbi into the policy framework he had sought to defend by drafting the letter to Michel in the first place. Let us see what that framework is, and how well Secretary Shultz has succeeded.

The issue in Angola is less complex than in Nicaragua. In 1975 the Soviet Union helped its client communist movement, the MPLA, to seize power by supplying an invasion force of some 20,000 Cuban troops. That number today is closer to 30,000, augmented by the usual contingents of East German internal security specialists, Bulgarians, Yemenis, etc. The Soviet Union devotes fully one third of its airlift capacity to supplying the expeditionary force in Angola. A Soviet hospital ship is permanently stationed off Luanda to care for the wounded.

On the other side of this war, Jonas Savimbi's UNITA controls one third of the country and actively contests another third. It has sanctuaries in Zambia and South Africa, and receives most of its aid from Europe, principally France. Although it once accepted aid from Communist China, UNITA is thoroughly pro-Western. The canard of the extreme left in the United States and Europe — that Savimbi is somehow the tool of South African racism — is clearly just that. In fact, UNITA is a thoroughly black movement, while its opponents, the leaders of the MPLA, are obviously dependent on white Cubans, Soviets, East Germans, etc.

The Soviet Union is determined to prevail in Angola. In 1985 Cuban forces under the direction of a Soviet general launched an attack across nearly a thousand miles of wilderness that inflicted heavy losses on UNITA and reached within 100 miles of its capital, Jamba. The Cubans used armor and aircraft to break through the defenses, and helicopters for enveloping movements. UNITA was saved by the remoteness of its capital, as well as by excellent fighting.

Yet, the 1985 attack foretold that UNITA is being outclassed. Between 1975 and 1985, UNITA had laboriously built a native organization with just enough foreign guns, trucks and radios to challenge the forces which had fashioned the communist victory in 1975. But by 1985 the Soviets had obviously upped the ante. In 1986 the Soviet-Cuban buildup, especially of aircraft, had further outclassed UNITA. Without a quantum leap in foreign assistance, UNITA seems ultimately doomed.

The Negotiations Track in Southern Africa

The question for U.S. policy is obviously whether or not to give Savimbi's UNITA enough to contend for victory at this higher level of violence, and to prepare to meet any ulterior Soviet escalation with even more massive assistance, or perhaps to prepare to prevent Cuban reinforcements from going to Angola. If the United States decided to do none of these things, it would have to prepare to live with the consequences of a Soviet victory in Angola.

U.S. policy, insofar as it exists, has been to obfuscate this choice. Since 1981 Assistant Secretary of State Chester Crocker has pursued what the State Department fancies as negotiations between Angola's ruling MPLA and South Africa. The objective of the negotiations ostensibly is a scenario in which South Africa grants independence to Southwest Africa/Namibia under conditions acceptable to the MPLA, and cuts off all support to Savimbi; in exchange for this the MPLA would expel the Cubans, Soviets and other Bloc nationals, and form a coalition government including UNITA. Of course, the United States, although not a formal party to the agreement, would respect it and cease its own support to Savimbi. Hence, Angolans would solve Angola's problem without interference.

In order to believe in the feasibility of this arrangement, one would first have to accept a string of propositions. The first is that the MPLA is free to order the Soviet coalition out. The second is that the MPLA's leaders would feel themselves secure enough to dispense with Cuban troops. The third is that South Africa could agree to hand Southwest Africa/Namibia over to Sam Nujoma's communist Southwest African People's Organization (SWAPO), as the MPLA demands, and help to destroy UNITA, thus leaving its northwestern border in thoroughly unfriendly hands.

So committed has the State Department been to this negotiation that in 1984–1985 it agreed to, and pressed upon South Africa, the MPLA's escalation of demands: namely that at the end of the process, after Savimbi was cut off and Namibia was in SWAPO's hands, some ten thousand Cuban troops would remain in Angola. After unfavorable publicity, however, the State Department returned to its original negotiating position that all the Cuban troops had to leave.

The Soviet-Cuban offensive of 1985 also convinced some officials in the State Department that U.S. aid to UNITA might not be a bad means of putting some pressure on the MPLA, and that without it the Savimbi bargaining chip might not last much longer. Moreover, by the winter of 1985–1986 Jonas Savimbi's prestige in the United States was high. In the wake of the furor over his letter to Congressman Michel, Secretary Shultz was not in a position to oppose aid to UNITA, which was supported by the Secretary of Defense as well as the Director of the CIA.

When President Reagan received Savimbi at the White House, the only question besides how much and what kind of aid he would receive was whether the aid would replace negotiations or be subordinate to them. Secretary Shultz seemed to ensure that aid would be subordinate to the negotiations by taking the initiative away from the Congress. He proposed that Savimbi receive $15 million of covert aid, administered by the CIA. The use of the covert mechanism tends to forestall the painful process of formulating U.S. policy in any given area.

ABIDING QUESTIONS ABOUT U.S. ANGOLAN POLICY

By agreeing to give some aid to Savimbi, the U.S. Government had satisfied one set of pressures. The President's authority, after an intervention by several Senators, was enough to overcome resistance within the Administration — notably in the higher echelons of the CIA — to supplying some Stinger missiles to UNITA. But no one at the higher levels of the U.S. Government has (publicly) addressed the question: What will our $15 million a year do in Angola against a combined Soviet Bloc investment of over $1 billion?

The answer from the State Department would be, of course, that the U.S. aid is designed to keep pressure on the MPLA to accept the negotiated arrangement pushed by Assistant Secretary Crocker. But that answer cannot stand up to questions concerning its premises. Why should the MPLA and the Soviets-Cubans abandon one another so long as there is no serious prospect of disastrous defeat? Even if the communist side agreed to a deal, who would enforce it? Given what each of the sides in the affair is trying to do, and the means they are employing, what will the situation be in a few years hence? What are the likely consequences of a Soviet victory? Just how much should the United States be willing to commit in order to prevent it?

The decision to supply $15 million in covert aid to Savimbi was above all a decision not to confront those questions and to indulge a while longer the State Department's hope, at the same time satisfying pressures to do something in support of Savimbi. Meanwhile, the Soviets are pursuing a steadfast policy in Angola and Southern Africa.

INDECISION OVER AFGHANISTAN

Because the issue in Afghanistan is clearer than even in Angola, its obfuscation in the Administration is all the more conspicuous. In December 1979, the Soviet Army invaded Afghanistan. The Soviets have changed the government in Kabul three times since the invasion. That government has absolutely no standing in the country other than as an agent of the Soviet Union. It is a foreign, atheistic abomination among devout, xenophobic Muslims. Perhaps one million Afghan civilians have been killed, and some three-and-one-half million have fled the country. The Mujahideen fighters are the only representatives of the Afghan people. Pakistan — especially its conservative Muslim ruling elite — has placed itself in great danger by acting as a conduit for foreign aid to the Mujahideen.

Yet, President Reagan, having invited the leaders of the Mujahideen to the Oval Office in May 1986, resisted their request that he withdraw recognition from the puppet government in Kabul. "Administration sources" explained that the President wants to maintain the U.S. embassy in Kabul in order to gather intelligence. This is in line with his decision to maintain recognition of the Sandinista regime in Managua, but it begs the question. Intelligence is information useful for implementing policy. In fact, the U.S. Government has not decided what it wants to do about Afghanistan.

What makes this indecision all the more poignant in the case of Afghanistan is that there is little, if any, opposition in the U.S. domestic arena to the proposition that the United States should help the Afghan freedom fighters drive the Soviets out of their country. Indeed, each year since the Soviets invaded and the CIA began to funnel arms to the Mujahideen, the Congress has *increased* the Administration's requests for funds for this purpose.

In 1984 the Congress, led by the liberal Democratic Senator from Massachusetts, Paul Tsongas, passed a resolution requesting the Administration to supply aid to Afghanistan that would allow the Afghans to do more than fight and die. The resolution's original draft used the words that President Reagan later made the touchstone of the Reagan Docrine: "enough to win." Ironically, because the Administration, in the persons of Secretary George Shultz and CIA Deputy Director John MacMahon, lobbied so hard against these very words, Senator Tsongas reluctantly agreed to change them to "advance the cause of freedom."

LACK OF ASSISTANCE POLICY TO THE MUJAHIDEEN

Even as Congress has sought to increase the flow of aid to the Afghans, it has asked the Administration to set a policy for using it. This the Administration has seemed unable and/or unwilling to do. The CIA, for example, has consistently demonstrated refusal to admit what every observer of the Afghan scene has noted about Soviet strategy there: namely, that the Soviet Union is waging a devastating war against the civilian population. By the same token, the CIA has refused to acknowledge the broad Afghan population's (not just the main-force Mujahideen's) need for competent defenses against indiscriminate and pervasive strafing by Soviet aircraft. Indeed, even under pressure from Congress the CIA has resisted providing competent portable air defenses to the main-force Mujahideen.

Finally, the CIA has refused to address the Afghans' need to have the quantity and quality of weapons delivered to them tailored to the requirements of operations, and the need to have operations tailored to a winning strategy. For years CIA officials insisted that the Afghans were not to be trusted either with money or sophisticated weapons, and/or that Pakistan would not allow either more or more effective weapons or tactics. Finally, within the U.S. Government the CIA has argued against setting a policy toward Afghanistan more specific than one simply of delivering aid to the Resistance.

But as members of Congress came to see — and the Defense Department demonstrated within the NSC — that the CIA's contentions about Afghanistan were inaccurate, the NSC approved — and the President signed — a National Security Directive stating that henceforth the actions of the United States shall be tailored to help drive the Soviets out of Afghanistan. The first practical fruit of this NSDD was the decision finally to send a token number of Stinger missiles to the Afghans.

STILL ANOTHER NEGOTIATIONS TRACK

Nevertheless, as the current year fades and another hungry winter faces the Afghans, the United States has made no plans to provide the general staff work, the weapons and training, the food and money, and the support to Pakistan without which the new NSDD will be a dead letter. On the contrary, as the Soviets further consolidate their position on the ground, while waging a scorched-earth offensive throughout the countryside, the State Department is encouraging negotiations among the Soviet Union, Pakistan and the Kabul puppet regime, the objective of which is to exchange the withdrawal of Soviet troops from Afghanistan for Pakistan's cessation of its role as sanctuary to the Mujahideen. Once again, the United States is not an official party to the negotiations, would sign nothing, but would stop all aid to the Afghan Resistance were the parties to reach an accord.

The State Department advertises the negotiations as a door kept open to encourage the Soviets' face-saving exit from Afghanistan. It is difficult to imagine that the Department's high officials do not realize that the negotiations are allowing an even more face-saving exit for Pakistan — indeed, that they allow Pakistan's internal opposition to offer itself as the fashioner of a deal that would rid their country of millions of aliens and of a dangerous enemy at its doorstep. In Pakistan as elsewhere, not only do the negotiations tend to destabilize the Resistance's sanctuary, but they offer yet one more excuse in the intragovernmental debate over U.S. foreign policy not to take the Reagan Doctrine seriously.

THE MIRRORS OF DECLARATORY POLICY

The Reagan Doctrine is one more species of that present-day American phenomenon: the *declaratory* policy. In normal parlance, policy is the reasonable orchestration of action to achieve certain goals. The qualifier "declaratory" attached to so many U.S. policies, on matters ranging from nuclear targeting to liberation movements, reflects a widespread recognition that they are not policies at all, but rather rhetoric that satisfies some domestic political needs and may contribute to decisions regarding discrete actions in a particular field.

The Reagan Doctrine of helping anticommunist liberation movements to win sprouts from the political conscience of President Reagan — and from values deeply embedded in the American ethos. Perhaps the most salient effect of that conscience and those values is that those within the U.S. Government who do not share them find themselves compelled to pay lipservice to them even while they pursue their own policy preferences. This has given rise, among other things, to a new type of diplomacy — one that might be dubbed "surrogate" diplomacy, in which representatives of the United States try to bring their country's influence to bear on third and fourth parties to strike covenants among themselves to which the United

States is not a signatory — covenants which are never submitted to the scrutiny that the U.S. Constitution prescribes, but which bind the United States nonetheless. In other words, the political consciousness of which the Reagan Doctrine is an expression has led its opponents to seek through diplomatic legerdemain abroad the leverage they lack in the U.S. political process.

This and other declaratory policies may demonstrate that many of those responsible for the fate of the United States in the world, having ceased to be competent creators and executioners of policy, have become more clever at bureaucratic infighting.

16 Why Not a Kennedy-Reagan Doctrine?

JOHN R. SILBER

On May 9, 1984, addressing the nation on the situation in El Salvador, President Reagan cited President Kennedy's words on communist penetration of the Western Hemisphere: "I want it clearly understood that this Government will not hesitate in meeting its primary obligations, which are to the security of our nation."

John F. Kennedy, President Reagan noted, had referred to the "long twilight struggle" to defend freedom in the world. As a matter of fact, President Kennedy was far more than a phrase-maker with regard to Soviet ambitions in Latin America. Indeed, if there is today a single key to the situation in Central America — and to America's policy in that region — it lies in the 1962 exchange of letters between Kennedy and Nikita S. Khrushchev, and more generally in the set of principles that can be characterized as the Kennedy Doctrine.

THE KENNEDY DOCTRINE

The goals Kennedy pursued in the crisis of 1962 were consistent with his inaugural statement that the United States under his leadership was prepared to "go anywhere and pay any price in the defense of freedom." Perhaps that promise was overly ambitious in global terms; surely it applied, however, to the defense of freedom in the American hemisphere. Kennedy pledged in 1962 that Cuba would not be invaded so long as it did not threaten the peace or the freedom of the United States or the other nations of the hemisphere. He thus recommitted the nation to a set of principles that are as relevant today as they were at the time they were enunciated.

This chapter appeared as an article, entitled "The Kennedy Doctrine: Principles for a Settlement in Central America," in the Fall 1984 issue of Strategic Review.

The position John F. Kennedy adopted in 1962 represented, in fact, a reaffirmation of the principles of the Truman Doctrine and their application to the Western Hemisphere, as well as a responsible extension of the Monroe Doctrine into our own era. Fundamental to the Truman Doctrine was the principle that U.S. interests require the protection and preservation of democracy. As President Truman declared in 1946, when communist insurgency was threatening the fragile postwar foundations of democracy in Greece: "It must be the policy of the United States to support free peoples who are resisting attempted subjugation by armed minorities or outside pressure."

The Monroe Doctrine, when it was proclaimed in 1823, was cast in a form appropriate to Nineteenth Century colonialism. It addressed itself principally to the direct acquisition of territories abroad; it did not address, nor could it anticipate, the indirect methods of Soviet imperialism in the latter part of the Twentieth Century: the use of satellite and surrogate forces trading on the instruments of subversion, terror and insurrection against its colonial targets in the guise of a "liberation struggle" directed from and subservient to Moscow. In these circumstances, the principles that President Kennedy set forth in 1962 constituted a restatement of the Monroe Doctrine appropriate to the contemporary situation, combined with the U.S. commitment, under the Truman Doctrine, to the defense of democratic societies.

From the beginning of the Cuban Missile Crisis, it was the goal of the U.S. Government not merely to compel the removal of Soviet intermediate-range ballistic missiles from Cuba, but to prevent the Soviet Union, and Cuba, from threatening Central and Latin America with the export of totalitarian revolution. In his proclamation of October 23, 1962, implementing the quarantine on arms shipments to Cuba, President Kennedy declared:

> The United States is determined to prevent by whatever means may be necessary, including the use of arms, the Marxist-Leninist regime in Cuba from extending, by force or the threat of force, its aggressive or subversive activities to any part of this hemisphere, and to prevent in Cuba the creation or use of an exter-

nally supported military capability endangering the security of the United States.

In this sense, the historical label that has been placed on the events of October 1962 — "the Cuban Missile Crisis" — is misleading. That crisis was not merely about Soviet missiles in Cuba: it was about the transformation of Cuba into a forward base of Soviet military power and into an aggressive and destabilizing force in the hemisphere.

Even in the brief letter that President Kennedy sent to Nikita Khrushchev enclosing his speech of October 22, 1962, he noted that the United States objected not only to Soviet IRBMs but also to "other offensive weapons systems in Cuba." That his demand was fully understood — and accepted — by the Kremlin was clearly demonstrated by subsequent events. In the months following the missile crisis, the Soviets withdrew from Cuba far more than just their IRBMs. They also pulled out some 10,000 to 15,000 Soviet combat and support troops, all nuclear weapons of whatever description, as well as the IL-28 bombers stationed there.

Even so, the Kennedy Administration was never satisfied that the terms of the understanding had been fully carried out by the Soviet Union. President Kennedy's letter to Khrushchev of October 28, 1962, unequivocally stated that the U.S. pledge not to invade Cuba would be in force only *after* the Soviets had lived up to their side of the bargain. At his news conference on November 20, 1962, the President repeated this condition and observed:

> Nevertheless, important parts of the understanding of October 27th and 28th remain to be carried out. The Cuban Government has not yet permitted the United Nations to verify whether all offensive weapons have been removed, and no lasting safeguards have yet been established against the future introduction of offensive weapons back in Cuba.

And he went on to warn that there would be peace in the Caribbean only "if all offensive weapons systems are removed from Cuba and kept out of the hemisphere in the future, and if Cuba is not used for the export of aggressive communist purposes."

BREACHES OF THE 1962 UNDERSTANDING

What might have transpired if John F. Kennedy had lived to serve two full terms is one of history's moot questions. But it is a fact that, in the intervening period, the Soviets have systematically transgressed, circumvented and otherwise flouted the principles of the 1962 understanding. They have done so methodically and patiently, making small and ostensibly "marginal" moves and measures that, if undiscovered and/or unchallenged, have been followed by new incremental moves. This has led to a steady buildup of power on the island of Cuba and to the projection of that power into other parts of the hemisphere.

I do not mean here — nor would it serve a useful purpose — to point an accusing finger at successive American administrations for permitting this buildup in contravention of the 1962 understanding. Forcing the Soviet Union to fulfill its international obligations has required, under the best of circumstances, unwavering vigilance, determination and large measures of political courage on the part of leaders of democratic governments. The formal deficiencies of the 1962 understanding further tended to inhibit U.S. challenges to Soviet, and Cuban, violations of the agreed-upon ground-rules. Moreover, the attention of U.S. governments in the 1960s and 1970s was diverted elsewhere, in particular to Vietnam, and later to Watergate.

In any event, the legacy of these years is the crisis that now confronts us in Central America. Cuba, supplied, trained and supported by the Soviet Union, has been allowed to grow into a power with major offensive capability. It has built a standing army of 230,000 men — by far the largest in Latin America except for Brazil (the population of which is nearly thirteen times larger than that of Cuba). On a per capita basis, the Cuban Armed Forces are ten times the average for all of the Caribbean Basin. Thanks to Soviet support, they are also by far the best-equipped. Cuba has the capability to deliver by air massive military forces anywhere in the world. It has extensive combat experience on foreign soil, sophisticated weaponry and a high level of training. It is rated, by the International Institute for Strategic Studies in London, as second in this hemisphere only to the United States in military capability. In addition, Cuba has paramilitary and reserve formations totaling some 780,000.

Propped up economically and militarily by the USSR, Cuba has been able to finance, train, advise and participate in insurgent movements in Guatemala, Nicaragua, Honduras, El Salvador, Bolivia, Colombia, Venezuela and elsewhere in the hemisphere. It has, with Soviet aid, erected a powerful radio communications facility which is being used to relay the orders of insurgent leaders based in Nicaragua to their troops in the field in El Salvador and Honduras.

Moreover, the Soviets have constructed in the port of Cienfuegos a base capable of tending and repairing nuclear submarines. Such a facility is crucial to supporting the Soviet submarine fleet now prowling the waters of the South Atlantic and Caribbean — a force already twice the size of the German fleet which sank 50 per cent of U.S. shipping during the first six months of 1942. In the event of war, this fleet could effectively block the needed U.S. supplies and reinforcements from reaching NATO battlefields.

In 1979 the Carter Administration discovered that a fully equipped Soviet combat brigade was based in Cuba. Despite protest, that brigade of some 2,600 men is still there, still combat-ready, still supported by at least 500 additional Soviet military personnel.

The patient, methodical effort by the Soviet Union since 1962 to undermine, circumvent and erode the Kennedy Doctrine is seen most clearly in airpower. First, the Soviets introduced into Cuba the Bear (TU-95C), a reconnaissance plane. These were then replaced by the modernized TU-95F, which can be used not only for reconnaissance, but also in antisubmarine, or anti-antisubmarine, warfare. Now airfields have been built in Cuba that can accommodate the supersonic Backfire, a bomber equipped to deliver nuclear weapons and capable of flying from the Soviet Union across the United States to bases in Cuba.

In fighter aircraft the pattern is the same. To the MiG-21 was added the MiG-23. Because it is virtually impossible, short of inspecting the cockpit, to distinguish the MiG-23 from the MiG-27, the Soviets may well have supplanted the MiG-23 with this newer and improved aircraft, which is capable of supersonic delivery of nuclear weapons.

REACTIVATING THE KENNEDY DOCTRINE

Thus, the clear plan that President Kennedy projected in 1962 has given way to the very situation that the Kennedy Doctrine sought to prevent. In 1962 it appeared that Cuba, through an exercise of American will and projection of American strength, would be neutralized as a springboard for Soviet military power and as a threat to the developing countries of Central and Latin America. Now the threat is being reasserted — and in forms far more dangerous to the stability of the region than was signified by the Soviet IRBMs of the 1960s.

If the United States seriously intends to stop the threat posed by the Soviet Union and its regional surrogates to the Caribbean Basin and Central America, it must act to hold both the USSR and Cuba to the understandings reached twenty years ago. But it must be recalled that the principles of the Kennedy Doctrine expressed a bipartisan consensus that freedom should be preserved and defended, and that in 1962 both the Executive Branch and the Congress were in agreement that U.S. power should be used, if necessary, in support of those principles.

In implementing the Kennedy Doctrine, the United States must, first and foremost, use diplomacy and economic incentives rather than military force. Yet, there is little doubt that the projection of U.S. military power in some form will be essential in preserving the interests of the United States and those of other free nations in the region. Diplomacy can be effective only if it is understood that there are circumstances in which, as a last resort, the commitment of military power — by the United States or by others — may become necessary in order to protect valid national interests.

A political strategy designed to protect our interests must be based upon healthy economies and strong economic relations within Central America, coupled with our own willingness to commit significant resources to the betterment of the region. For example: the Kissinger Commission recommended that 10,000 college scholarships for study in the United States be provided to young Central Americans. In 1983, 7,500 Central American youths were given scholarships in the Soviet Union and the Communist Bloc, while fewer than 30 were thus educated in the United States. If this trend continues, virtually all politicians and government officials in Central America will, within the next fifteen years, have received their education at Soviet hands.

U.S POLICY IN EL SALVADOR

Let us now look at the two countries that are at the focus of the Central American crisis: El Salvador and Nicaragua. What are the choices available to American policymakers?

In El Salvador, we can try to maintain basically the present situation and the present methods for dealing with it. Unfortunately, this means continuing a debilitating stalemate in which insurgents destroy electric power systems, blow up bridges, raze crops, engage in urban and rural terrorism and so destabilize the economy that eventually the people of the region, and the American electorate as well, will call for peace at any price. And because the Salvadoran insurgents are organized and supplied from outside the country, they can be sustained in the absence of strong popular support within the country.

We can be reasonably sure, since it was freely elected, that the government of Jose Napoleon Duarte has the general support of a large majority of its citizens. But El Salvador historically has little tradition of strong and effective government. Until recently, it has been weak: the judiciary is not independent, the military has been divided, and what is left of the oligarchy wants to preserve the past and to protect itself from what it perceives as the threat of confiscation of its property.

Events in more recent times, however, give grounds for qualified optimism. In an election in which 70 per cent of those eligible participated, Duarte was returned to the presidency that was stolen from him after the election of 1972. Working in harmony with General Vides Casanova, the Commander of the Armed Forces, President Duarte has sent the former head of the Treasury Police, General Carranza, into virtual exile abroad and disbanded the intelligence unit of the Treasury Police. That organization is to be turned into a non-uniformed service on the model of the Internal Revenue Service in the United States. It is now accurate to say that official involvement in the so-called death squads is at an end and that personal involvement on the part of those in authority is dropping sharply.

The rebels themselves now face serious problems in recruitment and have begun to resort to impressment and to shooting deserters. Lacking the support of the people, they are no longer able to confront the army in the field and have been reduced to operating purely as terrorists. They remain a disruptive and destabilizing force, but they no longer pose a strong, direct threat to the government. Among the lingering myths of the Vietnam War in the United States is a belief in the invincibility of Marxist insurgencies; yet, the true measure of their vulnerability can be found in their defeat in such countries as Greece, Malaya and Venezuela.

The deep internal divisions in El Salvador are caused in large part by the violent reaction of the former ruling classes to the potentially confiscatory consequences of land reform. Although this reaction is not justified, it is comprehensible. In El Salvador, a comparatively weak central government has been threatening the economic interests of the large landowners, and it is not reasonable to expect them to view this threat with complacency.

In considering the problem of land reform in El Salvador, we in the United States tend to forget a tragic chapter in our own history. In 1860 and afterward, the Southern slave-holders, protecting their property rights in slaves — an interest that was morally compromised as property rights in land are not — defied a powerful central government and required it to spend four years fighting the first modern war, which reduced the South to desolation before it capitulated. In 1862 Abraham Lincoln had proposed that the Federal Government buy all the slaves in the country from their owners and free them. His proposal died in the Congress because the abolitionists argued successfully that to purchase the slaves, even for the purpose of freeing them, was to recognize a property right in slaves and therefore represented an unacceptable compromise with the South. Others argued that the cost — approximately $15 billion in current dollars — was too high. And so the war went on, at a cost of $150 billion and nearly a million lives in a nation of only 30 million people.

No such considerations of moral compromise or cost would arise in the case of El Salvador if the United States were to underwrite genuine compensation for those Salvadorans whose land is being taken and distributed under the land reform programs. We should offer to do so by guaranteeing 50 cents on the dollar to those who wish to divest their holdings and leave El Salvador. To those who are prepared to remain and invest their money in building the infrastructure and in financing El Salvador's economic development, we should offer 80 or 90 cents on the dollar. This investment should take the form of municipal and utility bonds to build bridges, roads, power networks, waterworks, sewage systems, schools, etc. The bonds themselves, bearing a dividend of perhaps 10 per cent for as long as twenty years, should be guaranteed by the Government of the United States.

Such a program would remove one of the strong motivations to resist land reform and to support right-wing terrorism. The acceptance of a U.S.-backed bond would constitute a quit-claim to the land being distributed and would clear the way for prompt issuance of valid title to the farmer or cooperative receiving the land. Such arrangements will also be decisive in ensuring that land reform, so essential to building popular support in El Salvador, be consolidated. Whether or not land reform is to go further than its present stage, the plan offers a practical means both of reducing violence by disgruntled landowners and of providing development funds to improve the lot of the poor.

We must confront the unpleasant fact that, even if all U.S. military aid were to be withdrawn from El Salvador, the remnants of the oligarchy have it in their power to frustrate land reform and deny any hope of freedom and prosperity for the majority of the people of that country. We must ensure that land reform, which is in the interests of the *campesinos*, is also in the interest of the oligarchs. Even if the decision of the Salvadoran National Assembly to suspend the later stages of land reform is not rescinded, the proposed approach can be used retroactively in order to solidify the land reform already completed. If we assume that half the landowners left the country and half stayed and reinvested their compensation, the total cost would be about $166 million, plus accumulated interest over 20 years of $332 million. The total cost of all land reform programs would be less than $1 billion — the cost, in current dollars, of fighting the Vietnam War for just ten days.

The United States should also substantially increase military aid to El Salvador. Continuing only the present level of outlays provided by the Congress — which is approximately one-third to one-fifth of the funds deemed necessary by the Department of Defense for the effective defeat of the insurgents — ultimately will weary the Salvadoran people in a protracted civil war, destroy the morale of the democratic center and lead eventually to victory for the insurgents.

Moreover, U.S. military assistance to El Salvador has not been spent to the best advantage. American advisers, rather than being assigned on a long-term basis, are being rotated in the same mindless way that characterized U.S. personnel policies in Vietnam. The commanding officer of the United States advisers in El Salvador, Colonel Joseph Stringham, was reassigned after only ten months, just when he had acquired the experience essential to his demanding task. Larger numbers of U.S. officers acquire the El Salvador ribbon, but the mission in El Salvador suffers. The Kissinger Commission repeatedly requested that the Defense Department provide it with the rosters of the American mission so that the turnover could be evaluated. The request was never granted.

Additionally, the Commission determined that the Defense Department has failed to adapt the material sent to El Salvador to the needs of its army. The American trucks that have been supplied are too large for the roads, bridges and small-statured Salvadoran drivers. A sophisticated heavy communications set costing $3,000 is sent when 100 inexpensive walkie-talkies could vastly extend the communications capability for the same price. These are some examples of our failure to adjust to the realities of counterinsurgency warfare in El Salvador. The DOD evidently is beginning to remedy these deficiencies.

If we are to support the legitimate government in El Salvador at all, we must do so at a level sufficient to permit that government to accomplish a prompt and decisive military victory over the insurgents. The key to such a victory lies in cutting the insurgents' supply and communications. Aid should be targeted to stop the insurgents' access to bases in Nicaragua and Honduras, to block their reinforcements and eventually to achieve their effective dispersal. With adequate support, this should take no more than one year.

The Kissinger Commission recommended that U.S. support be contingent on the Salvadoran Army using its power against the right-wing death-squads. With the election of President Duarte, the Army leadership under General Vides Casanova has now clearly ranged itself against the death-squads. Tutela Legal, the human rights office of the Roman Catholic Church in El Salvador, reported that in the first half of 1984 civilian deaths fell by nearly 75 per cent. It should be noted that the Salvadoran military, for all its defects, strongly supported the free elections held in the spring of 1984, and that it was the Salvadoran military which originated the land reform that accounts for much of the popularity of the present government. General Vides Casanova continues to be strongly supportive of the elected government. More generally, the behavior of the Salvadoran Army refutes the stereotyped notion that the military in any Latin American country favors and supports right-wing dictatorships.

As land reform is consolidated and made more effective, popular support for the Salvadoran government will continue to rise. Some of the Kissinger Commission's recommendations on economics, education and health, designed to help rebuild the country, can proceed as soon as funds are available. The other reforms can follow immediately upon the restoration of peace.

The Salvadoran Government's negotiating position is, and should be, to guarantee the insurgents' safe participation in future elections. It is one thing to invite insurgents to participate in free elections and to allow them access to the media; it would be quite another to permit them to join the government without having been elected and then to expect that they will allow the peaceful observance of due process and free elections. The history of communist takeovers, from Czechoslovakia and Hungary in 1948 to the present, attests to the futility of that hope. Power-sharing would give the Salvadoran insurgents a legitimacy unwarranted by their small base of popular support; it would simply present them and their external suppliers with the opportunity to defeat the ends of democratic politics. Wielding a monopoly in military power, the insurgents, with the full support of Nicaragua and Cuba, would seize control in El Salvador.

ALTERNATIVES VIS-A-VIS NICARAGUA

Let us now consider U.S. policy toward Nicaragua. In dealing with that troubled nation, the United States is confronted with basically three choices. The first is a continuation of the present situation, which in all probability will lead to the collapse and "Cubanization" of independent governments in El Salvador, Costa Rica, Panama, then Honduras and Guatemala, with the eventual subversion of Mexico. No one should dismiss this probable pattern with glib references to a "discredited domino theory." Developments after the collapse of the U.S. commitment in Vietnam have vividly demonstrated that the domino theory is more accurately described as an empirically tested and confirmed law of contemporary international relations. The fall of Cambodia and Laos followed precisely as had been predicted by the domino theorists. Thailand was left standing only because Communist China moved to block the Vietnamese, and thereby Soviet, expansionist drive in Southeast Asia.

If a diminutive country like Nicaragua is allowed to develop a fully equipped armed force in excess of 100,000 men, buttressed by an excellent structure of command, control, communications and intelligence, those forces — which exceed by far any conceivable "defensive" needs by Managua — will most certainly be used (along with Cuban forces) in military operations in the region.

A second alternative is a solution similar to that which the United States contrived at the close of the Korean War to contain North Korean aggression. This would involve the containment of Nicaragua through the militarization of all countries in the region with the possible exception of Costa Rica. The overwhelming disadvantage of this course is immediately obvious: it would entail the expenditure of billions of dollars in an effort to match the military buildup of Nicaragua without any real prospect of substantially reducing the dangers in the area.

Indeed, massive diversions of funds from the economic, social, medical and educational development of the region into military channels would exacerbate the problem of poverty and otherwise burden the fragile economies and social structures of the countries involved. Not only would the creation of a congeries of garrison states virtually guarantee the elevation of their armies into permanent ruling classes, but the very amassing of those armies, amid mounting stockpiles of arms, would also heighten the risks of regional conflict and thus sharpen the instabilities that U.S. policy is striving to dampen. In the process, the road of a true democratic revolution for the nations of Central America would be blocked indefinitely and perhaps forever.

ENCOURAGEMENT OF THE DEMOCRATIC REVOLUTION

The legitimate revolution for democracy is the only effective way for the societies of Central America to escape their oligarchic and quasi-feudal backwardness in order to join the community of modern democratic nations. It is the democratic revolution that inspired the rising against Somoza in Nicaragua but that was betrayed by the Sandinistas and perverted into their instrument for totalitarian power. And it is the presence of Soviet-financed and Cuban insurgents that hampers the United States in the encouragement of democratization in other countries in the region — for example, Guatemala — lest the temporary instabilities caused by that process open the doors to new Marxist takeovers.

Fortunately, recent developments in Guatemala suggest that democratization in that country is gaining a momentum of its own. Perhaps warned by the developments in Nicaragua, the Guatemalan junta has held an election for a constituent assembly that will write a new constitution. This election gained the massive participation (70 per cent) of the Guatemalan people. Guatemala is on the path toward representative democracy. If we were to try to prod this process beyond the internal tempo of Guatemalan society, we might not only jeopardize the process but intensify the instabilities that will be inevitably exploited by the totalitarians of the left.

As long as a Soviet-Cuban threat persists in the region, we shall be compelled to support governments not subject to the influence of the Soviet Union or Cuba, even though they do not measure up fully to our expectations of democracy or protection of human rights. We face the tragic limitation on our moral choice in that we do not always have the option of choosing between good and evil. It is perfectly moral to support the lesser of two evils. It is utterly immoral to abandon an inadequate democracy struggling to become an effective one, leaving it an easy prey to forces that are effectively totalitarian.

It is obvious, then, that a regional policy of containment is unlikely to be successful for the reasons cited. Moreover, such a policy would stand little chance of blocking Nicaraguan ambitions simply because it would need to be sustained over many years through annual Congressional budgets, through changes in administrations and against a background of probably enhanced instability in the region.

A POLICY FOR NICARAGUA

There is, however, a third alternative for U.S. policy: to impose direct pressure on Nicaragua in order to compel the Sandinista regime to divest itself of the means of regional destabilization and to conform to its own solemn pledges. In tangible terms, this would mean a reduction of the Nicaraguan Armed Forces to the levels that obtained in 1979, the departure of all foreign advisers and the dismantling of its massive intelligence and command and control centers. Nicaragua would be required also to observe the commitment it made to the Organization of American States in July 1979 to hold genuinely free and competitive elections. This requirement cannot be met by an empty propaganda exercise of the sort familiar under Marxist-Leninist regimes.

Such U.S. pressure on Managua would include open and effective support of the betrayed leaders of the anti-Somoza revolution who are now combatting the Sandinistas — the "contras" or "counter-revolutionaries" as they have been labeled by the Sandinistas and fellow-Marxists. The term is a perverse bit of propaganda contrived by the totalitarians because the men thus labeled — Pastora, Robelo, Chamorro, Cruz and others — were and are the true leaders of the democratic revolution against Somoza and the true freedom fighters, as they properly call themselves. They are striving to redeem the revolution and to attain its democratic objectives, including a free and democratic Nicaragua with a free labor movement, a free market economy, a free press, independent judiciary, free and contested elections, and the other requisites of a democratic society.

The United States can fully justify direct and open pressure on the Sandinista government and encouragement of the freedom fighters on the basis of the principles enunciated by President Kennedy in 1962. We respect the right of the people of Nicaragua to be free of both the tyranny of a Somoza and the yoke of a Castro. We respect the right of the Nicaraguan people to true democracy, and we oppose in the Western Hemisphere the imposition of a totalitarian rule and the occupation of a hemispheric country by the minions of foreign powers that have clearly proclaimed their objective of subverting the continent to their own imperialist aims. We rightly oppose the perversion of education in Nicaragua into a vehicle of mass indoctrination. In accordance with the Kennedy Doctrine, we also oppose Cuba's callous use of Nicaragua as a massive staging area for the further extension of totalitarian coups that would ultimately pose a tangible threat to the security and economic stability of the United States itself.

This alternative would entail, in addition to effective U.S. support of the freedom fighters, as much U.S. economic pressure on Nicaragua as could be mustered in order to push it toward meaningful negotiations. And Cuba itself must be made to understand that there are circumstances in which we would be prepared to use military force against its activities in the region.

What if Nicaragua rejects these conditions and continues on its course of not only oppressing its own people but also directing insurgency and military threats against its neighbors? The export of violent revolution by Nicaragua cannot be condoned by the United States. Where fundamental American interests are at peril, any U.S. President is not only justified — but, indeed, obligated under the responsibilities of his office — to consider the full range of options available to him in meeting the dangerous situation, including the application of direct military force.

President Kennedy was prepared to invoke this option in the crisis of 1962. As we have pointed out, the explicit alternative of U.S. military action was a keystone of the Kennedy Doctrine and the main incentive behind the U.S.–Soviet understanding that brought about a peaceful settlement — for the time — of the crisis. Today, when the challenge that triggered that crisis has reappeared in much broader and more ominous form, the Kennedy Doctrine offers a proven design for meeting it. But applying the Kennedy Doctrine effectively will require a revitalized political bipartisanship, an element that is essential to purposeful U.S. policy.

The Kennedy Doctrine is one side of such a purposeful U.S. policy design toward Central America. The other side must be a vigorous U.S. commitment to the revolution for democracy that is sweeping Central America. We must actively support the striving of the peoples of the region to erect free market economies and thus allow for the development of the middle classes on which democratic institutions depend. Above all, we must give full and active support to their quest for those democratic institutions, including independent judiciaries and free and open elections contested by unfettered political parties. And we must continue to champion the advancement of human rights, including the right to be free from terrorism and subversion of both the right and the left.

POSTSCRIPT

Since I wrote the above essay, the situation with regard to Cuba is essentially unchanged: Cuba, both in itself and as a satellite of the Soviet Union, remains a major threat to the peace of the hemisphere. But there have been dramatic developments in Central America. In two countries, El Salvador and Guatemala, these changes have been for the good.

The movement toward peace and democracy in El Salvador has picked up velocity: the administration of President Jose Napoleon Duarte has drastically reduced killing by right-wing death squads. A human rights official was quoted in the *New York Times:* "If you look at where the government started, it's pretty incredible what they've achieved." Politically motivated killings have dropped from an estimated 800 a month in 1980 to fewer than 30 a month in 1986, many carried out by leftist rebels who have resorted to increasingly brutal and haphazard forms of violence.

El Salvador has not reached perfection, but it has made exceptional progress. If we remember that thirty years ago Colombia, now a relatively stable democracy, was plagued with ideologically motivated massacres as grievous as anything in the recent history of El Salvador, we may be permitted considerable optimism.

In Guatemala the Kissinger Commission saw severe obstacles to progress toward democracy. Yet, four years later Guatemala has a civilian government, chosen in elections of exemplary fairness in which 70 per cent of the electorate took part. The Army remains committed to the constitutional process by which President Cerezo came to office. Guatemala remains oppressed by poverty, threatened by leftist guerrilla movements and ethnic tensions. But it has joined the third of mankind which lives under democracy. Here, too, a qualified optimism is now justified.

In Nicaragua, however, the situation has deteriorated sharply. The Sandinistas have moved to suppress the last vestiges of freedom. In October 1985, President Ortega suspended human rights in a proclamation even more sweeping than that by which Hitler ended the Weimar Republic. In June 1986, having long shredded the pages of *La Prensa* with the censor's shears, the government closed down this last independent newspaper. The campaign against the church has taken on new virulence with the expulsion of Bishop Vega and further restrictions on the freedom of church officials to speak out. A continuing propaganda campaign in the United States and Europe, orchestrated by a public relations firm, has led many to succumb to the Sandinista party line. Following the example of Castro, Commandante Ortega and the Sandinistas pose all too successfully as idealistic would-be democrats forced into repressive measures by U.S. hostility.

If the Sandinistas consolidate totalitarian control of the country with Soviet and Cuban support, the regime will be removable only by the means used to remove Hitler and Mussolini: armed invasion in force.

Time is running out in Nicaragua. If the democratic revolution which overthrew Somoza is to be restored, the democratic forces in Nicaragua will have to win a military victory. This seems a remote possibility, but there have been some hopeful developments: public support for the Sandinistas is eroding; the opposition groups, rapidly increasing in number, have come together in the Unified Nicaraguan Opposition; and the U.S. Congress has voted $100 million in aid to the democratic forces. The Contras can succeed if — and only if — the United States stays the course.

This will require further dollar aid and training to make the democratic troops a professional force able to win over the Soviet-equipped forces of the Sandinistas. As long as every detail of foreign policy is to be thrashed out in a divided Congress, the hopes for an effective Nicaraguan policy are slim. President Reagan was able to gain approval for the $100 million in aid to the democratic forces only by maximum exertion of his formidable lobbying skills and ability to compromise. Even now, delivery of this aid is threatened by further delays.

The President should be free to conduct foreign policy in Central America under a broad mandate from the Congress. That mandate can be developed only if the bipartisan consensus the Kissinger Commission hoped to generate comes about. Developments in Central America which directly and immediately threaten the United States might bring about such a consensus, but it is much wiser to achieve a coherent bipartisan policy before the crisis-point is reached. A Reagan-Kennedy Doctrine along the lines I have indicated offers such a policy — one which is a direct continuation of principles and understandings already established in the 1960s.

The Contributors

WILLIAM R. BODE has been a Special Assistant to the Under Secretary of State for Security Assistance, Science and Technology since 1983, after serving as an assistant to the Assistant Secretary of Defense for International Security Policy.

ANGELO CODEVILLA, before joining the Hoover Institution as a Senior Research Fellow in 1985, served for eight years on the staff of the U.S. Senate Select Committee on Intelligence.

ARTURO J. CRUZ in 1977 joined The Group of Twelve, a group of Nicaraguan citizens organized politically to support the Sandinistas. After the overthrow of Somoza in 1979 he served as a member of the ruling Junta, President of the Nicaraguan Central Bank, and Ambassador to the United States. He resigned in 1981, became a dissident, and in 1984 was nominated Presidential candidate by the largest opposition coalition, but refused to run on the grounds of lack of guarantees of a free election. Mr. Cruz now is one of three Directors of the Unified Nicaraguan Opposition and President of Democratic Action for Nicaragua.

H. EUGENE DOUGLAS served as Ambassador-at-Large and United States Coordinator for Refugee Affairs from 1982 to 1986. He is the Visiting Professor for the C.B. Smith Centennial Chair in U.S.-Mexico Relations at the Lyndon B. Johnson School of Public Affairs at the University of Texas at Austin.

DAVID C. JORDAN is Professor of Government and Foreign Affairs at the University of Virginia. He was U.S. Ambassador to Peru from 1984 to 1986.

JEANE J. KIRKPATRICK served as the United States Permanent Representative to the United Nations from 1981 to 1985, and is now Senior Fellow at the American Enterprise Institute and Professor of Government at Georgetown University.

H. JOACHIM MAITRE is Interim Dean of Boston University's College of Communications and Associate Director of the Center for International Relations at Boston University. He is the Foreign Affairs Editor of *Strategic Review.*

R. BRUCE McCOLM is Director of the Center for Caribbean and Central American Studies, Freedom House, New York. He also serves as a member of the Inter-American Commission on Human Rights of the Organization of American States.

DOUGLAS W. PAYNE is Assistant to the Director of the Center for Caribbean and Central American Studies, Freedom House, New York.

NESTOR D. SANCHEZ is U.S. Deputy Assistant Secretary of Defense for Inter-American Affairs.

SOL SANDERS, a freelance writer who has focused on Central American issues for the past several years, is the author of *Mexico: Chaos on Our Doorstep* (Macmillan, 1986).

JOHN R. SILBER is President of Boston University since 1971 and served as a member of the National Bipartisan Commission on Central America in 1983–1984.

JAIME SUCHLICKI is a Professor of History and Director of the Institute of Interamerican Studies, Graduate School of International Studies, University of Miami.

ASHLEY J. TELLIS is a Visiting Researcher at Georgetown University. He specializes in defense and security policy and has published extensively on those topics in various Indian journals.

MALCOLM WALLOP (R. Wyoming) is a member of the Select Committee on Intelligence of the U.S. Senate and Chairman of its Budget Authorization Subcommittee.